PONTIFICAL INSTITUTE OF MEDIAEVAL STUDIES

STUDIES AND TEXTS

32

THE THEOLOGY OF THE HYPOSTATIC UNION
IN THE EARLY THIRTEENTH CENTURY

WALTER H. PRINCIPE, C. S. B.

THE THEOLOGY OF THE HYPOSTATIC UNION
IN THE EARLY THIRTEENTH CENTURY

VOLUME IV

PHILIP THE CHANCELLOR'S
THEOLOGY
OF THE HYPOSTATIC UNION

THE PONTIFICAL INSTITUTE OF MEDIAEVAL STUDIES
59, Queen's Park, Crescent E
Toronto, Ontario, M5S 2C4
Canada

1975

This book was produced with a grant
in aid of publication from
the De Rancé Foundation.

232.15

P93b

v.4

200276

ISBN 0-88844-032-4
ISSN 0082-5328-1

Copyright
by
THE PONTIFICAL INSTITUTE OF MEDIAEVAL STUDIES

PRINTED BY UNIVERSA — WETTEREN — BELGIUM

Gloria et honor Deo
qui paschalis hostia
agnus mente, pugna leo
victor die tertia
resurrexit cum tropaeo
mortis ferens spolia.

Philip the Chancellor

TABLE OF CONTENTS

THE THEOLOGY OF THE HYPOSTATIC UNION
IN THE EARLY THIRTEENTH CENTURY

FOREWORD

This fourth volume of our series of studies completes publication of the first stage of our research. Although further research into later authors of the first half of the thirteenth century has been begun and will, we hope, be published before too long, the four authors studied thus far provide sufficient basis for a judgment about the theology of the Hypostatic Union in the early thirteenth century. Hence a general conclusion to these four volumes has been added after the study of Philip the Chancellor's doctrine and the edition of his texts. This general conclusion provides a synoptic view of the four theologians examined thus far together with an evaluation of their contributions to the theology of the Hypostatic Union.

For the study of Philip the Chancellor, a John Simon Guggenheim Memorial Foundation Fellowship gave me the opportunity to consult the original manuscripts of his works, which had first been read in microfilm, and to examine and include within the edition of his texts some additional manuscripts. For this opportunity I should like to thank the Directors of the Guggenheim Foundation.

I should also like to thank the various libraries whose directors allowed the use of their manuscripts and other resources, and all who have assisted in the publication of this volume.

W. H. P.
January 28, 1974

LIST OF ABBREVIATIONS

For PHILIP THE CHANCELLOR:

P 1ra; *T* 1ra; *V* 1rb.

— *Summa de Bono*; text established from *MS.* Padua, Antonianum, Scaff. VIII, 156 (= *P*) fol. 1ra, from *MS.* Toulouse, Ville 192 (= *T*) fol. 1ra, and from MS. Vatican *Latin* 7669 (= *V*) fol. 1rb. Only significant variants are noted in such texts.

De Anima [4(xxii)]; Keeler, p. 42.

— *Summa de Bono: Quaestiones de Anima*, q. 4 [of those questions on the soul edited by Keeler], q. 22 [of Philip's questions on the soul in the *Summa de Bono*]; ed. Leo W. Keeler, *Ex Summa Philippi Cancellarii Quaestiones de Anima* (Münster i. W. 1937) p. 42.

DeDiscrPers, 4; p. 156.

— *Summa de Bono: Quaestio de Discretione Personali*, no. 4; found on p. 156 of the edition given here in Part II, ch. 2.

De Fide, 1; Ceva, p. 35, ll. 609-617.

— *Summa de Bono: Quaestiones de Fide*, q. 1; ed. Victorius a Ceva, *De Fide: Ex Summa Philippi Cancellarii († 1236)* (Rome 1961), p. 35, lines 609-617. For his edition, Ceva uses the following MSS: Padua, Antonianum, Scaff. VIII, 156; Padua, Antonianum, Scaff. X, 214; Florence, Laurenziana, Plut. 36, déxt. 4; Naples, Bibliot. Nazion., VII, C. 37; Pisa, S. Caterina 143. In our study, texts from this section of the *Summa de Bono* are edited by us from *PTV* and a reference is then given to the corresponding place in Ceva's edition.

DeIncarn, 1-i, 1 (p. 158), & 1-ii, 2 (p. 158).

— *Quaestiones de Incarnatione*, question 1, redaction 1, paragraph 1 (p. 158 of our edition in Part II, ch. 3), and question 1, redaction 2, paragraph 2 *(ibid.*, p. 158). When the paragraph number is the same in both redactions, it is given only once, e.g.: *DeIncarn*, 1-i & 1-ii, 9: p. 162.

OTHER AUTHORS:

Alexander of Hales, *Glossa*; or *ProlGlossaAlex*

— See *infra, GlossaAlex*; or *ProlGlossaAlex*

Anselm, *Cur Deus Homo* II, 21; Schmitt II, 32.

— St. Anselm of Canterbury, *Cur Deus Homo*, Book II, ch. 21; in *S. Anselmi Cantuariensis Archiepiscopi Opera Omnia*, ed. F. Schmitt, 6 vols. (Seckau-Rome-Edinburgh 1938-61) II, 32. (All references to St. Anselm's works are to Schmitt's edition.)

Aristotle, *Physics* II, 3; 194b 26-27.

— Aristotle, *Physics*, Book II, sec. 3; in *Aristoteles Graece* ex recensione Immanuelis Bekkeri edidit Academia Regia Borussica, 2 vols. (Berlin 1831) p. 194, col. b, lines 26-27. (References to other works by Aristotle follow this pattern.)

Beiträge

— Beiträge zur Geschichte der Philosophie ([from 1927]: und Theologie) des Mittelalters. Münster i. W., 1891 ff.

Bettoni, "Filippo"
— E. Bettoni, "Filippo il Cancelliere (Rassegna bibliografica)," *Pier Lombardo* 4
(1960) 123-135.
Boethius, *ContraEut*, 3; Rand, p. 84.
— Boethius, *Liber contra Eutychen et Nestorium*, ch. 3; ed. E. K. Rand, in Boethius: *The*
Theological Tractates (London-New York 1918) p. 84.
Boethius, *DeHebdom;* Rand, p. 48, ll. 128-140.
— Boethius, *Quomodo Substantiae in Eo Quod Sint Bonae Sint Cum Non Sint Substantialia*
Bona; ed. E. K. Rand, in *Boethius: The Theological Tractates* (London-New York
1918) p. 48, lines 128-140.
BullThAncMéd
— *Bulletin de Théologie ancienne et médiévale*. Louvain, 1929 ff.
Callus, "Philip"
— D. Callus, "Philip the Chancellor and the *De Anima* Ascribed to Robert
Grosseteste," *Mediaeval and Renaissance Studies* 1 (1941-43) 105-107.
Ceva
— Victorius a Ceva, *De Fide: Ex Summa Philippi Cancellarii († 1236)* (Rome 1961).
CorChrSerLat
— Corpus Christianorum: Series Latina. Turnhout, 1954 ff.
Damascene, *DeFideOrth* III, 6; PG 94, 1005B; Buytaert, p. 188.
— St. John Damascene, *De Fide Orthodoxa*, Book III, ch. 6; in PG 94, 1005B; Latin
version of Burgundio in *St. John Damascene: De Fide Orthodoxa: Versions of Burgun-*
dio and Cerbanus, ed. E. Buytaert (St. Bonaventure-Louvain-Paderborn 1955) p.
188.
Denis, *DeDivNom* 4, 23; PG 3, 724D; PL 122, 1142A; *Dionysiaca* I, 274.
— Pseudo-Denis (or Dionysius) the Areopagite, *De Divinis Nominibus*, ch. 4, no. 23;
in PG 3, 724D; Latin translation by John Scotus Erigena, *Versio Operum S. Dionysii*
Areopagitae III: *De Divinis Nominibus*, in PL 122, 1142A; *Dionysiaca: Recueil donnant*
l'ensemble des traductions latines des ouvrages attribués au Denys de l'Aréopage, edd. [Ph.
Chevallier *et al.*], 2 vols. (Bruges [1937-1950]) I, 274.
Englhardt, *Glaubenspsychologie*
— G. Englhardt, *Die Entwicklung der dogmatischen Glaubenspsychologie in der mit-*
telalterlichen Scholastik vom Abaelardstreit (um 1140) bis zu Philipp dem Kanzler (gest.
1236), Beiträge 30, 4-6 (Münster i. W., 1933).
Firmin-Didot II, 278
— Aristoteles, *Opera Omnia Graece et Latine cum Indice Nominum et Rerum Ab-*
solutissimo, 5 vols. (Paris: Firmin-Didot, 1848-1873) II, col. 278.
Gillon, *Théorie des oppositions*
— L.-B. Gillon, *La théorie des oppositions et la théologie du péché au XIIIᵉ siècle* (Paris
1937).
Glorieux, *Répertoire*, 129; I, 293.
— P. Glorieux, *Répertoire des Maîtres en Théologie de Paris au XIIIᵉ siècle*, 2 vols. (Paris
1933) nᵒ 129; I, 293.
GlossaAlex [or Alexander, *Glossa*] III, 2, 10 (A); p. 25.
— *Magistri Alexandri de Hales Glossa in Quatuor Libros Sententiarum Petri Lombardi*,
Book III, dist. 2, par. 10, Redaction A [(L) = Redaction L]; edd. PP. Collegii S.
Bonaventurae, 4 vols. (Quaracchi 1951-1957) III, p. 25.
GlossaOrd in Luc 10, 30; Lyranus V, 153ra.
— *Glossa Ordinaria in Lucam*, ch. 10, verse 30; in *Biblia Sacra [Bibliorum Sacrorum* in

some volumes] *cum Glossa Ordinaria ... et Postilla Nicolai Lyrani ...*, 7 vols. (I, III, VI: Paris 1590; II: Venice 1603; IV, V: Lyons 1545; VII: Lyons 1590) V, folio 153ra. (This edition is used when the text of the *GlossaOrd* in PL 113-114 is incomplete.)

HypUnion I, 94.

— W. Principe, *The Theology of the Hypostatic Union in the Early Thirteenth Century*, Vol. I: *William of Auxerre's Theology of the Hypostatic Union* (Toronto 1963) p. 94.

HypUnion II, 110.

— W. Principe, *The Theology of the Hypostatic Union in the Early Thirteenth Century*, Vol. II: *Alexander of Hales' Theology of the Hypostatic Union* (Toronto 1967) p. 110.

HypUnion III, 33.

— W. Principe, *The Theology of the Hypostatic Union in the Early Thirteenth Century*, Vol. III: *Hugh of Saint-Cher's Theology of the Hypostatic Union* (Toronto 1970) p. 33.

Keeler

— see *supra*, Philip the Chancellor, *De Anima*.

Künzle, *Verhältnis*

— P. Künzle, *Das Verhältnis der Seele zu ihren Potenzen: Problemgeschichtliche Untersuchungen von Augustin bis und mit Thomas von Aquin*. (Freiburg [Schweiz] 1956).

Landgraf, *Dogmengeschichte* II/2, 162.

— A. Landgraf, *Dogmengeschichte der Frühscholastik*, 4 parts, each of 2 vols.(Regensburg 1952-56) Part II, Vol. II, p. 162.

Lombard, *Coll in Rom* 1, 7.

— Peter Lombard, *Collectanea in Omnes D. Pauli Apostoli Epistolas: In Epistolam ad Romanos*, ch. 1, verse 7.

Lombard, *Sent* II, 41, 2; Quaracchi³, 564.

— Peter Lombard, *Sententiae in IV Libris Distinctae*, Liber II, distinctio 41, capitulum 2; edd. PP. Collegii S. Bonaventurae ad Claras Aquas, 3rd ed., Vol. I (Grottaferrata 1971) p. 564. (This edition is used for Books I and II: its second volume, containing Books III and IV, has not appeared as this volume goes to press.)

Lombard, *Sent* III, 6, 3; p. 576.

— Peter Lombard, *Libri IV Sententiarum*, Liber III, distinctio 3, capitulum 3; edd. PP. Collegii S. Bonaventurae, 2nd ed., Volume II (Quaracchi 1916) p. 576. (This edition is used for Books III and IV only).

Lottin, *PsychMorale* IV, 849.

— O. Lottin, *Psychologie et Morale au XIIᵉ et XIIIᵉ siècles*, 6 tomes in 8 vols. (Louvain 1942-1960) Tome IV, p. 849.

Meylan

— H. Meylan, "Les 'Questions' de Philippe le Chancelier," *Positions des thèses: École Nationale des Chartes* (Paris 1927) pp. 89-94. (An offprint was graciously furnished by the author.)

PG 3, 724D.

— *Patrologiae Cursus Completus: Series Graeca*, accurante J.-P. Migne, 161 vols. in 166 (Paris 1857-1866) Vol. III, col. 724, sec. D.

PL 114, 650D.

— *Patrologiae Cursus Completus: Series Latina*, accurante J.-P. Migne, 221 vols. (Paris 1844-1864) Vol. CXIV, col. 650, sec. D.

Pouillon, "Premier Traité"

— H. Pouillon, "Le premier Traité des Propriétés transcendantales: La 'Summa de bono' du Chancelier Philippe," *Revue Néoscolastique de Philosophie* 42 (1939) 40-77.

ProlGlossaAlex III, 31*.

— *Prolegomena* to *GlossaAlex* [q.v.], Vol. III, p. 31*.

QuaestAlex [or Alexander, *Quaest*], 15, 64; I, 213.

— Alexander of Hales, *Quaestiones Disputatae 'Antequam Esset Frater'*, quaestio XV, num. 64; edd. PP. Collegii S. Bonaventurae, 3 vols. (Quaracchi 1960) p. 213. (The pagination for the three volumes is continuous.)

Richard of Saint-Victor, *DeTrin* IV, 13; Ribaillier, p. 175.

— Richard of Saint-Victor, *De Trinitate*, Liber IV, cap. 13; ed. J. Ribaillier (Paris 1958) p. 175.

SummaAlex III, 58; IV, 85.

— Alexander of Hales, *Summa Theologica* ([Vol. IV adds]: *seu Sic ab Origine Dicta "Summa Fratris Alexandri"*), Liber III, num. 58; edd. PP. Collegii S. Bonaventurae, 4 vols. (Quaracchi 1924-1948) IV, 85.

William of Auxerre, *DeInc* 9, 32; Principe, p. 290.

— William of Auxerre, *Summa Aurea: Quaestio de Incarnatione*, cap. 9, num. 32; ed. W. Principe, *The Theology of the Hypostatic Union in the Early Thirteenth Century*, Vol. I: *William of Auxerre's Theology of the Hypostatic Union* (Toronto 1963) p. 290.

William of Auxerre, *DeStatu* 3, 3; Principe, p. 299.

— William of Auxerre, *Summa Aurea: Quaestio de Statu Christi in Triduo*, cap. 3, num. 3; ed. W. Principe, *ibid.*, p. 299.

INTRODUCTION

1. PHILIP THE CHANCELLOR

The forceful but enigmatic person known as Philip the Chancellor united ecclesiastical administration with extensive preaching and theological study and writing in such a way that he became one of the most influential clerics of the church of Paris in the early thirteenth century.[1] Philip was born between 1160 and 1185. He studied at the University of Paris and became a Master in Theology perhaps about 1206.[2] We know that in 1211 he was already Archdeacon of Noyon. In 1218 he became Chancellor of Notre Dame of Paris and thereupon became engaged in many of the conflicts that troubled the Church and the University of Paris in the years following. Among these was the dispersion of masters and scholars from the University of Paris in the years 1229 to 1231, during which time the Dominicans obtained a chair of theology at the university. Philip retained his chancellorship until his death on December 23, 1236.[3] Leaving aside both the story of his often stormy administration and detailed examination of his numerous extant sermons,[4] we shall center our attention on his influential *Summa de Bono*

1 On Philip's life, works, and activity see the following: P. Feret, *La faculté de théologie de Paris et ses docteurs les plus célèbres*, 4 vols. (Paris 1894-97) I, 232-237 (under the name "Philippe de Grève," a different person from the Chancellor); Meylan, pp. 89-94; Glorieux, *Répertoire*, 119 (I, 282-284); M. de Wulf, *Histoire de la philosophie médiévale*, 6th ed., II (Louvain 1936) 72-74; Callus, "Philip," pp. 105-107; A. Landgraf, *Einführung in die Geschichte der theologischen Literatur der Frühscholastik* (Regensburg 1948) pp. 132-133; A. Meier, "Filippo il Cancelliere," *Enciclopedia Cattolica* 5 (1950) cols. 1315-16; N. Wicki, "Philip der Kanzler und die Pariser Bischofswahl von 1227/1228," *Freiburger Zeitschrift für Philosophie und Theologie* 5 (1958) 318-326; Bettoni, "Filippo," pp. 123-135; Ceva, pp. 1-4; J. B. Schneyer, *Die Sittenkritik in den Predigten Philipps des Kanzlers*, Beiträge 39/4 (Münster Westf. 1962) pp. 1-8; N. Wicki, "Philipp der Kanzler," *Lexikon für Theologie und Kirche*, 2nd ed., 8 (1963) cols. 452-453; N. Wicki, "Philip the Chancellor," *New Catholic Encyclopedia* 11 (1967) 274-275.

2 Glorieux, p. 282, and Callus, p. 105, who are followed by later authors.

3 On the biased opinions expressed about his personal life see Callus, p. 106, n. 1.

4 The most authoritative studies of Philip's sermons are the relatively recent works of J. B. Schneyer, whose *Sittenkritik* (see n. 1), pp. 9-26, gives a good introduction to Philip's preaching, and whose *Repertorium der lateinischen Sermones des Mittelalters für die Zeit von 1150-1350 (Autoren L-P)*, Beiträge 43/4 (Münster Westf. 1972) pp. 818-868, lists individually 723 sermons by Philip together with indications of the MSS and editions. See also the same author's "Philipp der Kanzler — ein hervorragender Prediger des Mittelalters," *Münchener Theologische Zeitschrift* 8 (1957) 174-179, and "Einige Sermoneshandschriften aus der früheren Benediktinerbibliothek des Mont Saint-Michel," *Sacris Erudiri* 17 (1966) 150-211, esp. 163-187.

Some earlier works on his sermons: A. Lecoy de la Marche, *La chaire française au moyen âge* (Paris 1886) pp. 94-95, 524-525; Meylan, pp. 91-92; M. Davy, *Les sermons universitaires parisiens de 1230-1231*

and even more, for the theology of Hypostatic Union, on several of his
theological questions.

2. THE SUMMA DE BONO AND THE QUAESTIONES DE INCARNATIONE

Philip's major theological work, the so-called *Summa de Bono*,[1] is
generally thought to have been written in the early 1230's: it was cer-

(Paris 1931) pp. 125-128; Glorieux, *Répertoire* 119 (I, 283); Th. Kaepelli, "Un recueil de sermons
prêchés à Paris et en Angleterre," *Archivum Fratrum Praedicatorum* 26 (1956) 161-191. Editions of his
sermons: three by Davy, pp. 153-177; one by Wicki, "Philipp der Kanzler und die Pariser Bischofswahl," pp. 323-326; one by V. Doucet, "A travers le manuscrit 434 de Douai," *Antonianum* 27 (1952)
553-557; one by J. Leclercq, "Sermon de Philippe le Chancelier sur S. Bernard," *Cîteaux* 16 (1965)
208-213. Schneyer gives some extracts in his *Sittenkritik*.

Philip is considered a gifted poet. His known poems are edited in *Analecta Hymnica Medii Aevi* XX
and XXI, ed. G. Dreves (Leipzig 1895), and L, edd. G. Dreves and C. Blume (Leipzig 1907). See vol.
L, 528-535, for the notice on "Philippus de Grevia, Cancellarius Parisiensis, † 1236," for the list of
his poems printed in vols. XX and XXI, as well as for six additional poems. The editors' confusing
Philippe de Grève and Philip the Chancellor has been rectified by later studies: see F. Raby, *A
History of Secular Latin Poetry in the Middle Ages*, 2 vols. (Oxford, 1957, 1967, reprint of 1934 edition) II,
227-235; see also the same author's *A History of Christian Latin Poetry from the Beginnings to the Close of the
Middle Ages*, 2nd. ed. (Oxford 1953) pp. 395-401; Callus, "Philip," p. 106, n. 2. See also Bettoni,
"Filippo," pp. 25, 27, for references to some further poems.

A French translation of sixteen of Philip's poems, together with the Latin texts and some commentaries, has been recently provided by Henry Spitzmuller, *Carmina Sacra Medii Aevi Saec. III-XV /
Poésie latine chrétienne du moyen âge* (Bruges 1971), pp. 752-797; 809-812 (commentaries); 1816-18 (on
the author). Although Spitzmuller is aware of the problem of two or even three Philips (p. 1817), he
continues to speak of "Philippe (le Chancelier) de Paris ou de Grève," (p. 753) and mixes the names
"Philippe le Chancelier" and "Philippe de Grève" indiscriminately in his notes.

1 Although the work is generally referred to as the *Summa de Bono*, at least some of the MSS call
it *Summa Quaestionum*. Meylan refers to the treatise as *Tractatus de bono nature et de bono in genere* (p.
89) or simply as *Questions* (pp. 89, 93). N. Wicki, who is preparing the critical edition, names it *Summa
quaestionum theologicarum (Summa de bono)*, "Philipp der Kanzler," *Lexikon für Theologie und Kirche*, 2nd.
ed. 8 (1963) col. 453, and "Philip the Chancellor," *New Catholic Encyclopedia* 11 (1967) 274. O. Lottin,
in *BullThAncMéd* 1 (1929-32) 623, p. 343*, says that in spite of the title *Summa Quaestionum* the work
"ne suppose aucunement des questions disputées antérieures"; in some instances, however,
disputed questions of Philip have been found that cover material in the *Summa* and that seem
preparatory to it. For the sake of convenience we shall continue to employ the generally-used title,
Summa de Bono.

For MSS of the work see Landgraf, *Einführung*, p. 133, and F. Stegmüller, *Repertorium Commentariorum in Sententias Petri Lombardi*, 2 vols. (Würzburg 1947) 698; I, 340 (the Florence MS should
be numbered 36 instead of 26, and the Toledo MSS, according to a personal communication to me
from H. Meylan, do not seem to contain the *Summa de Bono*).

Extensive passages from the work have been edited by the following: Englhardt, *Glaubenspsychologie*, pp. 185-187 (n. 49), 427-444; Thomas Graf, *De Subiecto Psychico Gratiae et Virtutum secundum
Doctrinam Scholasticorum usque ad Medium Saeculum XIV* I (Rome 1934) pp. 151-178 passim; Keeler (see
Philip, *De Anima*); Lottin, *PsychMorale*, passim; Landgraf, *Dogmengeschichte*, passim (especially in Parts I
and II); Künzle, *Verhältnis*, pp. 226-229; Ceva, pp. 17-118; J. Gründel, *Die Lehre von dem Umstanden der
menschlichen Handlung im Mittelalter*, Beiträge 39/5 (Münster Westf. 1963) pp. 368-373; L. Hödl, *Die
neuen Quästionen der Gnadentheologie des Johannes von Rupella OM († 1245) in Cod. Lat. Paris 14726*
(Munich 1964) pp. 81-90.

tainly composed after Alexander of Hales' *Glossa* since the Chancellor used this work.[2] The discovery that in some parts of his *Summa* Philip copied extensively from Alexander's *Glossa* has tended to diminish his previous reputation for great originality.[3] In other sections the *Summa de Bono* also follows the so-called *Summa Duacensis*. However, because some scholars maintain that Philip may be directly or indirectly responsible for the *Summa Duacensis*, no judgment about his originality can be drawn from his use of it.[4] In any event, because the *Summa de Bono* was

2 The date is fixed variously as follows: From an indefinite *terminus a quo* to 1236, the year of Philip's death (Meylan, p. 94; de Wulf, II, 72, n. 5); between 1228 and 1236 (Landgraf, *Einführung*, p. 132); after 1228 (Glorieux, *Répertoire*, 119; I, 282); between 1230 and 1236 (Callus, p. 107); about 1232 (Lottin, *PsychMorale* IV, 849; *ProlGlossaAlex* III, 31*: both use extensive studies of the interrelationships of authors). The *Summa de Bono* is certainly later than the *Summa Aurea* of William of Auxerre and the *Glossa* of Alexander of Hales, both of which it uses. Neither the *Summa de Bono* nor the *Scriptum* of Hugh of Saint-Cher show evidence of knowledge of one another: they may well have been written at the same time.

3 For a study of the copying from Alexander's *Glossa* in both the *Summa de Bono* and in some of Philip's separate theological questions, and for comments on Philip's originality, see *ProlGlossaAlex* I, 111*; II, 12*, 12*-18*; III, 8*-15*; IV, 28*-34*.

4 The *Summa Duacensis* was first given this title and presented as an integral work within the questions of *MS*. Douai 434 by P. Glorieux, "La Summa Duacensis," *Recherches de Théologie ancienne et médiévale* 12 (1940) 104-135, who later edited it: *La "Summa Duacensis" (Douai 434): Texte critique avec une introduction et des tables* (Paris 1955). In the article and on pp. 10-11 of his edition Glorieux maintains that this *Summa* is anterior to Philip's *Summa de Bono*, was extensively used by Philip for his *Summa*, and is the work of some unknown author other than Philip. In 1948 Lottin, *PsychMorale* II, 432-434, supported Glorieux on these points, as did A. Meier, "Filippo il Cancelliere," *Enciclopedia Cattolica* 5 (1950) 1315.

V. Doucet, "A travers le manuscrit 434 de Douai," *Antonianum* 27 (1952) 541-542, preferred to see in the *Summa Duacensis* a sketch or first draft written by Philip himself in preparation for his *Summa de Bono*. His hypothesis seems to be supported by N. Wicki, "Philipp der Kanzler," *Lexikon für Theologie und Kirche*, 2nd ed., 8 (1963) 453. R. Gauthier, *Magnanimité* (Paris 1951) p. 272, n. 4, suggests the hypothesis that the *Summa Duacensis* represents a careful redaction by someone other than Philip of notes taken at Philip's lectures, these lectures being Philip's own preparation for his *Summa de Bono*, just as other lectures preserved in *MS*. Douai 434 were his preparation for the final version of the *Summa de Bono*. O. Lottin, *BullThAncMéd* 7 (1954-57) 2143, p. 565, modifies his earlier position by suggesting a similar hypothesis. More radically, C. Vansteenkiste, after noting imperfections in Glorieux's edition of the text, questions whether the material edited as the *Summa Duacensis* is really one work at all: see his review in *Angelicum* 34 (1957) 331-334.

In the meantime Glorieux's position about the author being someone other than Philip was supported against Doucet by P. Künzle, "Hat Philipp der Kanzler die Summa Duacensis verfasst?" *Freiburger Zeitschrift für Philosophie und Theologie* 2 (1955) 469-473. Bettoni, "Filippo," pp. 132-135, gives a good summary of the debate and concludes that Glorieux's hypothesis is "più ragionevole." Gründel, *Umstanden* (cit. supra, sec. 2, n. 1) pp. 362-367, having compared the doctrine of the *Summa Duacensis* with that of the *Summa de Bono* on his topic, treats the former as the work of an independent author.

In a dissertation defended in 1973 at l'Université de Montréal and entitled *La connaissance prophétique dans le manuscrit de Douai 434: Édition critique et commentaire des textes*, Eugène J.-P. Torrell gives a thorough review of the debate and carefully compares questions 107-113 from *MS*. Douai

so greatly influential on subsequent authors, who used it in preference
to either the *Glossa* of Alexander or the *Summa Duacensis*, it retains great
importance in the history of the development of theological thought.[5]
Furthermore, so far as is known, this copying occurs only in certain sections of the huge work and is not necessarily characteristic of the whole;
we shall see, moreover, that in the questions on the Hypostatic Union
Philip remains quite independent of Alexander in many respects, and
apparently strikes out on his own. New sources of Philip's works may
yet appear, but one gets the impression that far from being servile,
Philip is quite as independent in his theological thought and judgment
as he was in his administration as Chancellor of Notre Dame of Paris.[6]

434 (questions on prophecy forming part of the so-called *Summa Duacensis*) with the questions on
prophecy in Philip's *Summa de Bono* and with the other questions on prophecy in the Douai
manuscript (pp. 177-231 and 479-489 of the thesis). From this detailed study of one section Torrell
concludes that at least here the *Summa Duacensis* is anterior to the *Summa de Bono*, was used by Philip
for his *Summa*, and could not have been written by Philip even as a preliminary sketch. At the same
time he shows that the divergencies between Philip's text and that of the *Summa Duacensis*, as well as
the additions Philip makes to the discussion of prophecy, are so considerable that it is erroneous to
speak of plagiarism or even of servile dependence on Philip's part. Torrell rightly calls for further
detailed studies of other parallel sections in the two works.

For our part we wonder if still another hypothesis should not be investigated. Given the considerable and significant divergencies of terminology and even at times of doctrine within a
similarity of order and thought, should it not be asked whether the so-called *Summa Duacensis* and
Philip's *Summa de Bono* both derive from some unknown common source, whether an actually written work or the lectures of a professor heard by the two authors? Would not such a common
source better explain both the similarity of order and material and the divergencies within two
works subsequently written independently of each other?

5 On Philip's influence see Lottin, *PsychMorale* IV, 849-850; VI, 149-169. Speaking of Philip's use
of Alexander's *Glossa*, Lottin, in *BullThAncMéd* 7 (1954-57) 1052, p. 258, says: "Faut-il pour autant
mésestimer l'influence du Chancelier? Non certes; et le P. D[oucet] reconnaît que les maîtres fran-
ciscains du temps se sont inspirés de préférence du Chancelier, parce que précisément ils y recon-
naissaient, quoique mieux élaborées, les vues du premier maître franciscain (p. 12* de l'édition du
livre II [of the *GlossaAlex*]). Dans ce cas peut-on encore parler d''influence littéraire' du Chancelier,
comme je l'ai fait jadis (voir *Bull.* I, n° 484)? En revoyant les textes que j'avais cités alors, j'ai con-
staté que, dans son traité *De virtutibus*, Jean de la Rochelle et le compilateur de la Somme
théologique d'Alexandre se sont adressés, non pas à la Glose d'Alexandre qu'ils connaissaient, mais
au texte même du Chancelier. Odon Rigaud utilise lui aussi le texte de Philippe, mais, dans les textes cités, rien ne prouve qu'il ait connu la Glose. Si par 'influence littéraire' on entend une influence
qui se traduit dans les textes, on peut donc continuer à parler d''influence littéraire' de Philippe;
mais on soulignera l'influence 'doctrinale' d'Alexandre sur ses confrères, s'exerçant, en partie du
moins, par le truchement du Chancelier." Cf. the reply to this in *ProlGlossaAlex* IV, 34*: Referring to
Philip's copying of Alexander, the editors say: "Cancellarii sane scripta nedum minoris, quinimmo
maioris inde facimus; nec alia ratione citra dubium explicatur eorum influxus in Scholam fran-
ciscanam ab O. Lottin saepissime meritoque notatus. At simul fatendum est quondam elatam huius
auctoris originalitatem non parum iam exsufflatam fuisse." See also Lottin's remarks in a revised
study on the subject in *PsychMorale* VI (1960) 149-169.

6 Cf. the following remark of V. Doucet, "A travers le manuscrit," p. 542: "... Il nous est im-

Except for its question *De Discretione Personali*, edited here,[7] the *Summa de Bono* treats of the Hypostatic Union only indirectly and in passing; it is uncertain whether the work, which may be incomplete, was intended to have a section on the Incarnate Word. As it stands, the *Summa de Bono* organizes around the concept of the good various tracts on God, creation (angels, bodies, man), grace in angels and men, the virtues both theological and cardinal, and the gifts of the Holy Spirit.[8] Besides its incidental references to the Hypostatic Union the *Summa* furnishes the indispensable philosophical and theological background for understanding Philip's questions dealing with the Hypostatic Union. These separate questions, found in the famous *MS.* 434 of the Bibliothèque de la Ville at Douai, are roughly contemporary with the *Summa de Bono*; indeed, one may ask whether they were not the product of classroom discussions preparatory to a final incorporation into the *Summa* itself.[9] In any case, they provide a valuable complement to the *Summa* and reveal an important development in the theology of the Hypostatic Union at this period.

possible de voir en lui [Philip] le roi des plagiaires et de comprendre en même temps l'énorme influence de sa Somme ..."

7 See *infra*, pp. 155-157.

8 A brief outline of the work is given by Keeler, p. 7, and Ceva, p. 14; a more detailed analysis is provided by P. Minges, "Philosophiegeschichtliche Bemerkungen über Philipp von Grève († 1236)," *Philosophisches Jahrbuch* 27 (1914) 22-23.

9 This appears to have been the case with at least one of Philip's questions (*De Fortitudine*) contained in *MS.* Douai 434; see Gauthier, *Magnanimité*, pp. 271-272, n. 4.

PART ONE

STUDY OF
PHILIP THE CHANCELLOR'S
THEOLOGY OF THE
HYPOSTATIC UNION

CHAPTER I

THE PHILOSOPHICAL BACKGROUND

1. INTRODUCTION

Philip the Chancellor's *Summa de Bono* reveals the steadily-growing penetration into the West of the philosophy particularly of Aristotle and Avicenna. Although Avicenna is not named, he is an important influence and indeed probably the main channel for Philip's knowledge of Aristotle;[1] however, Philip also knew Aristotle directly and he quite regularly quotes or refers to most of the Stagirite's works.[2] The Chancellor appears to have had some acquaintance, whether directly or indirectly, with the thought of Avicebron and of the *Liber de Causis*; Averroes, too, is mentioned at least three times.[3] This does not mean, however, that the outlook of *Summa de Bono* is predominantly philosophical; the work, according to the author's declared intention, is

---

1 See Minges, "Philos. Bemerkungen," pp. 29-30. H. Pouillon, in *BullThAncMéd* 3 (1937-40) 384, p. 169*, says: "Penseur originel, personnel et vigoureux, Philippe s'est assimilé tout le *De anima* d'Aristote, mais surtout à travers Avicenne, son vrai maître en péripatétisme et qu'il ne nomme pourtant jamais, quoiqu'il l'utilise souvent." Lottin, *PsychMorale* I, 534, likewise says: "Si l'on étudiait dans ses sources la psychologie du chancelier Philippe, on verrait de même sur le vif l'influence d'Avicenne sur le célèbre professeur de théologie."

Cf. also Callus, "Philip," p. 107: "The Chancellor's knowledge of Aristotle, whom he calls *summus philosophus*, was derived from Avicenna rather than from the works of Aristotle himself, though he quotes the *Physics*, the *De Generatione et Corruptione*, the *De Anima*, the *Metaphysics*, and the *Ethics* from the Graeco-Latin version and the *De Caelo et Mundo* and the *De Animalibus* from the Arabic-Latin translation." Pouillon, "Premier Traité," pp. 51-54, 59-60, indicates several areas of thought in which Avicenna influenced Philip.

2 Minges, "Philos. Bemerkungen," pp. 25-29, gives a detailed account of the use of the different books of Aristotle. E. Filthaut, *Roland von Cremona O.P. und die Anfänge der Scholastik im Predigerorden: Ein Beitrag zur Geistesgeschichte der älteren Dominikaner* (Vechta i. O. 1936) p. 61, counts 177 uses of Aristotle in the *Summa de Bono*. Often Philip does not name the author or work; among those named the *Ethics* predominates (32 citations), followed by the *Physics* (7 citations), the *De Anima* (5 citations), and the *Metaphysics* (4 citations). Cf. also the quotation from Callus in the preceding note and M. Grabmann, *Forschungen über die lateinischen Aristotelesübersetzungen des XIII. Jahrhunderts*, Beiträge 17/5-6 (Münster i. W. 1916) pp. 32-34.

3 Callus, "Philip the Chancellor," p. 107 (Algazel is also included). For Avicebron see Keeler, p. 22; for the *Liber de Causis* see Minges, p. 30, and Filthaut, *Roland*, p. 76; for Averroes see Minges, p. 30, and Filthaut, pp. 74-75 (n. 119), as well as Keeler, p. 65 (in two of these texts only the name "Commentator" is used).

theological.[4] St. Augustine, St. Hilary, Denis, Boethius, St. Gregory, St. John Damascene, St. Anselm, St. Bernard, and many other ecclesiastical writers constantly appear as authorities and, in some cases, secondarily as transmitters of a neo-Platonic current of philosophy. Particularly noteworthy are Philip's use of St. John Damascene and Denis, his numerous citations of the *Glossa* (of Peter Lombard), his frequent, precise references to Lombard's *Sentences*.

The growing philosophical maturity of theologians of the first part of the thirteenth century, already observable in Alexander of Hales, is set in sharp relief by Philip the Chancellor's *Summa de Bono* in its opening section, a series of twelve questions that has been hailed as "the first treatise on the transcendental properties."[5] Although William of Auxerre and Alexander of Hales had already dealt with the transcendental properties, their treatment was neither complete nor systematic. For his part Philip the Chancellor expressly undertakes a thorough, ordered study of the good and the true in their relationship to being and to each other; although he does not study unity so thoroughly as the good and the true, and although he neglects *res* and *aliquid*, his treatise marked a clear path that was to be followed and completed by his successors.[6] Since this treatise has already been

---

4 See the texts in Minges, p. 22, and in Pouillon, "Premier Traité," p. 42. Cf. also the following text from the *Summa de Bono*: "... Et quia patientia principaliter spectat ad theologum, magnanimitas magis ad moralem, dicendum est prius de patientia" (*P* 151vb; *T* 107va; *V* 113rb).

A clear distinction "de differentia inter theologum et moralem quantum ad praedictarum virtutum considerationem" is given on *P* 165vb, *T* 116va, and *V* 122rb; see the full text *infra*, p. 48.

For our method of referring to the *Summa de Bono* and the *Quaestiones* of Philip see *supra*, p. 13. Of the different MSS of the *Summa de Bono*, MS. Padua, Antonianum 156 (our *P*) is generally considered the best; cf. *infra*, p. 152, and n. 10 thereto.

5 Pouillon, "Premier Traité," esp. pp. 71-73. The *Summa Duacensis*, at least according to the plan that its editor, P. Glorieux, has drawn up from internal references, does not seem to have had a special tract on the transcendental properties in relation to *ens*, so that the missing parts (if there are such: cf. C. Vansteenkiste's review of Glorieux's edition, *Angelicum* 34 [1957] 331-334) seem unlikely to have provided a source for Philip.

Besides works already mentioned, the following may be consulted for various aspects of Philip's philosophical thought: Englhardt, *Glaubenspsychologie*, pp. 321-398 and passim; M. H. Vicaire, "Les porrétains et l'avicennisme avant 1215," *Revue des Sciences Philosophiques et Théologiques* 26 (1937) 475-482; Gillon, *Théorie des oppositions*, pp. 45-54; C. Fabro, "La distinzione tra 'quod est' e 'quo est' nella 'Summa de Anima' di Giovanni De La Rochelle," *Divus Thomas (Piacenza)* 41 (1938) 508-522 (John copies Philip on this subject); Lottin, *PsychMorale*, passim; J. Vande Wiele, "Le problème de la vérité ontologique dans la philosophie de saint Thomas," *Revue Philosophique de Louvain* 52 (1954) 535-540; Künzle, *Verhältnis*, pp. 108-110.

6 It was undoubtedly Philip's concern to combat the pessimism of the Albigensians that led him not only to organize his whole treatise around the concept of the good, but also to stress the transcendental property of good in relation to being and truth. Cf. Pouillon, "Premier Traité," pp. 42, 73-77.

thoroughly examined elsewhere,[7] we shall content ourselves with a few remarks on Philip's teaching concerning *ens*, and then move on to consider the related terms *esse* and *existere*. Then we shall consider his doctrine of essence and nature, his analysis of the compositions found in creatures, his concepts of substance, individual, hypostasis, and person.

2. Ens, Esse, and Existere

According to Philip, *ens*, along with the one, the true, and the good, is a most common notion; at times it is predicated commonly of all things, but at other times it is made proper to one subject, as we see from Scripture:

> Communissima autem haec sunt: ens, unum, verum, et bonum de quibus, quantum ad speculationem theologiae pertinet, disserendum est. Ens enim communiter modo dicitur de omnibus, modo appropriatur. Primo communiter dicitur, ut in Is.: *Qui ... vocat ea quae sunt tamquam ea quae non sunt*;[1] appropriatur, ut in Ex. 4: *Qui est misit me,* etc.;[2] *Ego sum qui sum,* etc.[3]

In one passage Philip distinguishes sharply between *ens* and *id quod est*; in another he says that *ens* includes *id quod est* along with *esse*. The first passage reads as follows: "Solutio: Ad primum dico quod alia est ratio entis et alia ejus quod est ...; et ens et id quod est ens non equivalent, quia cum dicitur 'id quod est,' tria secundum rationem designantur: id, et esse, et articulatio ..."[4] Of the three elements designated, the second, which is distinguished from *id*, is *esse*, so that it appears that in this text *ens* is really equivalent to *esse*;[5] hence the distinction made between *ens*

---

7 Especially by Pouillon, "Premier Traité," and also, with special reference to *verum*, by Vande Wiele, "Le problème de la vérité," pp. 535-540.

1 Cf. Rom 4, 17: *Qui ... vocat ea quae non sunt tamquam ea quae sunt.*

2 Ex 3, 14.

3 Ex 3, 14. Text from *P* 1ra-rb; *T* 1ra-rb; *V* 1rb. Cf. also the following passage: "... Cum ens potentiâ minime sit ens, quantum ad esse nihil addit [additur *T*] supra *ens communiter dicta*" (*P* 55rb; *T* 46va; *V* 48va: emphasis mine); cf. also the text ("Ad secundum") quoted *infra*, p. 31.

4 *P* 2ra; *T* 1vb; *V* 2ra.

5 This becomes clearer from the context, which is concerned with a discussion of two definitions of *verum*, viz., "Verum est clarificativum esse," and "Verum est id quod est." An objection argues: "Item, de alia quaeritur: 'Verum est clarificativum esse,' et 'Verum est id quod est.' Ergo id quod est est clarificativum esse. Ergo non est esse, cum nihil se ipsum clarificet" (*P* 1bv; *T* 1bv; *V* 2ra). The *esse* of the first definition becomes *ens* in Philip's reply ("Ad primum," just quoted in part), showing that the terms in some cases are identical, although in others they lack equal comprehension. On the definition of *verum* see Pouillon, "Premier Traité," pp. 58-59.

In another text, however, Philip agrees with the distinction of *ens* and *esse* in creatures, this time making *ens* equivalent to *id quod*; see the texts quoted *infra*, p. 35 ("Dicit") and p. 35 ("Quod autem").

and *id quod est* is in fact the familiar Boethian distinction of *esse* and *quod est*. Thus there is no real contradiction between this first text and the second, which includes within *ens* both *id quod est* and *esse* by saying:

> Respondeo: Dico quod verum simpliciter prius est intellectu quam bonum et hoc patet ex definitionibus: verum enim dicitur "habens indivisionem esse et ejus quod est." Non nominatur his quod non sit ex parte entis, scilicet ipsum esse et id quod est.[6]

When Philip discusses the opposition of good and evil, he states that their opposition differs from that between being and non-being; good and evil are opposed according to privation, being and non-being according to contradiction:

> Respondeo quod advertendum est quod malum relinquit possibile; unde non dicitur de unoquoque non-esse vel non-ente[7] indifferenter. Unde non est talis oppositio boni et mali qualis est entis et non-entis, sed haec secundum privationem, illa secundum contradictionem.[8]

Thus the most radical opposition is that between being and nonbeing.

The foregoing text leads us to the various divisions of being, among which Philip most frequently mentions the division into potential and actual being. A clear statement of this division occurs when he studies whether mortal sin is a species of the genus, sin. As a parallel case he introduces being, saying that it is divided into potential and actual being, and that since potential being is least in being, it adds nothing to common being (*ens communiter dictum*) in reality, but only in concept; similarly imperfect being adds nothing to being, whereas perfect being does. He then applies these analogies to mortal sin:

> ... Sicut cum dicitur ens dividitur in ens potentiâ et ens actu, cum ens potentiâ minime sit ens, quantum ad esse nihil addit supra ens communiter dictum, sed quantum ad rationem (sicut ens imperfectum nihil addit supra ens, sed potius ens perfectum), sic et posset dici quod mortale addit supra peccare quod egreditur ab eo per id quod magis notat et plus habet de malo quam peccare.[9]

---

6 *P* 2vb; *T* 2va; *V* 2vb. On the definition of *verum* given here see Pouillon, "Premier Traité," pp. 57, 60-62, and Vande Wiele, "Problèmes de la vérité," pp. 536-539.

7 *Om.* non-esse vel non-ente *PTV; mg. T1, V2.*

8 *P* 3vb; *T* 3rb-va; *V* 3va. The text is studied by Gillon, *Théorie des oppositions,* p. 48.

9 *P* 55rb-va; *T* 46va; *V* 48va. Cf. *P* 1va; *T* 1va; *V* 1vb: "Sic loquitur Philosophus de divisione entis cum dividit ens potentiâ, ens actu."

In describing the various ways in which one thing can come from something else, Philip states that potential being is at the source of some kinds of "coming from another": "Esse de divina essentia est primum esse ab alio; secundum vero est esse de nihilo; tertium vero de ente potentiâ in ens actu; quartum vero de ente actu, quodammodo ens potentiâ illud quod fit."[10]

Elsewhere an objection similar to one occurring in Alexander of Hales tries to prove that God did not create all things simultaneously or fully formed; it bases its proof on a twofold opposition, the first between nothingness and being in potency, the second between non-being in act (equivalent to being in potency) and being in act. Things, it argues, "primo factae sunt de nihilo in esse potentiâ aut in esse materialiter, demum de non-esse actu in esse actu ..."[11] In replying to the full argument Philip accepts these divisions (nothingness, potential being or actual non-being, actual being) and their twofold opposition; but, he argues, because a thing has potential being through its matter and actual being through its form, God's simultaneous creation of a thing's matter and of its form in the matter overcomes both oppositions at once: his creation of the matter overcomes the opposition between nothingness and potential being; his creation of its form in the matter overcomes the opposition between actual non-being (or potential being) and actual being:

> Ad sequens vero dicendum est quod licet prima oppositio sit inter ens potentiâ et non-ens potentiâ, non tamen secundum hanc solam exivit creatura in esse, immo secundum hanc, et hanc: esse in actu et non-esse in actu. Nam quia creavit materiam et formam simul in materia, quantum ad hoc quod creavit materiam, creavit secundum hanc oppositionem "esse potentiâ rem et non-esse potentiâ"; quantum autem ad hoc quod creavit formam in materia, creavit secundum hanc oppositionem "esse actu et non-esse actu." Nam per materiam est res in potentia, per formam est res in actu.[12]

10 *De Anima* [4(xxii)]; Keeler, p. 42.

11 *P* 17va; *T* 15va; *V* 16ra; the words quoted are introduced as follows; "Praeterea unus exitus est in esse de non-esse, alter vero de esse potentiâ in esse actu. Sed exitus de non-esse in esse potest intelligi duobus modis: vel in esse potentiâ et non in actu, vel in actu. Sed prima oppositio est inter non-esse materialiter sive in potentia et esse materialiter sive in potentia; secunda vero quantum ad esse actu et non-esse actu. Ergo res primo factae," etc. (*locis citatis*). For the similar argument in Alexander of Hales see his *Glossa* II, 12, 4d (p. 122), quoted in *HypUnion* II, 29.

12 *P* 17va-vb; *T* 15vb; *V* 16ra. The text concludes by asserting the universal creation of things by God from nothing; thus there was no pre-existing matter, which would be opposed to creation: "Et licet fiat forma in materia, a Deo tamen est creatio: non enim fit de materia prae-existenti, quod oppositum esset creationi, sed utrumque ex nihilo" (*P* 17vb; *T* 15vb; *V* 16ra).

That is, God's creation of matter raises a thing from nothingness to the state of potential being; his creation of its form and his uniting of the form to the matter makes the thing to be actually. And all this happens simultaneously. Besides this text's clear statement of the divisions of potential and actual being, it also indicates, by interchanging them, the same equivalence of the terms *ens* and *esse* that has already appeared in a text quoted previously.[13]

The reference to creation in the foregoing text recalls another division of being mentioned by Philip, that into *ens creatum* and *ens increatum*.[14] In connection with this we find that Philip frequently designates God as *Primum Ens* or *Summe Ens*,[15] designations that indicate an order of priority and posteriority in being. Thus Philip agrees with these words of an objection:

> ... "Ens" dicitur diversis modis secundum prius et posterius de ente impermutabili, ut est Primum Ens, et ente permutabili, ut est creatura ... Sic dicitur: "Hoc est vere ens," demonstrato vere ente impermutabili, et "Illud non est vere ens," demonstrato ente permutabili ...[16]

Within created being itself, Philip declares, there is an order of priority either according to dignity, as when a thing is an end for a less important being, or according to composition, as when a thing is an element out of which something is made, or a foundation for something superimposed on it, or a place for something located in it:

> ... Dicendum est quod duplex est ordo: est enim ordo secundum dignitatem vel nobilitatem, et secundum hunc modum posteriora sunt quae facta sunt propter aliquam quam ea propter quae facta sunt, et in hac ordine dignior est homo omni creatura sensibili ... Est autem alius ordo secundum viam compositionis, in qua principium est prius eo quod fit ex illo, et fundamentum eo quod superadditur, et locus locato, et per hunc modum, licet omnia sint simul facta, tamen secundum prius et posterius sunt entia ...[17]

---

13 *Supra*, p. 27. For other clear texts on potency and act see *infra*, pp. 53-55, and also *infra*, n. 22; p. 82.

14 E.g., in *P* 114rb; *T* 89ra; *V* 94rb: "Item, diligitur ens bonum increatum, scilicet Deus, ens creatum, ut beatitudo, virtutes, proximus [proximi *T*]."

15 E.g., for *Primum Ens*: *P* 3vb *mg.*, *T* 3vb, *V* 4ra (quoted *infra*, p. 33: "Ad hoc"); also *P* 3ra, *T* 2vb, *V* 3ra; *P* 4rb, *T* 4ra, *V* 4rb; *P* 12vb, *T* 11ra, *V* 11va. For *Summe Ens* see *P* 4rb, *T* 4ra, *V* 4rb.

16 *P* 124vb; *T* 95rb; *V* 101vb. The objection tries to draw a parallel between *ens* and charity. Philip rejects the parallel, but implies his acceptance of the statement about *ens*: "Ad aliud respondeo quod non est simile de ente et de caritate nisi quis loquitur de caritate increata et creata ut de ente increato et creato, sed de hoc modo non agitur" (*P* 125ra; *T* 95va; *V* 101ra).

17 *P* 18ra; *T* 16ra; *V* 16va.

The order of priority and posteriority reappears in another basic division of being mentioned by Philip, that according to substance and accidents or according to the predicaments. *Ens*, he says, is predicated *secundum prius* of substance and *secundum posterius* of the accident that exists through the substance and is therefore indirectly understood in it:

> Bonum enim de Deo dicitur quia finis, bonum de creatura quia ad finem ordinationem habet, sicut ens secundum prius dicitur de substantia quae est per se ens, secundum posterius de accidente quod est per sub-stantiam et ita indirecte intelligitur in illo.[18]

Again, *ens* is said in common, but according to an order of priority and posteriority, of substance, quantity, and quality: "Ad secundum respondeo quod bonum non dicitur aequivoce, sed multipliciter secundum prius et posterius de bono naturae et bono moris vel gratiae, et ita de aliis, et ideo communiter sicut ens de substantia et quantitate et qualitate."[19]

In another discussion an objection argues that *bonum* should, like *ens*, be multiplied according to the predicaments of substance, quantity, and the rest.[20] In his reply Philip rejects the parallelism of the argument, but at the same time shows that for him *ens* is formally multiplied according to the ten predicaments or categories. He first distinguishes between material and formal multiplication. The good, the one, and the true are multiplied materially according to the multiplication of *ens*, but this is not a formal multiplication in their case. This is most clear in the one and the true, which are multiplied (formally) only according to four modes:

> Respondeo: Est multiplicatio materialis et formalis. Secundum multiplicationem materialem multiplicat bonum sicut et ens, sed non secundum multiplicationem formalem, et hoc manifestum in uno et vero similiter, quia etsi multiplicantur materialiter, non tamen secundum eas differentias secundum quas multiplicatur ens formaliter multiplicantur unum et verum, immo multiplicantur tantum secundum quattuor modos ...[21]

18 *P* 3va; *T* 3rb; *V* 3va.

19 *P* 3ra; *T* 2vb; *V* 3ra.

20 "Cum igitur bonum sequatur ens, ergo videtur quod in quot multiplicetur ens tamquam in species, in tot multiplicetur bonum tamquam in species: multiplicari enim est 'multotiens plicari.' Sed ens multiplicatur secundum praedicamenta: aliter enim de substantia dicitur, aliter de quan-titate, et ita de aliis. Ergo et bonum" (*P* 4va; *T* 4rb; *V* 4va).

21 *P* 4va; *T* 4rb; *V* 4va.

After detailing the four modes of formal multiplication of the one, Philip concludes that it is multiplied not formally, but only materially according to ten modes:

> ... Unum enim dicitur secundum substantiam, scilicet idem, secundum quantitatem aequale, secundum qualitatem simile, secundum situm[22] et ubi dicitur simul, et ita non secundum decem multiplicatur formaliter; tamen materialem habet multiplicationem secundum decem.[23]

It is in this last statement that he states indirectly that *ens* is formally multiplied according to the ten modes or categories of being: the one is not multiplied formally as *ens* is, he has said previously, and here he concludes that the one is not multiplied formally according to the ten modes; again, he has said that the one is multiplied materially according to the divisions of *ens*, and here he concludes that it is multiplied materially according to the ten modes.

A final division of *ens* that may be noted here is that into simple and composite being: "... Omne ens aut simplex est aut compositum, et anima non est ens[24] simplex, quia tunc idem esset in anima quod est et quo est ..."[25] We shall see more of this division later.[26]

"Esse"

As in the other authors studied here, so in Philip the term *esse* most readily appears when he writes about the different aspects of being. Although the particular meaning he intends to give the term is not everywhere clear, the same three general usages of *esse* appear in his work as did in the *Glossa* of Alexander of Hales.[27] Philip knew and used this *Glossa*, but he does not seem to have copied some of its clearest passages concerning *esse*; hence we must study other texts in Philip to see his doctrine.

The three general uses of *esse* found in the *Summa de Bono* are, then, *esse* as being in general, *esse* as essence or form in the Boethian sense (or as *quo est* according to later terminology), and *esse* as existence, particularly the existence caused in creatures by God (often called the "First," under Avicennian influence). Quotations of texts could be

22 statum *TV*.
23 *P* 4va; *T* 4rb; *V* 4ra.
24 *Om. Keeler;* ens is given here in *P* 23vb, *T* 21ra, and *V* 21va.
25 Philip, *De Anima* [1(i)]; Keeler, p. 21.
26 See *infra*, pp. 34-40.
27 Cf. *HypUnion* II, 30-32.

multiplied to illustrate these different uses of the term; the ones that follow are selected as those most clearly indicative of one or the other of these three general meanings.

The use of *esse* to refer to being in general is most evident where Philip interchanges the terms *esse* and *ens* without differentiating their meaning. Besides passages already seen where this occurs,[28] Philip replaces *ens* with *esse* in the following passage concerned with "reflex predication," that is, in expressions like "Bonitas est bona":

> Respondeo: Aliter est in primis et in eis quae sunt sub primis: non enim dicitur justitia justa, prudentia prudens, sed dicitur bonitas bona, et hoc est quia *ens* et unum et verum et bonum sunt prima. Nam ipsum *esse* est, et veritas est verum, et unitas est unum.[29]

Again, when an objection says: "Sed quaeritur: Quoniam ipsa habitudo est *ens*, ergo est in specie, modo, et ordine,"[30] Philip replies: "Respondeo quod habitudo non dicit novum *esse* ..."[31]

In several other texts the transcendental properties are similarly linked with *esse* rather than with *ens*, which shows that the terms are synonyms. Thus when Philip associates the efficient, formal, and final causes with the one, the true, and the good respectively, he speaks of being mainly in terms of *esse*, saying twice that unity, truth, and goodness are conditions accompanying *esse*:

> Ad hoc dicendum est quod sunt tres conditiones concomitantes *esse*: unitas, veritas, et bonitas. Unitas autem est prima illarum, secunda veritas, tertia bonitas. In idem enim possunt concidere efficiens, formalis, et finalis, sed materialis non. Unde unaquaeque essentia habens has tres rationes causarum tres habet conditiones quae concomitantur *esse* ejus secundum quod est a Primo Ente, ut a Primo Ente secundum rationem unius efficiatur unumquodque ens unum; ab ipso secundum quod est causa formalis exemplaris, verum; secundum quod est finalis, bonum...[32]

In another passage he says that the one, the true, and the good together divide *esse*, which is prior to them: "... Modus praeponitur in

---

28 See *supra*, p. 27 ("Solutio: Ad primum"); p. 28 ("Sicut cum dicitur"); p. 29 ("Ad sequens").
29 *P* 4va; *T* 4rb; *V* 4va; Emphasis mine.
30 *P* 50vb; *T* 42vb; *V* 44va. Emphasis mine.
31 *P* 50vb; *T* 42vb; *V* 44ra. Emphasis mine.
32 *P* 3vb *mg.*; *T* 3vb; *V* 4ra. Emphasis mine. Cf. this similar text: "Respondeo: Esse [essentia *TV*] sive esse unum ordinatur ante esse verum, et esse verum ante esse bonum: esse enim unum cum Deo est secundum causam efficientem, esse verum secundum causam formalem, esse bonum secundum finalem, et non valet: 'Unumquodque sicut se habet ad esse, ita ad verum,' etc., quia licet species se habeat ad esse verum, non tamen ad esse vel ad esse unum quia prius est et differens ratione" (*P* 51ra; *T* 43ra; *V* 44vb).

ordine, quemadmodum et *esse*, inter sua condividentia praeponitur quae
sunt unum, verum, et bonum."[33]

That the term *esse* signifies general being is also evident when Philip
qualifies it in various ways; although, with the qualification, being of a
particular kind is signified, in these compound phrases the term *esse* itself stands for being in general. For example, Philip says: "Nunc enim
loquimur communiter, ut esse divinum ... et rationale et naturale et
morale comprehendamus."[34] The combination, *esse* and *bene esse*, occurs
frequently.[35] Again, *esse* is qualified as generic, specific, and individual.[36]
Elsewhere Philip speaks of a threefold division of *esse* in terms that partly
match the fundamental distinction made by Alexander of Hales: "Et
nota quod distinguendum est triplex esse: esse naturale, esse morale,
esse gratuitum."[37] With reference to the angels, Philip speaks of their
esse exemplare and *esse spirituale*.[38] Finally, some connotation of essence is
already added to the notion of being in general when Philip speaks of
the *esse virtutis*,[39] the *esse caritatis*,[40] the *esse miraculorum*,[41] or the *esse
latriae*.[42]

Philip's second general use of the term *esse*, according to which it is
equivalent to the essence or *quo est* and is composed with the subject or
quod est, shows the persisting influence of Boethius' essentialist thought
in Philip's own analysis of the metaphysical structure of the individual.
In the *Summa de Bono* the *quod est-esse* couplet occurs frequently, and
since at times it is referred explicitly to Boethius, it seems that Philip in-

---

33 *P* 51ra; *T* 42vb; *V* 44vb. Emphasis mine. In another passage, when comparing unity and eternity, he says: "Unitas enim est dispositio quae convertitur cum esse, aeternitas vero in minus est
quam esse secundum ambitum, eo quod non quicquid est, aeternum est, sed quicquid est, unum
est" (*P* 7vb; *T* 7ra; *V* 7rb).

34 morale comprehendamus] mortale comprehendamus *PT; P* 2ra; *T* 2ra; *V* 2ra.

35 E.g., in *P* 5ra; *T* 4vb; *V* 5ra: "Respondeo quod modus, species [*om. P*], et ordo pertinent ad
esse, ut dictum est, quandoque ad bene esse." Cf. also *P* 50vb, *T* 42vb, *V* 44vb; *P* 14ra, *T* 12ra, *V*
12va; *P* 29ra, *T* 25rb, *V* 25vb.

36 *P* 16va; *T* 14vb; *V* 15ra-rb: "Item, res prodierunt in esse secundum esse generale et speciale
et individuum." This division, it is true, occurs in an objection, but Philip does not reject this aspect
of the objection in his reply.

37 *P* 168va; *T* 118rb; *V* 124rb. He refers back to this division again on *P* 169vb, *T* 119ra,
V 125rb. For Alexander's division see *HypUnion* II, 31. *Esse gratiae* is used by itself on, for example, *P*
56rb, *T* 47rb, *V* 49rb; *P* 88ra, *T* 71rb, *V* 75vb.

38 *P* 38rb; *T* 32vb; *V* 33va (text *infra*, p. 79, n. 12).

39 *P* 85va (*bis*), *T* 69va (*bis*), *V* 74va (*bis*); *P* 135 rb (*bis*), *T* 97vb (*bis*), *V* 104ra; *P* 151va, *T* 107va (ap-
proximately: foll. 107va-108rb are missing from the microfilm copy of *T* at my disposal), *V* 113rb.

40 *P* 113vb; *T* 88vb; *V* 94ra.

41 *P* 75vb; *T* 62va; *V* 66rb.

42 *P* 179ra; *T* 126va; *V* 133rb.

terprets it in the Boethian manner. One such reference occurs in a discussion whether one can say "Bonitas est bona" with reference to a creature. An objection argues that such "reflex predication" may not be used of creatures because, as Boethius teaches, it is not validly used of those in whom *id quod est* and *esse* differ: "Dicit Boethius in libro *De Hebdomadibus* quod in quibus id quod est et esse differunt, non est reflexa praedicatio.[43] Sed in creaturis ens et esse differunt. Ergo in illis non est reflexa praedicatio."[44] Philip accepts the principle of the argument, and with it the Boethian interpretation of *quod est* and *esse*; but he rejects the conclusion by introducing a distinction in kinds of simplicity. There is the simplicity of the divine essence, in which *quod est* and *esse* are identical, and the simplicity of first intentions such as *bonitas*, which cannot be resolved into any simpler concepts; the latter simplicity, he indicates, suffices for reflex predication concerning such terms:

> Quod autem dicit Boethius hujusmodi praedicationem esse in solis sim-
> plicibus, respondeo quod simplex dicitur duobus modis: vel sicut divina
> essentia est simplex, scilicet quia[45] idem est esse et quod est; vel sicut
> primae intentiones simplices, et in his et in illis per hunc modum est
> dicere.[46] Primae intentiones simplices dicuntur quia non est ante ipsas in
> quae[47] fiat resolutio.[48]

The Boethian metaphysics is often invoked by Philip when he explains his preferred definition of truth, *Verum est indivisio esse et ejus quod est*, which contains the *quod est-esse* couplet. We have already seen a text in which, speaking of this definition, he implies that *ens* is coterminous with *id quod est* and *esse*: "Non nominatur hic quod non sit ex parte entis, scilicet ipsum esse et id quod est."[49] Elsewhere an objector tries to find a fallacy in the definition by arguing that it involves an infinite series.[50] Philip replies that this does not follow because in God there is no distinction of *esse* and *quod est*: "Respondeo quod non sequitur 'Ideo quod esse habeat esse, et ita in infinitum,' quia in Primis non est

43 Cf. Boethius, *DeHebdom*; Rand, p. 48, ll. 128-140.

44 *P* 4va; *T* 4rb; *V* 4rb-va.

45 quod *P*.

46 debet est *T; add.* quod *T*.

47 qua *TV*.

48 *P* 4va; *T* 4rb; *V* 4va.

49 *Supra*, p. 28 ("Respondeo").

50 *P* 2rb ; *T* 2ra; *V* 2rb: "Item, esse est. Sed quicquid est, est verum. Ergo esse est verum. Sed verum est indivisio esse et ejus quod est; ergo esse, etc."

dividere inter esse et quod est."[51] When the objector insists that Philip's reply makes the *esse* of the definition of truth as simple as God, Philip, in a reply reminiscent of Alexander of Hales, declares that outside of God *esse*, although not itself composed of two elements, lacks perfect simplicity because it is composed with *quod est*:

> Sed contra: Ergo esse est aeque simplex Primo. Respondeo: Primum dicitur simplex eo quod privat omnem compositionem, quia non est ex hoc et hoc; item, quia non est positum cum hoc. Sed esse, licet non sit ex hoc et hoc, tamen est compositum, id est, cum alio positum: quod non Primum, cum sit abstractum.[52]

In another text Philip explicitly states that this definition is to be understood in terms of Boethius' metaphysics of being. He then applies it to God and to creatures: God is the supreme truth, that is, the "indivision of act and potency in reality and in thought," in that his *esse* and *id quod est* are identical; in creatures truth is concerned with a composition because in them *esse* and *quod est* are different:

> Illa autem definitio: "Veritas est indivisio esse et ejus quod est," explicatur per hoc quod dicitur[53] a Boethio in libro *De Hebdomadibus: Omni simplici idem est esse et quod est; omni vero composito aliud est esse et quod est,*[54] et intelligatur alietas rationis, ut homo "animal rationale." Sic ergo summa veritas est indivisio actus[55] et potentia re et ratione, unde dicitur in ea: "Esse est id quod est." Unde Hilarius: *Esse non est accidens in Deo, sed subsistens veritas.*[56] In aliis vero, in quibus esse et quod est differunt, est veritas circa compositionem.[57]

A passage from Peter Lombard's *Sentences* regarding the attributes of angels gives Philip, as it did Alexander of Hales, the occasion to comment on the meaning of *quod est* and *esse;*[58] in this commentary Philip's

51 *Locis citatis.* In this text the word *ideo* is probably a scribal error for *in Deo; P, T,* and *V,* however, read *ideo.*

52 *P* 2rb; *T* 2ra-rb; *V* 2rb.

53 *Om.* quod dicitur *P.*

54 Boethius, *DeHebdom;* Rand, p. 42, ll. 45-48.

55 actu *P.*

56 *De Trinitate* VII, 11; PL 10, 208B: "Esse enim non est accidens nomen, sed subsistens veritas ..."

57 *P* 2ra; *T* 1vb-2ra; *V* 2ra. The text goes on to show that in created things truth varies according to the type of composition involved: "In quibusdam est re separare, ut ubi utrumque per se subsistat vel alterum sine altero, ut lux est aer, vel actio est id quod passio in physico motu: agendo enim patitur; in quibusdam ratione, ut in definitione et definito; in quibusdam potentia, ut in omnibus contingentibus quae sunt possibilia ad finem. Propter hoc, cum idem sit quod est et esse in Deo, maxime ibi est indivisio et maxime veritas, sicut maxima bonitas, quia indivisio potentiae et finis" (*P* 2ra; *T* 2ra; *V* 2ra).

58 For Alexander see his *Glossa* II, 3, 3; p. 25. Cf. *HypUnion* II, 35.

essentialist interpretation of *esse* stands forth. The four attributes listed by the Lombard are *essentia simplex, discretio personalis, ratio naturaliter insita*, and *liberum arbitrium*.[59] Philip, investigating the number and order of these attributes, begins by asserting that the first two refer to the angelic substance, the other two to the angelic power. The angel, he adds, was created perfect in both substance and power, as befits a spiritual creature:

> Jam dictum est de substantia et in parte de numero, sed propter quid quattuor sunt, et quo ordine se debeant habere, quaestio est. Hujus autem solutio est quod duo referuntur ad substantiam angelicae creaturae, alia vero pertinent ad posse ejus. Creata fuit perfecta in substantia et perfecta[60] in potentia, sicut spirituali creaturae competebat.[61]

The angel, Philip continues, is, like all creatures, distinct from God because in angelic being *esse* and *quod est* differ. Angelic *esse* refers to the first of the four attributes listed by Lombard, *essentia simplex*, or, as Philip describes it, "to be simply and to be immaterial according to a comparison to the First"; angelic *quod est* refers to the second attribute, *discretio personalis*. Of these two attributes pertaining to angelic substance (as opposed to angelic power), *esse* is first in order, *quod est* second: the former, he implies, has an affinity with the divine substance; the latter, he states expressly, is like the divine person:

> Quia vero creatura omnis in hoc differt a prima essentia quod in ea differt esse et quod est, ex parte esse sumitur esse simpliciter et immateriale secundum comparationem ad Primum, ex parte vero ejus quod est sumitur personalis distinctio, cum sit rationalis creatura: quod enim in aliis creaturis est individualis distinctio, hoc in rationabilibus est personalis distinctio ... Ex quo potest patere ordo, ut primum sit quod ad substantiam pertinet, demum quod ad potentiam. Cum vero quod ad substantiam pertinet quantum ad esse sit primum, quod vero pertinet ad id quod est, in quo habet similitudinem cum persona divina, secundum.[62]

From these two quotations we can see that for Philip, as for Alexander of Hales, *esse* and *quod est* are the two principles of a spiritual substance. *Esse* is to be interpreted with reference to the substance considered in its simplicity and immateriality, *quod est* with reference to the substance as a subject or, in a rational creature, a person. Although the

59 *Sent* II, 3, 1; Quaracchi³, 341.
60 imperfecta T.
61 *P* 10vb; *T* 9rb; *V* 9vb.
62 *P* 10vb; *T* 9rb-va; *V* 9vb.

statement about *esse* refers this term to essence less explicitly than Alexander of Hales' text did,[63] Philip's association of *esse* with angelic substance and the simplicity of angelic being indicates that in this context he interprets *esse* of essence rather than of existence.

That the *quod est-esse* couplet, or its equivalent, *quod est-quo est*, is to be understood in terms of the Boethian metaphysics of subject and form rather than in terms of essence and existence is especially evident from a remarkable passage of the *Summa de Bono* that has already been edited and studied elsewhere.[64] This passage deals with the simplicity of angelic substance. In investigating the problem Philip rejects any kind of matter in angels and therefore any kind of hylomorphic composition in them;[65] he discerns in their being a more fundamental composition, that of *quod est* and *quo est*, which he relates to the metaphysical order by express contrast with the composition pertaining to the natural or physical order, that is, the composition of matter and form:

> Item materia dicitur substantia; forma dicitur substantia; quod est dicitur substantia; et quo est dicitur substantia. Secundum hoc, diuerse sunt compositiones: una que est ex materia et forma, cuius consideratio pertinet ad naturalem; alia que est eius quod est ad id quo est, et hec non ad naturalem, sed ad metaphisicum; et huiusmodi est in intelligentiis.[66]

In the next paragraph Philip sees in man a twofold relationship of *quod est* and *quo est*: one, body and soul, is on the natural level; the other, man and humanity, is on the metaphysical level. On this latter level *homo* is identical with *quod est* and humanitas with *quo est*:

> Et attende quod inuenitur in quibusdam duplex id quod est siue duplex subiectum et duplex quo est. Verbi gratia in omnibus in quibus fit coniunctio corporee et incorporee substantie, ut corporis et spiritus, uerbi gratia in homine, anima quidem perficit corpus et est id quo est; corpus

---

63 Cf. Alexander of Hales, *Glossa* II, 3, 2; p. 25. Cf. *HypUnion* II, 35.

64 By Lottin, *PsychMorale* I, 432-438. A difference of opinion about the meaning of *quod est* and *quo est* in John of La Rochelle enters the picture here because John copies the passage in question almost *verbatim* from Philip the Chancellor. C. Fabro, "La distinzione tra 'quod est' e 'quo est' nella 'Summa de Anima' di Giovanni De La Rochelle," *Divus Thomas (Piacenza)* 41 (1938) 508-522, shows against G. Manser and O. Lottin's earlier position that *quod est* and *quo est* in John of la Rochelle (and therefore in his source, Philip) reproduce the usual Boethian doctrine rather than introduce the real distinction of essence and existence as this is understood by Thomists. Lottin, *PsychMorale* I, 443 and n. 2, accepts and follows Fabro's interpretation, saying that it applies equally to Philip.
Pouillon, "Premier Traité," pp. 61-62, likewise interprets the *quod est-esse* couplet according to the Boethian metaphysics; so, too, does J. Vande Wiele, "Le problème de la vérité," [*cit. supra*, sec. 1, n. 5], p. 536.

65 See text and commentary in Lottin, *PsychMorale* I, 435, 437.

66 Lottin, *ibid.* I, 436. In *P* 9vb; *T* 8vb; *V* 9ra.

perficitur et est id quod est; item humanitas perficit hominem et est id quo est homo id quod est. Unde ad duplicem pertinet considerationem; ex parte enim corporis magis se tenet ex parte materie, et pertinet ad con- siderationem naturalem; secundum perfectionem autem que est humanitas, magis se tenet ex parte forme, et pertinet ad considerationem metaphysici.[67]

By identifying *homo* with *quod est* and *humanitas* with *quo est*, and by placing this composition on the highest level of being, the metaphysical, Philip reveals that he has retained the basic pattern of Boethian thought. Although he does not mention *esse* in these paragraphs, he ap- pears to have substituted for it, as was commonly done, the term *quo est*; that this is so is shown when, at the end of the following paragraph in which he explores the multiple relationships of subject and matter, he says that matter and subject differ in that "de materia nunquam dicitur forma, sed de subiecto dicitur forma uel *esse*."[68]

Perhaps the most evident linking of *esse* with *essentia* occurs in a passage that can be best understood in the light of the previous ones. An objector argues that the good has priority of nature over the true because the good is related to the final cause, and the final cause is the cause of all causes, including the formal cause from which the true is taken: "Item, bonum sumitur a causa causarum, scilicet a finali, verum autem sumitur ab aliqua causa, ut a formali per quam est esse. Sed finalis prior est naturâ. Ergo bonum prius quam verum."[69] In his reply Philip distinguishes the *esse* that comes after the union of the form to matter from the *esse* "that is through the mode of *essentia*." If, he begins, the true were taken from this first type of form, which is ordained to an end and is the term of natural generation, the good, if taken from the final cause (the end), would indeed be prior to the true, as the objector argues:

> Ad sequens dico quod aliud est esse, aliud forma. Forma est ut anima in homine, esse quod consequitur post conjunctionem formae ad materiam, ut animae ad corpus. Et verum est quidem quod in fieri rem finalis causa habet ordinationem ad formalem ut prior intellectu, et si sumitur verum a forma hujusmodi et bonum a finali, a priori sumeretur bonum[70] quam verum.[71]

67 Lottin, *loc. cit.* In *P* 9vb; *T* 8vb; *V* 9ra. Cf. the text quoted *infra*, n. 73; p. 40.

68 Lottin, *loc. cit.,* In *P* 10ra; *T* 8vb; *V* 9ra-rb. Emphasis mine.

69 *P* 2vb; *T* 2va; *V* 2vb.

70 verum *P.*

71 bonum *P. P* 2vb; *T* 2va-vb; *V* 2vb. Another example is found in a text quoted *infra*, p. 53, in which *esse formale* is equivalent to the fact that grace is grace.

But, he continues, the true is not taken from the form, but from the *esse* that is through the mode of essence, and so it has no order to the final cause nor is it the terminus of a thing's generation, as is evident in non-material things. To make his meaning abundantly clear, Philip repeats what he has said: a form caused by the end is ordered to the end, is the terminus of the thing, is posterior to the final cause; but the true is not taken from this form, but from the essence, and this has no order to the final cause:

> Sed verum non a forma sumitur, sed ab esse quod est per modum essentiae, et sic non habet ordinationem ad finalem, nec est terminus fieri, ut patet in non-materialibus. Secundum quod forma causatur a fine, ordinationem habet ad illam ut posterior ad suam causam: haec est forma quae est terminus fieri. Et non sumitur verum ab ea, sed sumitur verum ab essentia, et hoc nullam ordinationem habet ad causam finalem.[72]

In the light of the previous passages distinguishing the levels of natural or physical consideration from the level of metaphysical consideration, we can see that Philip here is distinguishing an *esse* of the natural or physical order from an *esse* of the metaphysical order. The former is attained at the end of a process of generation, for example, when the soul is united to the body in man so that he then begins to be in his natural, physical existence; the latter is of the order of essence. This text thus confirms our interpretation of the *quod est-quo est* and *quod est-esse* couplets, and at the same time introduces, with its teaching about physical *esse*, the third general use of *esse* found in Philip, that according to which *esse* signifies existence. This is an existence, we already see from the present text, that is thought of by the Chancellor as something of the concrete, natural, physical order as distinct from and even in opposition to the essential *esse* of the metaphysical order.[73]

---

72 *P* 2vb; *T* 2vb; *V* 2vb.

73 The same distinction of *esse* on the natural level from *esse* on the metaphysical level is implicit in Philip's reply to an objection arguing as follows: The definition of the true means nothing other than the joining of form to matter, and this joining "facit esse; ergo idem est ac si dicat verum est ens" (*P* 1vb; *T* 1vb; *V* 2ra).

Philip's reply is as follows: "Ad tertium dicimus quod non est idem esse quod forma, et quod est non idem quod materia, quia materia non dicitur de forma nec e converso, sed esse dicitur de eo quod est, ut alibi. Sed in naturis dicitur esse forma: unde veritas secundum philosophiam naturalem est indivisio formae a materia. Nunc enim loquimur communiter, ut esse divinum, quod est sine materia, et rationale et naturale et morale, comprehendamus. Unde dicere quod 'verum est indivisio esse et ejus quod est' non est dicere 'verum est habens conjunctionem formae cum materia' quia alicubi est esse ubi non est conjunctio" (*P* 2ra; *T* 2ra; *V* 2ra). Cf. also the text *infra*, p. 46 ("Et sicut"), in which Philip says that the object of "divine philosophy" (metaphysics) is the essence, and that of natural philosophy is the operation.

Philip the Chancellor constantly uses the term *esse* when he speaks of the contingent beings that come from non-being to being or that have a possibility of returning to non-being. Keeping in mind the influence of Avicenna and Alexander of Hales on Philip, and judging from the tenor of the texts, one has the impression that in these cases *esse* refers to the existence of these contingent beings.

For example, in discussing the kind of truth involved in certain expressions, Philip says that the statements "Antichrist does not exist" or "Antichrist will be" are true with a real truth (*veritas rei* as opposed to *veritas signi* or *veritas prima*) because Antichrist has an ordination towards *being* according to matter and a possibility to *be* in nature; but that he is actually in the world is not a real truth: "... Hoc enim: 'Antichristum non esse vel fore' verum est a veritate rei, cum habeat[74] ordinationem ad esse secundum materiam et possibilitatem ad esse in natura; ut sit actu in mundo non est veritas rei."[75] This text means that in really-existing matter there is potency for a generation whereby Antichrist will come into being; also, his existence in the world of natures is possible. Since his existence is only possible, his being actually (*ut sit actu*) is not really true at this moment. The coupling of possibility with being, the reference to being actually, the time-element: all these seem to indicate, in the terms *esse* and *sit*, the notion of existence.

We have already seen a text in which Philip speaks of the opposition between *esse in actu* and *non-esse in actu*;[76] the same distinction occurs in a passage in which Philip explains the different ways by which multiple beings go forth from God, who is one. The first mode of going-forth, he says, is the generation of the Son from the Father: this produces no opposition or disparity. The second is creation: this produces a multitude from the one, the possible from the necessary, the composite of *quod est* and *quo est* from the simple. Whence arise these imperfections in the creature? Not from God, the principle of creation, but from the non-being out of which the creature was drawn. Hence, Philip concludes, being and non-being are mixed in a creature: it has actual being and potential non-being; hence it can be changed into non-being:

> Ad secundum dicimus quod est primus egressus, scilicet secundum generationem, qui nullam habet oppositionem vel disparitatem, secundum quod Filius a Patre est; secundus per creationem, et secundum hoc ab uno

74 habet *T*.
75 *P* 2va; *T* 2rb; *V* 2va.
76 *Supra*, p. 29 ("immo").

multum, a necessario possibile, a simplici compositum, quia non idem est id quo est et id quod est, et hoc non est ex parte principii a quo sed de quo, scilicet quia de non-esse. Unde esse et non-esse miscentur: esse actu, non-esse potentiâ; quare vertibile[77] in non-esse.[78]

In such texts, in which *esse* and *non-esse* are opposed and the potency-act relationship is introduced with reference to being, the term *esse* seems to refer to the existence or non-existence of the thing in question. The same is true of other texts that speak of *esse* coming after *non-esse*, as when Philip, perhaps in dependence on Avicenna and his notion of a possible, says: "Omne enim quod exit de non esse in esse est possibile, et ... vertibile est,"[79] or again: "... In quantum habent esse post non esse, sic sunt corruptibiles animae et intelligentiae; alio autem modo non."[80]

In assigning the reason for a creature's freedom to do both good and evil, Philip begins by locating in the creature's *exitus* from *non-esse* to *esse* the fitting source of both its likeness (in *esse*) to the Supreme Being from whom it flowed and of its unlikeness to him in that it was drawn from nothing. Thus he says:

> ... Duplicem est assignare rationem illius libertatis quae est faciendi bonum et malum: nam ex parte finis et ex parte subjecti secundum exitum in esse: cum enim exitus sit creaturae hujusmodi de non-esse in esse a Summo Ente, conveniebat ut similitudinem haberet cum ipso a quo fluxit aliquam, et dissimilitudinem quantum ad hoc quod ex non-esse ...[81]

Here again the passage from *non-esse* to *esse* appears to be a passage from non-existence to the state of actual existence.

As has been said with respect to the authors previously studied here, if *esse* sometimes refers to existence, this does not mean that the authors who so use it are speaking of a real composition of essence and existence within the created being; they are simply contrasting the non-existence of a creature with its contingent existence. As seems most evident from the texts of Philip quoted above,[82] they think of existence as a fact of the natural, physical order rather than as a metaphysical principle of the being of a thing.

---

77 convertibile *TV*.

78 *P* 6rb; *T* 5vb; *V* 6ra.

79 *De Anima* [8(xxvi)]; Keeler, p. 62.

80 *Ibid.*; Keeler, p. 72.

81 *P* 29va; *T* 25va; *V* 25vb.

82 See *supra*, pp. 39-40.

"Existere"

The terms *existere* and *existentia*, which occur much more frequently in Philip the Chancellor than in William of Auxerre or Alexander of Hales, appear to have this same meaning of physical existence; they seem, in other words, to express simply the common-sense notion of existence. The technical meaning of *sistere ex alio*, found in Richard of Saint-Victor and in others dependent upon him,[83] does not appear in Philip's writings. A good example of Philip's use of the terms *existere* and *existentia* occurs when Philip, speaking of the union of body and soul, shows how these two opposites can "have coexistence." Although two opposites, he says, cannot be in the same thing and still less in each other as informing principles, nevertheless, if one is simple and the other composite, nothing prevents their having coexistence, because then they are not opposed qualities. This is so with the soul and body: as a substance, the soul has coexistence with the body; hence, like the body and more truly than the body, the soul exists. And since it can exist through itself, it is not united to the body as if it needed the body to be supported in being:

> ... Quia duo opposita non sunt in eodem, multo magis nec oppositum in opposito, per modum informationis. Sed duo opposita nihil impedit habere coexistentiam, quorum unum sit simplex, alterum compositum, quia non sunt opposita sicut oppositae qualitates. Secundum ergo quod anima est substantia habet coexistentiam; quare quemadmodum corpus, immo etiam verius, existit, nec applicatur corpori ut per ipsum fulciatur in esse, cum per se possit existere.[84]

Elsewhere Philip rejects the possibility of God's making the soul or any spiritual substance of any pre-existing matter: "de aliqua materia praeexistenti."[85]

Most frequently, however, Philip uses the term *existere* to designate not simply existence, but existence somewhere or in some state. Thus he says that the soul "non potest videre Trinitatem, ut est existens in corpore corruptibili";[86] again, that "... omne quod intelligitur ut

83 Cf. *HypUnion* I, 30, 179, and II, 41.

84 *De Anima* [10(xxviii)]; Keeler, p. 80.

85 *De Anima* [4(xxii)]; Keeler, p. 42, ll. 30-31. Cf. *ibid.*; p. 42, ll. 16-17. Cf. also *ibid.* [5(xxiii)]; Keeler, p. 47: "Item existenti ante, melius esset non coniugi quam coniungi ... Hoc autem melius, non existere prius ..."

86 *Ibid.* [3(xvii)]; Keeler, p. 31.

universale, abstrahitur a materia per aliquid existens in anima ..."[87] Elsewhere he states that "jacere est infirmorum et existentium in peccato,"[88] or he speaks about a "causa intrinseca existente in ipsis virtutibus."[89] Such examples could be multiplied in every direction. They show the development within a few years of the meaning of a term that was to take on great technical significance in a later period.[90]

The Analogy of Being and the Degrees of Being

In examining the various divisions of being made by Philip, we have seen that although being (*ens*) is said in common, this predication is according to the priority and posteriority of uncreated and created being, or, in created being itself, according to the priority and posteriority of substance and accidents; the good, we have also seen, is said of God and the creature according to a similar order.[91] In other words, these are analogous concepts. Philip expressly says in one text that predication according to priority and posteriority is the same as predication "according to analogy." The common notion of liberty, he declares, is not applied univocally to the various definitions of liberty (freedom from force, freedom from sin, etc.), but according to priority and posteriority or according to analogy; it is not a genus with respect to these definitions because it does not apply equally to each, but rather according to an order of priority and posteriority:

> Si vero quaeratur qualiter ratio communis libertatis per appropriationem sumatur, ... libertas ... non dicitur aequivoce de his (tunc enim non diceretur haec magis libertas illâ ...), sed secundum prius et posterius sive secundum analogiam; sed non dicitur ut genus quia non aequaliter, sed secundum prius et posterius.[92]

The terms *analogia* and *analogice*, along with their Latin equivalents *proportio* and *proportionaliter*, occur more frequently in Philip's writings than in Alexander of Hales'; an exceptionally frequent use of the former terms is found towards the end of the *Summa de Bono* in Philip's study of the definition of virtue.[93] For example, he says that justice or

---

87 *Ibid.* [8(xxvi)]; Keeler, pp. 60-61.

88 *P* 165va; *T* 116ra; *V* 122rb.

89 *P* 201va; *T* 142va; *V* 150rb-va.

90 Cf. *HypUnion* III, 33-34, where a similar development in the use of this term was observed in Hugh of Saint-Cher's *Scriptum*, roughly contemporary with Philip's *Summa de Bono*.

91 See the texts *supra*, pp. 30-32.

92 *P* 29ra; *T* 25rb; *V* 25vb.

93 In *P* 199va-201rb; in *T* 140vb-142rb; in *V* 148vb-149vb.

any cardinal virtue can be understood according to the proper act of its proper power concerned with its proper matter, or the acts of any of these virtues can be understood analogically and as concerned with a matter understood analogically:

> ... Potest enim sumi justitia vel aliqua alia cardinalis virtus dupliciter: potest enim sumi prout accipitur secundum actum propriae potentiae et circa materiam[94] propriam illius potentiae ita quod se non extendat analogice ad actum alterius potentiae ... Item, potest esse quod actus uniuscujusque istarum virtutum analogice sumantur[95] et circa materiam analogice sumptam ...[96]

Again, the force of an argument about chastity that he considers depends on whether or not the accident *castus* is understood analogically or not:

> Notandum tamen quod accidentium quaedam analogice sumuntur et quaedam non, et cum accidens non dicitur analogice, non sequitur: 'Castitas est bonitas; ergo habens castitatem sive castus est bonus.' ... Si[97] autem 'castus' sumatur[98] analogice, bene sequitur: 'Est castus; ergo bonus.'[99]

Closely connected with such analogical predication, indeed standing behind it, are the various degrees of being. As we have seen in preceding authors, the degrees of being distinguished by them, as well as the intellectual disciplines corresponding to these degrees of being, are important to the understanding of our authors' theology of the Hypostatic Union. Hence Philip the Chancellor's thought on these matters should be noted.

As has been seen, Philip distinguishes a threefold good: the natural good, the moral good, and the good of grace.[100] When speaking of the good *in genere*, he introduces the same distinction with respect to *genera*, saying:

> Item, cum forma generalis dicatur genus, et est genus naturae, moris, et gratiae, genus naturae pertinet ad essentiam et respicit causam ef-

94 naturam *TV*.

95 sumatur *P*.

96 *P* 199vb; *T* 141ra; *V* 149ra. In *P* folio 199 has apparently been renumbered as folio 200, but it is followed by the true folio 200.

97 Cum *P*.

98 sumitur *P*.

99 *P* 200va; *T* 141vb; *V* 149va. The word *analogia* occurs on *P* 64rb; *T* 53va; *V* 56va: "... secundum uniuscujusque divinitus illuminatorum analogiam [anologiam *T*]." The terms *proportio* and *proportionaliter* are used even more frequently than *analogia* and *analogice*.

100 See *supra*, p. 31 ("Ad secundum").

ficientem. Secundum hoc omnia sunt bona in genere, sed de hoc non est intentio quantum ad propositum, sed de genere moris vel gratiae.[101]

The same distinctions, he indicates, are found in *esse* itself: "Et nota quod distinguendum est triplex esse: esse naturale, esse morale, esse gratuitum."[102] And the first two of these are found, along with the *esse individui*, in a division of *esse* obviously copied from Alexander of Hales and applied to the Trinity and Incarnation in order to show the difference between subject (*esse naturae*), hypostasis (*esse individui*), and person (*esse morale*).[103]

Another division of the being of things is according to their essence, power, and operation; a division of philosophy corresponds to each. Thus "divine" philosophy or metaphysics looks to the essence, moral philosophy to the virtues or powers of operation, natural philosophy to the operations themselves:

> ... Et sicut dicitur in libro *De Materia et Forma,* haec tria determinant tria secundum quem cadit res in triplicem philosophiam, scilicet, divinam secundum essentiam, moralem secundum virtutem, et naturalem secundum operationem,[104] et si quaeritur[105] cujusmodi[106] sit haec divisio, dicendum est quod est secundum principia rei in quantum est in effectu ordinata in suum finem. Nam ad hoc quod consequatur finem, oportet quod sit essentia cujus est finis, et virtus per[107] quam possit secundum[108] melius exire in finem, et operatio secundum quam est exitus.[109]

The last of these divisions, natural philosophy, seems to advert to the very physical energy exerted in operation; this is a confirmation of our interpretation of the third meaning of *esse* in Philip.[110]

In other texts Philip divides philosophical inquiry into the metaphysical, physical or natural, and logical or "demonstrative" consideration of things. Speaking of the study of substance, he says that as an active or efficient principle, substance is considered in metaphysics; as a passive principle, namely matter, it is considered in physics; substance, too, is the first principle in the logical order because conclusions

---

101 *P* 52vb; *T* 44rb-va; *V* 46rb.
102 *P* 168va; *T* 118rb; *V* 124rb.
103 *DeIncarn,* 2, 30; p. 177.
104 I have found no work with this title. On these divisions see *HypUnion* I, 32-33, and II, 60-64.
105 quaeratur *T.*
106 cujus *T.*
107 secundum *T.*
108 *Om.* T.
109 *P* 65ra-rb; *T* 54ra-rb; *V* 57rb.
110 See *supra*, p. 40; cf. *infra*, pp. 49-50 ("Sed aliter" and our commentary).

of proofs are ultimately reducible to the genus of substance, as are propositions to the first predicament, which again is substance:

> ... Est substantia activa et est substantia passiva. Activa est ut principium efficiens, ut scilicet Primus,[111] quod pertinet ad rationem metaphysici; substantia passiva, scilicet materia, quae ad considerationem physici. Demonstrativa etiam ad substantiam resolvitur, quia conclusiones ad principia et definitiones, definitiones ad genus et differentias; genus autem dicitur substantia. Item, propositiones ad praedicabilia et omnia ad decem praedicamenta, et quae in aliis decem ad primum, quod est substantia.[112]

When speaking of charity as a form, Philip introduces an objection that divides forms into physical, logical, and metaphysical forms. Although he rejects the application of this division to charity as a form by showing that there are other ways than these of considering forms, he appears to accept the validity of the division itself, which is presented as follows:

> Forma dicitur quae cum materia producit compositum, et haec est forma physica; et est forma universalis, sicut animal est forma hominis, et haec dicitur materia respectu differentiae, et haec est forma logica; et est forma quae dicitur exemplaris, et haec est forma metaphysica.[113]

The important text already seen concerning physical and metaphysical composition should also be recalled at this point.[114] And in at least one other text Philip distinguishes between "speaking logically" and speaking "according to nature."[115]

Finally, the theologian and the moralist are distinguished by Philip in a manner corresponding to the above-mentioned distinction between the order of grace and the moral order. Speaking of the virtue of modesty as considered by the two, he says that the moral philosopher intends to teach an "art" concerning the virtues, and since such an "art," as taught, deals with universals, the moral philosopher remains in the realm of the universal and eternal rather than descending to singulars and corruptibles. (By "art," especially as taught, Philip means

---

111 Primus *TV*, Primum *T2*, *V2*.

112 *P* 93rb-va; *T* 75ra; *V* 79va. Cf. *De Fide*, 1; Ceva, p. 35, ll. 609-617.

113 *P* 116vb; *T*90vb; *V* 96ra. Near the beginning of the *Summa de Bono* Philip himself had made a similar division of forms; the text is given *infra*, p. 56 ("Respondeo").

114 See *supra*, p. 38 ("Item materia").

115 "Non enim est eadem illi secundum formam speciei, logice loquendo, sed secundum formam generis; vel loquendo secundum naturam, eadem est quantum ad speciem secundum rationem, non quantum ad speciem in subjecto" (*P* 34vb; *T*30ra; *V* 30vb).

a knowledge about virtuous activity that, as a knowledge, remains
speculative.) The theologian, however, examines particular actions
because he is concerned with their merit or lack of it. Hence moral
philosophy is speculative, theology practical (*activus*), concerned with
the merit or demerit of actions:

> Solutio ad primum quod quaeritur de differentia inter theologum et
> moralem quantum ad praedictarum virtutum considerationem, dicendum
> est quod magna est diversitas, quia philosophus in morali philosophia in-
> tendit[116] tradere artem de virtutibus; ars autem circa universalia et de
> universalibus: artifex enim, in quantum tradit artem, non descendit ad
> singularia quia corruptibilia, sed stat in universalibus quae perpetua.
> Theologus vero versatur circa opera, attendens in eis meritum vel
> demeritum. Unde plus tendit ad specificationem theologus quam moralis:
> consideratio enim moralis secundum viam speculationis est; theologus
> autem activus est et circa opera attendit meritum vel demeritum.[117]

Thus the Chancellor, by discerning various aspects or degrees of
being, distinguishes as disciplines metaphysics, logic, natural philosophy
or physics, moral philosophy, and, with respect to the supernatural order, theology.

3. ESSENCE AND NATURE

Philip the Chancellor seldom speaks directly about the meaning of
essence. In one passage, however, he gives unmistakable indications of
his thought about it. Discussing the relationship between the condition
of an object of knowledge and the subject knowing it, he argues as
follows: The intellect is a power whose nature is to know simple, incorruptible objects such as the quiddity or *essence* of a thing. But since
these objects of knowledge are incorruptible, so too must be the power
that knows it, and hence, too, the substance or *essence* to which the
power belongs: for, he reasons, if an essence has an incorruptible
power, the essence itself must be incorruptible:

> Sed intellectus est potentia nata cognoscere incorruptibilia, ut quid-
> ditatem rei vel essentiam, quae simplex est et incorruptibilis. Et sic ex con-
> ditione obiectorum cognoscitur conditio potentiae, et ex conditione
> potentiae conditio substantiae, quoniam est incorruptibilis. Ergo essentia,
> cuius est illa potentia, est incorruptibilis; cuius enim essentiae potentia est
> incorruptibilis, ipsa est incorruptibilis.[1]

---

116 intenderit *T*.
117 *P* 165vb; *T* 116va; *V* 122rb.
  1 *De Anima* [8(xxvi)]; Keeler, p. 58.

Thus in this text Philip identifies an essence with both the quiddity of a thing making it an object of knowledge and the substance of the soul, which is distinct from its powers or faculties and from the acts proceeding from these.[2]

Elsewhere Philip associates essence with nature, as when he says: "Dicitur enim naturale quod naturam et essentiam rei consequitur,"[3] or: "... Genus naturae pertinet ad essentiam et respicit causam efficientem."[4]

We have already seen that for Philip one branch of philosophy is "divine" philosophy, that is, metaphysics, whose object is the essences of things.[5] In another text Philip, following Aristotle, identifies the essence (*quae quid erat esse*) with the formal cause:

> ... Artifex cognoscit artificiatum per speciem priorem quae est paradigma vel exemplar vel ratio, et haec est causa formalis secundum quod dicit Aristoteles in II *Physicorum: Causa formalis est quae quid erat esse et ratio et species et exemplar.*[6]

In another passage the essence is distinguished from the exemplar cause: the essence is a formal cause in the thing; the exemplar cause is separated from it: "Ad alterum respondeo quod duplex dicitur formalis causa: dicitur enim *quae quid est esse* ipsius rei,[7] et verum est quod ipsa posita, ponitur causatum; item, dicitur exemplaris, et tunc non sequitur ad ejus esse causatum, quia separata est ..."[8]

With respect to the term "nature," some indications of how it is used have already been seen.[9] Aristotle's definition of nature appears several times in the *Summa de Bono*. At one point nature is said to be a form that is a principle of operation and not of knowledge, and Aristotle is quoted to corroborate this meaning; in this sense it is opposed both to the exemplar form, which is a principle of knowledge and operation and is really God, and to the intellectual form, which is a principle only for knowing things:

2 The essence-power-act relationship is frequently mentioned; see, for example, in Keeler, pp. 21, 35, 58, 76, 77, 97.

3 *P* 11va; *T* 10ra; *V* 10ra.

4 *P* 52va; *T* 44rb; *V* 46rb. The full text is given *supra*, pp. 45-46 ("Item, cum").

5 See *supra*, p. 46 ("Et sicut dicitur").

6 *P* 11va-vb; *T* 10rb; *V* 10vb. See also the text quoted *infra*, pp. 56-57 ("Respondeo"). For Aristotle's text see his *Physics* II, 3; 194b 26-27. On the translations of Aristotle used by Philip see *supra*, sec. 1, n. 1.

7 Aristotle, *Physics*; see preceding note.

8 *P* 7vb; *T* 7ra; *V* 7rb. Cf. the text quoted *infra*, pp. 56-57 ("Respondeo").

9 *Supra*, pp. 38-40.

> Sed aliter procedendum et dicendum secundum quod forma triplex est, scilicet, quae est exemplar cognitionis et operationis, et operationis tantummodo, et cognitionis tantummodo; operationis et cognitionis secundum exemplar quod est ipsum Primum: est enim cognoscens res et creans; operationis et non cognitionis, scilicet forma quae est natura, secundum quod dicit Aristoteles in II *Physicorum: Natura est principium motus et status*, etc.;[10] de hac autem intendit auctor et ostendit in eodem quod sit forma et exemplar; cognitionis tantummodo, scilicet in intelligentia quae cognoscit res et non causat.[11]

The same definition of nature stands behind a later statement that "nature" can be put in the definition of a supernatural virtue if "nature" is understood as an intrinsic principle inclining towards the work of that virtue: "Nihil ... impedit quin natura ponatur in definitione virtutis gratuitae ut principium inclinativum intra ad opus virtutis illius."[12] Texts such as this and the one before it help to explain how in an earlier passage Philip could link natural philosophy with the operation of a thing, distinguishing it from metaphysics, concerned with the essence, and from moral philosophy, concerned with virtue.[13]

Elsewhere the notion of nature is broadened to include the four causes, the composite, and even privation: "... Natura dicitur multis modis. Dicitur enim natura efficiens et finis, forma et materia, et etiam compositum dicitur esse natura. Privatio etiam dicitur esse natura, quia privatio potest esse eadem cum composito et etiam cum materia."[14]

Philip, like the preceding authors, notes the drive of nature towards self-preservation:

> Item, natura in se curva est quia ad se reflectitur, quod apparet in naturalibus: prius cessat ab actu generativa naturaliter quam nutritiva eo quod haec sit propter subjectum conservandum, illa propter speciem, et hoc est quia natura plus intendit sibi, nisi sit ebria.[15]

10 Aristotle, *Physics* II, 1; 192b 13-14 & 21-22.

11 *P* 12ra; *T* 10rb-va; *V* 10vb-11ra. In another text the definition reads: "Natura est principium motus et quietis" (*P* 77ra; *T* 63vb; *V* 67va).

12 *P* 85vb; *T* 69vb; *V* 74rb.

13 See the text quoted *supra*, p. 46 ("Et sicut dicitur").

13 *De Anima* [8(xxvi)]; Keeler, pp. 71-72. Cf. Aristotle, *Physics* II, 1-4; 192b 8-196b 9. In comparing the virtues and gifts as to natural priority Philip speaks of nature as matter and as end: "Cum autem dicitur: 'Virtutes sunt priores donis naturaliter,' hoc dicitur ex parte suscipientis, secundum quod natura accipitur pro materia. Potest autem et natura accipi pro fine prout finis est movens, et cum finis sit beatitudo, manifestum est quod dona sunt propinquiora beatitudini quam sint virtutes" (*P* 210ra; *T* 147ra; *V* 155va).

15 *P* 12vb; *T* 11ra; *V* 11va.

From these basic meanings of nature and the natural Philip derives certain others to help answer particular problems. Thus he says that the natural place of spiritual substances is not to be understood according to the meaning of "natural" in natural philosophy, that is, a being of the same nature such that the natural place would be as spiritual as the substance it locates; rather it is to be understood as that kind of body more adapted to the nature of the spiritual substance or proportionately more like it:

> Dicendum est quod non est naturalis locus, sicut dicitur naturalis in philosophia naturali, tanquam ex eadem natura ens. Non enim est eadem natura corporis et substantiae incorporeae, sicut dicitur eadem natura partis et totius, vel sicut forma et eius quod est in potentia ad illam. Dicitur tamen naturalis quia de genere corporum plus naturae suae adaptatus, sive similior secundum proportionem.[16]

Elsewhere Philip speaks of the natural as that which "follows upon the nature and essence of the thing and is common to a thing of that species," and as that which "accompanies the nature itself by reason of God's benefits" to those to whom he wishes to give the good in question; the power of understanding in the soul is an example of the first, the particular perfections of knowledge in individual angels an example of the second.[17]

Again, nature is taken to mean either the natural course of events known to men, or the obediential potency given a creature by God, or, finally, "the highest law of nature, namely, God himself":

> Et est responsio quod natura accipitur multipliciter: dicitur enim quandoque naturalis cursus hominibus notus ...; quandoque dicitur natura possibilitas quaedam ipsius creaturae quam dedit ei Deus ut ex ea fiat quod ipse vult...; quandoque dicitur natura summa lex naturae, ipse scilicet Deus.[18]

Although these latter distinctions are of slight importance for our topic, they reveal a characteristic trait in Philip, that is, his extension by analogy of the technical meaning of a term in order to solve a particular theological problem.

---

16 *De Anima* [12(xxx)]; Keeler, p. 98.

17 "Naturale autem multipliciter accipitur: Dicitur enim 'naturale' quod naturam et essentiam rei consequitur, et commune est rei illius speciei, ut est animae potentia intelligendi et hujusmodi; naturale est etiam quod ipsam concomitatur naturam de beneficio Dei, non in omni, sed cui vult Deus dare, sicut dicuntur virtutes naturales ..., et non dico superadditas, sed simul natas et connaturales dici possunt, ut sunt quaedam habilitates in quibus ejusdem speciei res differunt, et sic est in angelis, et cognitio eorum dicitur naturalis" (*P* 11va; *T* 10ra; *V* 10vb).

18 *P* 74rb; *T* 61rb; *V* 65rb.

4. Various Kinds of Composition in Created Beings

Philip the Chancellor frequently affirms the simplicity of God and at the same time points out different types of composition in created beings. Affirmations of God's simplicity have already been seen;[1] in the following statement, where Philip says that the term *summum* is added to *bonum* with respect to God to indicate the created intellect's inability to know God's essence, he strongly asserts God's complete simplicity or lack of composition:

> Item, cum dicitur "summum," notatur ibi ex consequenti quaedam negatio, et sicut dicit Dionysius: *Negationes veriores sunt de eo quam positiones quia ostendunt non quid sit, sed quid non sit:*[2] non enim possibile est intellectum creatum intelligere quid sit: hoc enim est intelligere ipsum in omnimoda simplicitate sua.[3]

Alexander of Hales, in his *Glossa*, had listed five types of composition in created beings;[4] although Philip the Chancellor does not group them all together, in the course of his work he presents the same divisions as Alexander does. According to Philip the most fundamental composition, that of *quod est* and *esse* (or *quo est*), is metaphysical in character; texts concerning this composition have already been seen in our examination of the term *esse*.[5]

At times, in order to express the composition of things, Philip uses the relationship of subject and form. Sometimes this relationship refers to the previously-mentioned composition of *quod est* and *quo est,*[6] or to the equivalent composition of *quod est* and *esse*; the latter is involved when Philip says: "Item, de materia nunquam dicitur forma, sed de subiecto dicitur forma uel esse."[7] At other times the subject-form relationship refers to a second type of metaphysical composition, that of

---

1 *Supra*, pp. 35-37.

2 Denis, *De Caelesti Hierarchia* II, 3; PG 3, 140D-141A; PL 122, 1041B-C; *Dionysiaca* II, 757-759. John Scotus Erigena's translation reads as follows in *Dionysiaca*: "... et quae ex quibus non quid est sed quid non est significatur. Hoc enim (ut aestimo) potentius est in ipsa. Quandoquidem ... hoc quidem non esse secundum quid eorum quae sunt eam vere dicimus, ignoramus autem superessentialem ipsius et invisibilem et ineffabilem infinalitatem. Si igitur negationes in divinis verae, affirmationes vero incompactae obscuritati arcanorum, magis apta est per dissimiles reformationes manifestatio." Cf. Alan of Lille, *Theologicae Regulae*, 18; PL 210, 630A-C.

3 *P* 3rb; *T* 3ra; *V* 3rb.

4 Alexander, *Glossa* II, 3, 7e; p. 28. Cf. *HypUnion* II, 46.

5 *Supra*, pp. 38-39.

6 See the text quoted *supra*, pp. 38-39 ("Et attende").

7 Ed. Lottin, *PsychMorale* I, 436, ll. 181-182. In *P* 10ra; *T* 8vb; *V* 9ra-rb.

a substance with its properties or accidents. Thus Philip says that the essences of the soul and of the "intelligence" (an angel) are composed of substance and intellectual power: "Cum ergo essentiae animae et intelligentiae quadam compositione sint compositae : componuntur enim ex substantia et potentia intellectiva, quorum unum est sicut forma, aliud vero sicut formatum ..."[8] In the supernatural order, the relationship of free will and grace is likewise cast in terms of the subject-form relationship; although Philip does not speak of a "composition" in this case, he undoubtedly thinks of free will and grace as composed according to the manner of a subject and its accident. Grace, he says, is a form depending on its subject, free will, for its material *esse*; its formal *esse*, however, is had from God, that is, God makes it to be grace. Material *esse* is explained by Philip as the possession of existence by grace, which it has by being joined with free will as form to subject so that it can elicit meritorious acts:

> Et est responsio, cum quaeritur utrum gratia sit forma dependens a subjecto quantum ad esse suum, distinguendum est quod quantum ad quid dependet et quantum ad quiddam non. Nam quantum ad esse materiale dependet a subjecto, quantum ad esse formale non, quod solum trahit a principio efficiente: quod enim gratia est gratia, hoc habet a Deo; quod autem substet, ut actus meritorios eliciat, hoc habet ex conjunctione ad liberum arbitrium.[9]

In connection with metaphysical composition we should mention Philip's increased use of the potency-act relationship with reference to the being of creatures.[10] A survey of this relationship on all levels of being occurs in the question whether angels are composed of matter and form. In things that are generated and corrupted, Philip begins, there is potency prior to act; in heavenly bodies there is potency with act; in incorporeal substances there is act without potency: "Est igitur potentia ante actum, ut in generabilibus et corruptibilibus; et est potentia cum actu, ut in celestibus; et est[11] actus sine potentia, ut in in-

---

8 *De Anima* [8(xxvi)]; Keeler, p. 72. For more details on the substance-accident relationship see *infra*, pp. 57-59.

9 *P* 57ra; *T* 47vb; *V* 50ra. The relationship between matter and subject (at times one of identity, at times one of distinction) is treated in some detail by Philip in the question on angelic simplicity; text in Lottin, *PsychMorale* I, 435, II, 172-184.

10 See the text *supra*, p. 28 ("Sicut cum dicitur") as one example. Philip, of course, does not refer to potency and act as distinct principles within things, but he sees various principles in the things related as the potential to the actual.

11 *Add.* potentia sine actu uel *Lottin* (*PsychMorale* I, 435). The words are not found in *P* 9vb, *T* 8vb, or *V* 9ra. Lottin uses three Parisian MSS.

corporeis[12] substantiis."[13] But, he continues, incorporeal substances
must be subdivided. Although some are acts without potency, they are
the act of a potential being other than themselves: thus the soul is the
act of a bodily organ; others are acts that neither have potency nor are
the act of another potential being: thus the intelligences that are
separated substances. Among such completely separated substances
some, although wholly act with no potency, lack an identity of *quod est*
and *quo est*: such are the intelligences; but the First Being, God, is wholly
act with no potency and also has an identity in his being of *quod est* and
quo est:

> Sed subdiuiditur: est enim actus sine potentia, tamen est[14] actus
> alterius[15] potentie, ut est anima que est actus corporis organici; et est actus
> sine potentia et nullius potentie, ut in intelligentiis que sunt substantie
> separate; et iterum est huiusmodi in quibus actus sine potentia nec idem
> est quod est et quo est, ut in intelligentiis; in quibusdam est idem quod est
> et quo est, ut in Primo.[16]

Although it could be misleading to speak thus of separate substances
as beings in whom there is act without potency,[17] elsewhere Philip
clearly differentiates God from creatures by insisting that he is the only
one "for whom everything is act." This statement occurs within Philip's
explanation of his preferred definition of the good, namely, "The good
is that which has its act undivided from potency either without
qualification or in a certain respect." Act is undivided from potency
without qualification in the First Being, God, for in him potency (which
here seems to mean "power") is identical with act; he is preferably
called act without potency in so far as "potency" signifies a certain lack
of completion. God's having his act undivided from potency without
qualification means that for him everything is act; others have such a
non-division of act from potency only in a qualified sense because in
them there is some potency and incompletion:

---

12 corporeis *PTV e corr. V2.*
13 Ed. Lottin, *ibid.* I, 435, ll. 143-145.
14 *om. Lottin* and *V*; est *PTV2.*
15 alicuius *Lottin*; alterius *PTV.*
16 Ed. Lottin *ibid.* I, 435-436, ll. 145-151; cf. his commentary on this passage *ibid.* I, pp. 437-438.
Cf. also the *posse-esse* relationships expressed by Philip, *DeDiscrPers,* 4-5 (pp. 156-157), and *DeIncarn,* 1-
i & 1-ii, 11 (pp. 162-163).
17 Elsewhere Philip expresses it more carefully: "... In incorruptibilibus potentia numquam sine
suo particulari actu, nec ibi in materia alteratur [alternatur *TV*] actus et numquam sine actu ..."
(*P* 5va; *T* 5rb; *V* 5va). That is, the potency is always actualized; there is no matter to receive a new
act that would alter or corrupt the thing. This passage may be seen in its full context *infra,* ch. 2,
sec. 3, n. 22.

"Bonum est habens indivisionem actus a potentia simpliciter vel quodammodo." "Simpliciter" dico, ut in Primo: in divina enim essentia idem est potentia cum actu, et dicitur actus sine potentia secundum quod potentia sonat in quamdam incompletionem.[18] Et secundum hoc dictum est: *Nemo bonus nisi solus Deus,*[19] scilicet simpliciter indivisionem habens actus a potentia, sicut Primo qui totum est actus. Alia secundum quid habent hujusmodi indivisionem, sed non simpliciter, cum quid sit ibi de potentia et ita de incompletione.[20]

Philip then adds that God's lack of potency means he is absolute goodness, whereas other things are more or less good according to their likeness "to the First, who is purely act without potency":

In Primo ergo absoluta bonitas, in aliis secundum quid; et secundum assimilationem ampliorem cum actu qui est indifferens a potentia, id est, cum Primo, qui est pure actus sine potentia, dicetur magis bonum, et secundum minorem assimilationem minus bonum.[21]

In this text the designation of God as *pure actus* is particularly noteworthy.

In addition to metaphysical composition, Philip expressly mentions both the physical composition of matter and form and the logical composition of genus and difference. These two compositions are introduced together in a text dealing with the relationship in man of his intellectual powers: "Item, si ex voluntate et ratione componitur una potentia, non erit physica compositio, ut ex materia et forma, neque logica, ut ex genere et differentiis, et ita de aliis."[22] The two compositions, Philip shows, are found in man himself. Man is composed of two kinds of parts: body and soul, and genus and difference, that is, "animal" and "rational." The first parts make him a subject; the second ordain him to his end in that his rationality begets his highest act, reasoning:

Homo componitur ex duplici genere partium: componitur enim ex anima et corpore; item, ex genere et differentiis componitur, sicut ex animali et rationali. Per partes primas[23] est homo id quod est; per secundas[24] ordinatur ad finem suum. Optimus enim actus hominis est

18 *Add*. actus vero sonat in quemdam completionem *mg. V2.*
19 Lk 18, 19.
20 *P* 1va; *T* 1va; *V* 1va.
21 *Locis citatis.*
22 *P* 25rb; *T* 22rb; *V* 22vb.
23 primas] quae sunt anima et corpus *TV.*
24 secundas] genera vero et differentias *TV.*

ratiocinari: ad hunc autem actum ordinatur mediante differentia sua quae est rationale.[25]

The first of these compositions, that of matter and form, "whose consideration," Philip says, "pertains to the natural" rather than to the metaphysical order,[26] plays a considerable role in Philip's study of the union of soul and body in man.[27] The second, logical composition, is found, according to Philip, wherever there is some common essential element distinguished by some difference: "... In quocumque est commune essentiale cum aliqua differentia distinguente, necessario est compositio."[28]

The fifth kind of composition mentioned by Alexander of Hales, that of a whole from quantitative parts, is found in the *Summa de Bono*, at least by way of example. In speaking of the relationship of the powers of the soul to the soul itself, Philip summarizes a passage from St. Augustine's *De Trinitate* in which that Doctor denies that *mens, notitia*, and *amor* are three parts making up a whole in the same way that water, wine, and honey are combined as parts to make one drink.[29]

Since most of the types of composition that we have been examining involve forms of one kind or other, it may be convenient to gather together at this point Philip's various classifications of forms. We have just seen the subject-form composition as well as the composition of matter and form,[30] and a passage quoted earlier spoke of physical, logical, and metaphysical forms;[31] again, the formal cause, we have seen, is identified with the essence.[32] Several of these forms are listed by Philip in another text in which he says that the formal cause is appropriated to the essence (*quae quid est esse*), but is used in common of the form that is a part of a thing, of the form in the intellect, and of the exemplar form:

Respondeo quod intentio causae formalis quandoque appropriatur, quandoque communiter accipitur. Appropriatur cum dicitur causa for-

<hr>

25 *P* 5vb; *T* 5rb-va; *V* 5va-vb.
26 Text quoted *supra*, p. 38 ("Item, materia.").
27 See esp. *De Anima* [10b]; Keeler, pp. 81-83.
28 *P* 6rb; *T* 5vb; *V* 6ra.
29 "Nam nulla pars totum cujus est pars complectitur. Mens vero cum se totam novit, per totum est notitia ejus, nec se habent sicut aqua et vinum et mel ex quibus fit una potio: non enim unius substantiae sunt, quamvis ex illis fiat una substantia ..." (*P* 40ra; *T* 34rb; *V* 35ra). Cf. Augustine, *De Trinitate* IX, 4, 4-7; PL 42, 963-965; CorChrSerLat, 50, 297-300.
30 Cf. *supra*, pp. 52-53, for the first composition, and pp. 55-56, for the second.
31 *Supra*, p. 47 ("Forma").
32 *Supra*, p. 49 ("Artifex").

malis *quae quid est esse,*[33] ut anima hominis. Communiter accipitur cum in se continet formam quae est pars rei, et formam secundum rationem, et formam exemplarem quae simpliciter est extra. Prima vero est intra; media quodammodo est intra et quodammodo est extra; ultima ex toto est extra.[34]

In another passage Philip mentions self-subsisting forms along with the physical forms and the exemplar forms; all three, he says, are included in the notion of "species": "Intentio tamen speciei communior est quam intentio exemplarum: species enim comprehendit formam existentem in materia, formas etiam per se subsistentes, formas exemplares, si aliquae sunt."[35]

Finally, with respect to substantial and accidental forms, Philip presents an argument which states in passing that a substantial form is closer to the essence than an accidental form: "... Cum substantialis forma propinquior sit essentiae quam accidentalis."[36]

5. SUBSTANCE

Philip the Chancellor's doctrine of substance follows the general pattern of a simplified Aristotelian thought. In some instances Philip uses "substance" as the equivalent of "essence," for example, when he says: "... Dictum est quod scientia ad superiorem substantiam vel essentiam pertinebat ...,"[1] or when he says that *gratia gratum faciens* and *gratia gratis data* differ according to substance: "... Dona gratiae hujus et illius secundum substantiam differunt."[2] Again, he interchanges *substantia* for *essentia* when speaking of various types of *potentia*; one type is the very *essence* itself with a relationship to act: an example of this is the *potentia* in matter to receive the form. This *potentia*, he goes on to say, is the very *substance* of the matter: "... Est potentia quae est ipsa *essentia* adjiciens quamdam relationem ad actum, verbi gratia, ... potentia ... in materia recipiendi formam est ipsa *substantia* materiae."[3]

---

33 Aristotle; for the reference see *supra,* p. 49, n. 6.

34 *P* 7va-vb; *T* 7ra; *V* 7rb. The last three kinds of form correspond respectively to the physical, logical, and metaphysical forms mentioned in the text quoted *supra,* p. 47 ("Forma").

35 *P* 6va; *T* 6ra; *V* 6rb. In the study of the soul there occurs a different division of forms: *formae primae, ultimae, mediae.* See Philip, *De Anima* [10b]; Keeler, p. 83. The *forma corporeitatis,* taken from Avicenna, is mentioned as an example of a *forma prima (loc. cit.).*

36 *P* 9rb; *T* 8rb; *V* 8vb.

1 *P* 61va; *T* 51va; *V* 54rb.

2 *P* 48vb; *T* 41rb; *V* 42vb.

3 *P* 39vb; *T* 34ra; *V* 35ra. Emphasis mine. Full text in Lottin, *PsychMorale* I, 489. Cf. *supra,* p. 48. Cf. also the following text: "Ad primum ... dicendum est quod sicut dicitur [divina *mg. V₂*] sub-

For Philip the basic notion of substance is that of being or existing
per se; in this respect substance is opposed to accident, which exists
through the substance: "... Ens secundum prius dicitur de substantia
quae est per se ens, secundum posterius de accidente quod est per substantiam ..."[4] Philip lays great stress on this notion of substance when he
asserts that the soul is not only a form or perfection of the body, but a
substance. This assertion occurs in a discussion of a text from St.
Augustine about the creation of Adam's soul as being at the same time
as the angels and before its union to the body. Philip says that the point
of such a statement is to teach that the soul, although it differs from the
angels in that it is a "perfection" or form of the body and they are not,
is like the angels in being able to exist through itself and not only in
matter, as lower forms must; in other words, it is shown to be a substance:

> ... Cum anima sit ita substantia quod perfectio, ne putaretur esse sola
> perfectio, sicut ceterae formae quae a datore formarum dantur materiae
> praeparatae, quae est necessitas, per hoc quod Augustinus posuit eam
> creatam cum angelis qui sunt substantiae, ita quod non perfectiones, et
> per se existere antequam ad corpus accederet, ostendit esse substantiam.[5]

In another text he says that this independence of the soul from the
body "according as [the soul] is a *substance*" is a proof that it needs some
medium to be united to the body:

> Quod etiam secundum quod substantia aliquo medio unitur patet, quia
> per se est substantia separabilis a corpore, et etiam secundum operationes
> suas separabilis. Intelligere enim et reminisci sunt ipsius separatae. Ergo
> nec est dependens a corpore secundum substantiam, nec secundum
> operationes. Ergo secundum se non unitur corpori: quare indiget alio
> medio.[6]

---

stantia 'essentia' per appropriationem, licet aliis conveniat per posterius eo quod 'essentia' in illa
trimembri divisione prima [i.e., essence, power, operation] fuit nomen maximae dignitatis, ita
angelicae substantiae ... nominantur virtutes ..." (*P* 65ra; *T* 54ra; *V* 57ra-rb).

4 *P* 3va; *T* 3rb; *V* 3va.

5 *De Anima* [7(xxv)]; Keeler, pp. 51-52. Philip refers to this text later (*De Anima* [10(xxviii)]; Keeler,
p. 80), saying: "Solutio: Dicendum est quod anima (sicut dictum est) non est forma tantum sive per-
fectio, sed et substantia." In his explanation he includes the words quoted *supra*, p. 43 ("Quia duo");
these include another clear statement of the soul's perseity and independence of the body: "... Nec
applicatur corpori ut per ipsum fulciatur in esse, cum per se possit existere" (*locis citatis*).

6 *De Anima* [10b]; Keeler, pp. 83-84.

Thus for Philip the perseity of substance is opposed to the inherence of accidents;[7] in the case of the soul (or, we may add, of angels) its perseity is also opposed to the incompleteness of substantial forms of lower natures: these cannot exist independently of matter, whereas man's soul as a substance can exist per se.

Occasionally Philip the Chancellor lists different meanings of substance. Taking his lead from Aristotle, he includes under substance the following: matter, form, the composite of matter and form, and the genus or definition. Although this division of substance is enunciated most clearly in an objection, by his reply Philip shows that he accepts the division. The discussion concerns faith, and the objector says in part: "'Substantia' dicitur secundum quattuor modis, sicut in *Metaphysica* legitur: aut substantia materia, aut substantia forma, aut substantia conjunctum, aut sicut genus, aut sicut definitio."[8] Philip's reply implicitly accepts the division by saying that faith is substance as matter, that is, the first disposition of the subject.[9]

In a text quoted previously we have seen that among substances Philip lists matter, form, *quod est*, and *quo est*;[10] in doing so he appears to be combining Aristotle and Boethius. In the questions on the Hypostatic Union he also speaks of the *quod est*, which he calls the *habens naturam*, as substance.[11]

Finally, another text that we have seen orders these varying kinds of substance by referring matter as substance to physics, and genus and definition as substance to logic.[12] The same text speaks of the efficient principle as the substance that is the concern of metaphysics: perhaps this would involve the form and composite of Aristotle's list of sub-

---

7 The substance-accident relationship occurs frequently, as would be expected. Thus Philip says: "Sed duplex vertibilitas est: una secundum substantiam, et haec maior; altera secundum accidens, et haec minor" (*De Anima* [8(xxvi)]; Keeler, pp. 62-63). Again: "... Cum substantialis forma propinquior sit essentiae quam accidentalis ..." (*P* 9rb; *T* 8rb; *V* 8vb). And again: "Item, qui dicit hominem album duo dicit, et si quis poneret rationem hominis albi, poneret ex parte substantiae, id est, hominis" (*P* 26rb; *T* 23ra; *V* 23ra).

8 *P* 90va; *T* 73ra; *V* 77va. Cf. *De Fide*, 1; Ceva, p. 18, ll. 48-51. Cf. Aristotle, *Metaphysics*, Eta, 3, 1029a 27ff., 1028b 33ff.

9 "Secundum hoc responsio est ad objectum quod fides dicitur substantia sicut materia. Unde IV Damascenus, 2: *Fides est eorum quae sperantur hypostasis, id est, subsistentia, rerum redargutio quae non videntur* [*DeFide Orth* IV, 10; PG 94, 1128A; Buytaert, p. 298], et est materia in qua ipsa anima. Fides vero est primus habitus disponens in via, et nominatur substantia propter hoc quia de numero dispositionum subjecti est primus habitus aut dispositio" (*P* 91ra; *T* 73rb; *V* 77vb). Cf. *De Fide*, 1; Ceva, pp. 20-21, ll. 118-125.

10 *Supra*, p. 38 ("Item, materia").

11 *DeIncarn*, 3, 10; p. 179.

12 See *supra*, p. 47 ("Est substantia").

stances; certainly the *quod est* and *quo est* listed among substances would be included on this metaphysical level.[13]

6. The Individual

Although Philip the Chancellor has little to say in the *Summa de Bono* about individuation within a species, he treats the subject in greater detail in his *Quaestiones de Incarnatione*. Taking his lead, it seems, from Alexander of Hales and William of Auxerre, Philip discerns a twofold individuation, the first arising from a thing's particular or distinct *esse*, which is its own apart from and prior to properties and accidents, the second arising from the collection of accidents or properties peculiar to the thing and found in no other individual.[1]

The second of these types of individuation is the familiar one whose doctrinal origin goes back to Porphyry and Boethius.[2] Philip asserts that this kind of individuation comes now from a collection of accidents and now from a collection of properties; he appears to make no special distinction between the role of accidents and that of properties.[3]

As for the first type of individuation, Philip's teaching concerning it is less clear than with respect to the second. In one text he says that this first type is an individuation "as to an essential property" by contrast with individuation "as to the collection of accidents," which is the second type of individuation.[4] This concept of an essential property that individuates may be an echo of the teaching of William of Auxerre and, ultimately, of Gilbert of Poitiers; they maintained, we have seen, that properly speaking Socrates is not other than Plato because of his accidents but because of his singular humanity; William, speaking of Christ, calls this property of his singular humanity its *Jesuitas*.[5] Philip, however, seems to make this individuality more radical than William did, as we shall see especially in his theology of the Hypostatic Union. Here we shall simply gather his descriptions of it: this first type of individuation is "through particular *esse* alone without properties"; it is linked with the nature called by St. John Damascene "that which is bare

---

13 See *supra*, pp. 36-40.

1 On Alexander's possible influence see *infra*, pp. 61-62; for William of Auxerre's see *infra* on this page.

2 See *HypUnion* I, 48-51.

3 See *DeIncarn*, 2, 3 (p. 170: "quantum ad *collectionem accidentium quam in nullo alio est reperire*"), and *ibid.*, 3, 44 (p. 184: "per *collectionem proprietatum quas impossibile est in alio quolibet reperire*").

4 *Ibid.*, 2, 3; p. 170.

5 Cf. *HypUnion* I, 49-50.

(*nuda*)", that is, Philip comments, "[the nature] abstracted from accidents and properties;"[6] it is distinct from the second type of individuation found in the nature *in atomo*, that is, in the singular nature, along with its properties, existing in its hypostasis and constituted a singular by the collection of individuating properties;[7] it gives rise to the "individual in its distinct *esse*," and the three persons of the Trinity are called "three beings" according to this first type of individuality or distinct *esse*.[8]

Thus Philip conceives of a thing as individuated, that is, as distinct or particular in being prior to the advent of individuating properties and accidents. This prior individuality abstracts from properties and accidents, except that it seems to derive from an essential property, not otherwise identified: perhaps Philip, like his predecessors, would call it, in Peter, his *Petreitas*, and, in Socrates, his *Socrateitas* or *Socratitas*.[9] From certain arguments that Philip gives in his theology of the Hypostatic Union, it seems that for him this essential property, which gives a thing its particular or distinct *esse* prior to its second individuation by the collection of properties or accidents, comes to the thing by its origin in generation, that is, in its achievement of physical *esse*.[10]

This last point may perhaps be seen as well from a text of Alexander of Hales that helps understand Philip's doctrine of twofold individuation. In this text Alexander distinguishes two kinds of individual: one is "the first substance separated from another by ultimate separation"; the second is the individual constituted by the collection of properties. The first, Alexander adds significantly, is the same as a hypostasis "in naturalibus", that is, according to the doctrine we have seen, a substance on the level of concrete physical being.[11] In another text in Alexander, which seems to correspond to this doctrine in Philip, he says that if we abstract the properties of Paul, his substance or hypostasis still remains: "... Abstrahamus proprietates Pauli: remanet substantia, quae hypostasis est ..."[12] If Philip's doctrine of twofold individuation follows that of Alexander, then his first type of individual

6 *DeIncarn*, 3, 29; p. 182.

7 *Loc. cit.*

8 *Ibid.*, 3, 44; p. 184.

9 Cf. *HypUnion* I, 50-57; III, 49.

10 Cf. *infra*, pp. 80-85.

11 For the text see Alexander, *Glossa* I, 19, 24c; p. 203. It is quoted and studied in *HypUnion* II, 59-60. Alexander, however, also adds that the first kind of individual (first substance) "est individuum vel atomum," whereas in one text Philip links the *atomum* with the second type of individual (*DeIncarn*, 3, 29; p. 182). Although in this he definitely varies from Alexander's thought, it is still quite possible and even likely that his doctrine derives from Alexander's on the more essential points.

12 *Glossa* I, 25, 14; p. 249. Cf. *HypUnion* II, 54.

would be the first substance, conceived of as constituted in its singular, distinct, substantial being by an essential property that itself may derive from the origin of the individual by natural generation. Richard of Saint-Victor, who influences both Alexander and Philip by his doctrine of personal distinction through origin, may also be an influence at this point.[13]

The doctrine of twofold individuation, interpreted similarly to this, is found stated more explicitly in the so-called *Summa Fratris Alexandri*, which in other places appears to copy these very questions of Philip the Chancellor on the Hypostatic Union.[14] Although it is hazardous to rely on a derivative work for the interpretation of its source, and although in this case one cannot be certain that Philip is the direct source, a comparison of the text of the *Summa Fratris Alexandri* on this point will at least show the mentality of the times and thereby the reasonableness of our interpretation. With Philip, the *Summa Fratris Alexandri* makes a clear-cut distinction between two types of individuation, one by reason of a singular property, the other by a collection of properties:

> Et cum individuatio dicatur duobus modis, prima scilicet et secunda — prima individuatio est in hypostasi secundum se ratione proprietatis singularis, qua ab omni alia distinguitur se ipsa, secundum quod dicitur Petrus alius esse a Paulo; secunda vero individuatio est per proprietates advenientes consequenter ipsi hypostasi, secundum quod dicitur individuatio collectio proprietatum, quae nunquam in alio eaedem erunt ...[15]

---

13 Richard of Saint-Victor's influence on Philip is strongest with respect to the teaching on the three types of personal distinction found in beings. In both his *Summa de Bono* and in his *Quaestiones de Incarnatione* Philip teaches that personal distinction in the Trinity is according to origin or lack of origin, in angels according to quality (the *Quaestiones* say "essence" or "property of essence"), and in man according to both origin and quality. See *DeDiscrPers*, 3, 4 (pp. 155-156), and 6 (p. 157); *DeIncarn*, 1-i, 1 (p. 158, 1-i & 1-ii, 8 (p. 161), and 3, 22 (p. 181). Cf. also *infra*, p. 68.

For Richard's teaching see his *DeTrin* IV, 13-14 (Ribaillier, pp. 175-177), especially the following: "In humana pro certo natura, quam per experientiam novimus, personarum existentiam tam secundum personarum qualitatem quam secundum ipsarum originem variari videmus. Certe omni humane persone est qualitas singularis et propria, per quam absque omni ambiguitate differ[i]t a qualibet alia (IV, 14; Ribaillier, p. 176). "Differ[i]t" is the editor's emendation.

It may be that Richard's text, with its "singular and proper quality," influenced Philip's ideas concerning the first type of individuation by means of an "essential property" prior to individuating properties and accidents. Richard's emphasis on origin as a source of distinction may also have been influential on Philip if, that is, our interpretation of the role of origin with respect to Philip's first kind of individual is correct.

14 Cf. *SummaAlex* III, 30 (IV, 49), with Philip, *DeIncarn*, 3, 1-8 (pp. 178-179), and *SummaAlex* III, 35 (IV, 54-55), with Philip, *DeIncarn*, 3, 20-33 (pp. 181-182).

15 *SummaAlex* III, 52; IV, 75.

Here the first individuation is said, more expressly than by Philip, to be in the hypostasis taken in itself; the "essential property" of Philip's doctrine is described as "a singular property by which" the hypostasis "is distinguished from every other one"; it is by such a property that "Peter is said to be other than Paul." The other properties are said to "come to" the hypostasis already constituted. All this is evidently more precise than Philip's statements, but the two doctrines seem to be woven of the same cloth: indeed, Philip's may have influenced that of the *Summa*. This resemblance continues in the rest of the same text, in which the first individual is identified with the very substance itself, singular by reason of the singularity of substance and present even apart from those properties in Peter and Paul whose collection makes an individual in the second sense:

> ... Secundum hoc dicitur individuum duobus modis: individuum primo modo, scilicet hypostasis, id est ipsa substantia singularis ratione singularitatis substantiae; nam, si abstrahantur omnes proprietates quae sunt in Petro et in Paulo, adhuc tamen haec substantia est alia ab illa. Alio modo dicitur individuum ex collectione ipsarum proprietatum, quae nunquam in alio eadem est.[16]

In this text the most striking similarity to Philip's doctrine, and also to that of Alexander's *Glossa*, is found in the hypothesis of an abstraction of properties, which would still leave the first individual intact.[17]

Philip omits any discussion of matter as a principle of individuation; however, because this doctrine is mentioned in an objection, Philip must have been aware of it. Thus in a discussion of angelic orders an objector presents this argument: In beings that lack matter, one individual suffices in each species to preserve that species; hence there will be as many species among the angels as there are angelic intelligences:

> Item, cum ordo sit alicujus multitudinis distinctae, in unoquoque ordine erit multitudo distincta. Sed quae est causa multitudinis in singulis ordinibus? In non habentibus enim materiam sufficit in unaquaque specie unum individuum ad salvationem speciei. Quot ergo erunt intelligentiae angelicae, tot erunt species in angelis, et tot erunt differentes proprietates species consequentes.[18]

16 *Ibid.*; IV, 75-76.
17 Cf. Philip, *DeIncarn*, 3, 29 (p. 182), and Alexander, *Glossa* I, 25, 14 (p. 249).
18 *P* 65va; *T* 54rb; *V* 57va.

Although Philip agrees that multiplication of individuals is un-
necessary for the conservation of angelic species, he maintains that
many individual angels exist within species for the purpose of assisting
in the divine government and for showing forth the divine power:

> Solutio: Ad primum dicendum est quod multitudo essentiarum
> angelicarum est aut secundum numerum eorum quae reguntur, aut secun-
> dum numerum ostendentem potentiam divinam communicantem sapien-
> tiae... Neque necessaria est multiplicatio individuorum in angelis propter
> conservationem esse speciei (et sic intelligitur prior propositio), sed prop-
> ter diversitatem ministeriorum in quibus ministrant Summo Principi et
> Summo Dominatori.[19]

Although the expression "multitude of angelic essences" is ambiguous
in that it could refer to a multitude of specifically distinct angels, the
final sentence of the text seems to refer definitely to a multiplication of
individuals within a species. Philip, it will be noted, fails to state just
what constitutes the principle of individuation for angels within a
species; elsewhere, however, he indicates that there are certain connatural aptitudes (*habilitates*), given by God in varying degrees, according to which angels of the same species differ among themselves;
the same is true of human souls.[20]

19 *P* 65va; *T* 54va; *V* 57va. In the omitted section Philip explains that the number of angels in-
creases in the lower orders, which are closer to corruptible things and farther removed from the
supreme unity of God: "... ut infimus gradus angelorum sive ordo sit secundum numerum eorum
quae reguntur [regunt *P*] in superioribus et in inferioribus, scilicet principibus, gentibus, et
hominibus; superiores vero secundum diversitates [diversitatem *T*] operationum magis ac magis
unitas proportionaliter. Secundum enim quod fit recessus [*om. PB*] et [*om. PV*] accessus ad summam,
est major unitio; secundum autem quod est recessus et accessus ad res corruptibiles, major
multiplicatio" (*locis citatis*).

20 Speaking of the angelic orders, Philip says: "... Attendenda est duplex diversitas: est enim
diversitas ordinum, et in ipsis ordinibus diversitas individuorum. Plus autem differunt illi qui sunt
in diversis ordinibus inter se quam qui de uno ordine: diversi quidem ordines differunt et secundum simplicitatem essentiae et habilitates [habilitatis *P*]; qui autem in uno ordine non secundum
simplicitatem essentiae, sed secundum habilitates differentes, cum se habeant in latus, illi secundum
lineam. Sic multae animae differunt non secundum essentiam, sed secundum habilitates, et haec est
differentia quia in angelis est ordo et in animabus non, et ideo major est differentia, et differentiae
multiplicantur secundum sapientiam divinam.** Naturale autem multipliciter accipitur: Dicitur
enim 'naturale' quod naturam et essentiam consequitur, et ... [for the rest of the text see *supra*, n. 17
(p. 51).]" (*P* 11va; *T* 10ra; *V* 10vb).

(**At this point *T* adds a long digression that repeats much of the earlier discussion about personal discretion in men and angels and also speaks of the unitability of human and angelic natures
to the Son of God; concerning this latter problem see *infra*, pp. 77-87.)

Since the angels in question do not differ according to simplicity of essence, they must be of the
same essence or species: their difference, then, is according to certain aptitudes or connatural
properties given them by God in varying degrees.

Thus, although Philip, when he wrote the *Summa de Bono*, was aware of a doctrine of multiplication of individuals by matter, he does not accept it for angels or human souls: he sees the principle of individuation for them in a diversity of connatural aptitudes. These would undoubtedly correspond to the "collection of properties" of which he speaks in his *Quaestiones*; there are, moreover, indications in these writings that angels also have the first type of individuation prior to individuation by properties.[21] With respect to matter, from what has been seen of Philip's thought one would suspect that he might view matter as a source of individuation for purely material things on the level of physical being, but that it would not provide him with a metaphysical principle for explaining individuation.

7. Hypostasis and Person

Philip the Chancellor's teaching on individuation provides the background for his definitions of hypostasis and person, both of which he develops mainly for use in the theology of the Hypostatic Union. Here only the main definitions will be given, their application to the Hypostatic Union being left until later.

At times the term "hypostasis" is used as a synonym of either "person" or "substance" (understood as the *id quod* or *habens naturam*). In the *Quaestiones de Incarnatione* the equivalence of "hypostasis" and "person" derives from texts of St. John Damascene; thus, after speaking of the *personalis hypostasis* in Christ and saying that the two natures come together in one "hypostasis," Philip at once confirms these statements by quoting two texts from the *De Fide Orthodoxa*.[1] In several other places he interchanges the two terms in the course of his argument, thereby showing that in some cases they are synonyms.[2] The equivalence of "hypostasis" with "substance," understanding this as *id quod*, is implied when Philip lists the four terms "nature," "essence," "substance," and "hypostasis," and then goes on to speak about only the first three. In this text *substantia* is made equivalent to *habens naturam* and is opposed to *natura* and *essentia*;[3] thus it seems quite certain that in this case Philip means "hypostasis" to have the same signification as "substance."

---

21 See *DeDiscrPers*, 4; p. 156. There Philip says that "personal difference among the angels does not consist in a quality alone, but each hypostasis differs from another through itself, with no quality being understood ..."

1 *DeIncarn*, 2, 10; p. 172.

2 See *ibid.*, 1-i; 1 (p. 159); 2, 4 (p. 170); 2, 9 (pp. 171-172).

3 *Ibid.*, 3, 10; p. 179.

When Philip speaks most formally about the meaning of "hypostasis," he distinguishes it, in definition at least, from both "person" and "individual." In two different questions Philip asserts that the hypostasis holds a middle position between the person and the individual.[4] In one of these passages he says that three things are to be considered: the person, the hypostasis, and the individual as both distinct in being and as individuated by the unique collection of properties. Comparing hypostasis and person first, the Chancellor defines them in the same way except that the definition of person adds to the definition of hypostasis the distinction of dignity:

> Solution: Three things must be considered: person; hypostasis; the individual in its distinct being, and according to this the three persons are called three beings; the second individuation is through *the collection of properties that cannot be found in any other*. Now the hypostasis can be described as follows: A hypostasis is an incommunicable existence that is distinct according to a collection of properties; but a person is an incommunicable existence that is distinct according to the property of dignity. According to these designations the hypostasis is midway between a person and an individual ...[5]

What is the relationship of the hypostasis to the individual? This is somewhat obscure. One text says that the hypostasis has a universal nature in itself and is individuated by the twofold individuation already mentioned;[6] the conclusion of the foregoing text says that the hypostasis "regards the individual, and the individual *in atomo*."[7] It is uncertain whether this second text means to include the two kinds of individuation or to relate the hypostasis exclusively to the second, that is, to the individual *in atomo*, which is the same as the individual constituted by the collection of properties.[8] Judging from the first text, which explicitly mentions both kinds of individuation, it would seem that the second text likewise intends to include both of them.

Although these passages are somewhat obscure and although they are elaborated with special reference to the Hypostatic Union, their doctrine seems to amount to this: The hypostasis is identical with the person in a higher nature (man, angel, God) that enjoys the property of dignity, which itself may be connected especially with rationality and

---

4 See *ibid.*, 2, 11 (p. 172), and 3, 44 (p. 185).
5 *Ibid.*, 3, 44; pp. 184-185. Cf. *ibid.*, 2, 11; p. 172.
6 *Ibid.*, 2, 11; p. 172.
7 *Ibid.*, 3, 44; p. 185.
8 Cf. *ibid.*, 3, 29 (p. 182), and *supra*, p. 61, n. 11.

perhaps independence in action; the hypostasis is identical with the individual in a lower nature that lacks this property of dignity and that is constituted an individual by its distinct individual being of a lower order (first type of individuation) and by its unique collection of properties (second type of individuation).

That such a schematic interpretation is to be used cautiously can be seen from another text, similar to a passage in Alexander of Hales' *Glossa*, in which the hypostasis is linked with the *esse individui* and is distinguished not only from the subject, whose *esse* is of the order of nature, but also from the person itself, whose *esse* is of the moral order.[9] This last distinction, which seems to identify hypostasis and individual, corresponds, however, to a very particular problem and should hardly be thought to contradict Philip's teaching on the middle position of the hypostasis between the person and the individual, a teaching that he explicitly states twice in central passages of his questions on the Hypostatic Union.

Concerning personality, Philip mentions together with the "excellence of dignity" other characteristics of the person, namely, that a person is "one *per se*" and has "absolute *esse*";[10] the latter phrase seems to mean a being that is cut off from others and incommunicable with others — a person is not a part, but a whole. In the same passage Philip gives the Boethian definition of person, and interprets the words *individua substantia* as *quid* and *rationabilis naturae* as *quis*;[11] the first appears to point to the hypostasis; the second, with its note of rationality, denotes the property of dignity added to the hypostasis by which it becomes a *quis* or person.

Philip also expresses the perfection of personality by speaking of a person as "more complete" in being than the subject or individual.[12] He also says that at the terminus of creation of a person, the personal *esse*, if it is to be truly personal, must not be joined or be able to be joined to something else; it must be unjoined and be unable to be joined, and this both potentially and actually.[13] Here once again is expressed the incommunicability and distinction of a person, its perseity in being.

9 *Ibid.*, 2, 30; p. 177. Cf. *GlossaAlex* III, 2, 14i (L) (p. 30), quoted in *HypUnion* II, 150. If Redaction L of the *GlossaAlex* is the actual source used here by Philip, this would be of some importance because the editors of the *GlossaAlex* have found no places in Philip's *Summa de Bono* where the use of Redaction L can be seen; see *GlossaAlex* III; p. 15*.

10 *DeIncarn*, 3, 32; p. 182.
11 *Loc. cit.*
12 *Ibid.*, 2, 30; p. 177.
13 *Ibid.*, 3, 33; p. 182.

Finally, as has already been mentioned, Philip follows Richard of
Saint-Victor in assigning the causes of personal distinction or discretion
in God, angels, and men.[14] Although there are variations in the exact
wording of the different passages in which this topic is discussed, the
doctrine is basically the same. In addition to the texts already edited
here,[15] another passage from the *Summa de Bono* gives this teaching,
making explicit reference to its Victorine source. Is man or the angel
the image of the Trinity, Philip asks? Consider personal distinction, he
says: In God personal distinction is found according to origin or lack of
origin, but not according to quality; in an angel it is found according to
a property of qualities, but not according to origin; in man it is found
according to each. Since a human person has something by which he
imitates personality in God and the angel does not (that is, origin as a
source of personality), in man will be rightly found the image of the
Trinity.

> Sicut dicit Magister Richardus de Sancto Victore, cum persona in tribus
> inveniatur, Deo, angelo, et homine, in Deo reperitur distinctio personalis
> secundum habere originem et non habere,[16] et non secundum qualitatem;
> in angelo secundum proprietatem qualitatum, non secundum originem
> habere; in homine vero secundum utrumque. Cum ergo persona in
> homine habeat secundum quid imitetur personam in Deo *et non per*-
> sonam in angelo, recte imago quae in Trinitate personarum attenditur
> homini attribuenda[17] fuit.[18]

In the case of man, personal distinction by origin refers to his physical
birth from another, and so pertains to the order of nature; personal
distinction by a property refers to the logico-metaphysical order. Philip
the Chancellor makes an interesting application of this doctrine to the
problem whether a human nature is more suited than angelic nature to
be assumed in the Hypostatic Union. The application of this and of the
other philosophical concepts that we have surveyed may now be seen in
Philip's theology of the Hypostatic Union.

14 *Supra*, p. 62, n. 13.
15 See *DeDiscrPers*, 3, 4, 6 (pp. 155-156, 157), and *DeIncarn*, 1-i, 1 (p. 158), 1-i & 1-ii, 8 (p. 161), and
3, 22 (p. 181).
16 *Add.* originem et non habere *P*.
17 tribuenda *TV*.
18 *P* 38rb-va; *T* 32vb-33ra; *V* 33vb. On angelic individuation see *supra*, pp. 64-65, nn. 19-21.

CHAPTER II

THE THEOLOGY OF THE HYPOSTATIC UNION: INTRODUCTION

1. SURVEY OF PHILIP THE CHANCELLOR'S TEXTS ON THE HYPOSTATIC UNION

Before beginning an examination of Philip the Chancellor's theology of the Hypostatic Union, it would be helpful to survey briefly the various materials he provides on this subject. As has already been said, his main work, the *Summa de Bono*, contains no section dealing directly with the Hypostatic Union.[1] Its question *De Discretione Personali*, which is edited here, is nonetheless very important for our study; Philip himself says that it applies directly to our subject: "For this question holds true for the question of the union of divine nature with human [nature] and for the question of the non-union of divine nature with angelic [nature]."[2]

The *Summa de Bono* contains other texts that add to our knowledge of Philip's theology of the Hypostatic Union. Several brief texts touching the subject occur in passing within his examination of the problem of evil, the theology of original sin, and the question of miracles. More substantial developments concerning the theology of Christ are found in the following places: the discussion of angels, especially their relation to Christ; the treatment of grace, especially concerning adoptive sonship of ordinary men compared with the sonship of Christ, man as image and likeness of God through grace, and predestination with respect to ordinary man and to Christ; the examination of different aspects of faith, especially the articles of the creed and the place of the In-carnation among the mysteries of faith; the study of worship, and par-ticularly the role of Christ as an object of worship. All these discussions and the appropriate texts will be seen in their place within our study.

The main body of texts on our subject is found in the three questions on the Incarnation which we have edited here. It is uncertain whether

---

1 *Supra*, p. 21.
2 *DeDiscrPers*, 1; p. 155.

the order in which we have given them was Philip's order of disputation, although we do know at least that our question 1 preceded our question 2, which refers to our question 1 twice.[3] Question 1 has indeed some logical priority in that it asks which nature, angelic or human, was more suited for union. In passing, it compares the possibility of reparation for fallen man with that for fallen angels. The latter part of question 1 looks at the intellect or soul as medium of the union between divine nature and human nature and brings into the discussion the question of the potency in created nature to be united. Although at first glance this discussion of the intellect or soul as medium seems unrelated to the first part of the question, one can see on reflection that in Philip's mind the two parts are related because in the latter part he is concerned with the possibility of human nature being united and with certain conditions found in it that make it a possible subject for union by contrast with angels.

The second of our three questions is mainly concerned with debates about oneness, union, and unity. It opens with an examination of the kind of oneness or unity in which the union of the natures terminates, and then focuses on the hypostasis or person as that medium in which the union takes place ("medium" here has a different meaning from that in the first question). The third section, an important development on the grace of union, appears less directly related to the questions of union or unity examined in other parts of the question. The fourth section returns to the main theme by comparing the union or unity of the Incarnation with that of the Trinity and with examples of unity found in creation.

The third question, which the manuscript rubric rather misleadingly entitles *De Homine Assumpto*, begins with a discussion of the subject of the act of assuming, asking whether it was the divine nature or the divine person that assumed. Further queries are made about expressions such as "The divine nature is united to flesh," "The divine nature united human nature to itself," "The divine nature is man," and "The divine nature is incarnate." The second part of the question asks whether the divine person assumed a human person, a discussion that goes to the heart of the theology of the Hypostatic Union. The third part of question 3 is equally important for Philip's presentation of the mode of union in Christ: it is an extended treatment of the theme of the

---

3 *DeIncarn*, 2, 1 (p. 169) and 11 (p. 172). The importance of these references in establishing Philip's authorship of this question is presented *infra*, p. 153.

hypostasis composita in Christ, a treatment that starts from Damascene's use of this expression and goes into the questions of Christ as *totum* and the composition of parts.

Although there is no clearly detailed logical order in these three questions, one can discern a general pattern or order. The first question deals with the possibility and fittingness of the union of human rather than angelic nature, the second with the oneness and unity achieved by the union, and the third with the "elements" entering into the union, that is, the divine participant, the human reality assumed, and the resulting "composition" of these two. In a general way our own order of presentation of Philip's thought follows this broad pattern, but within it we have introduced a number of refinements and some rearrangements,[4] choosing a detailed division parallel to that in our first three volumes and seeing how Philip replies to the questions we raise according to this order. Such a procedure, we think, allows us better to incorporate the materials from the *Summa de Bono*, gives a clearer understanding of his doctrine by following it in a logical pattern, and at the same time facilitates comparison with the other authors examined in our series of studies.

2. THE INCARNATION AS A DOCTRINE OF FAITH

In his long investigations of the virtue of faith and the articles of the Creed, Philip the Chancellor frequently mentions among the objects of faith the mystery of the Incarnation. Thus in one place he says that faith is always concerned with the uncreated, but that in some cases along with the uncreated there is understood the created; the Incarnation and suffering of God are examples of such cases: "... Dicendum quod fides semper est de increato, sed quandoque cum cointellectu[1] increati, ut de Deo uno, trino, et hujusmodi; quandoque cum cointellectu[2] creati, ut de Deo incarnato, passo, et hujusmodi."[3]

Philip's concern with the problem of necessity and contingency in objects of faith leads him to consider the Incarnation as an object of faith.

---

4 The most significant rearrangements have been to consider the second and third parts of question 3 (no human person in Christ and the *hypostasis composita*) within our treatment of the mode of union. These parts, however, do enter into our discussion of the human nature assumed in the union (Part I, ch. 5).

1 intellectu *TV*.

2 intellectu *T; om. V, mg. V2*.

3 *P* 96va; *T* 77rb; *V* 81vb. Cf. *De Fide*, 3; Ceva, p. 59, ll. 104-107. Cf. Englhardt, *Glaubenspsychologie*, pp. 432, 436, for two texts that speak of the Incarnation as an object of faith.

In reply to an argument saying that because the Incarnation took place
in time, there is therefore an element of contingency in the object of
faith, Philip declares that if the phrase "Christ is to be incarnate" is understood to mean that "it was *ordained* that Christ will become incarnate," then the Incarnation is necessary; if it is understood to mean
"Christ will be incarnate," then the Incarnation will be shown to be
contingent in one respect and necessary in another. According to Philip,
faith regards the necessary aspect:

> Respondeo quod aliud est judicium de hoc: "Christum esse in-
> carnandum" secundum quod accipitur pro hoc: "Ordinatum est quod
> Christus incarnabitur",[4] et aliud secundum quod pro hoc: "Christus in-
> carnabitur".[5] Nam primum est necessarium; de secundo autem ostendetur
> qualiter contingens sit secundum quid et necessarium secundum quid, et
> ita fides semper erit vel de necessario simpliciter vel de necessario secun-
> dum quid. Non enim respicit fides illud ex parte contingentiae quam
> habet.[6]

From these words we see that Philip regards the Incarnation as an object of faith; at the same time he implies that the Incarnation did not
have to happen.

What are the various necessities that Philip refers to in the foregoing
text? He explains them immediately by relating these necessities to
either the absolute power of God or to this power linked with his
wisdom. Since the necessary, Philip says, is opposed to the impossible,
the necessary is diverse according as impossibility is diverse. Now the
impossible and possible refer to power, and power is either "first
power, that is, [power] without qualification," or it is "ordered power."
According to either of these powers it is necessary that Christ be incarnate so long as this means that it is *ordained* that Christ be incarnate:

> Nota ergo quod necessarium, cum opponitur impossibili, diversificatur
> secundum quod diversificatur impossibile. Impossibile autem et possibile
> respicit potentiam; potentia autem dicitur vel potentia prima sive sim-
> pliciter, vel potentia ordinata. Quocumque autem modo accipitur poten-
> tia, necessarium est Christum esse incarnandum secundum quod accipitur
> pro hoc: "Ordinatum est quod Christus incarnabitur".[7]

However, he continues, if the phrase means "Christ will be incarnate,"
a distinction is necessary. Philip had already said that this event would

---

4 incarnabatur *P.*
5 incarnabatur *P.*
6 *P* 99vb; *T* 79vb; *V* 84vb. Cf. *De Fide,* 4; Ceva, p. 79, ll. 322-329.
7 incarnabatur *P; locis citatis.* Cf. *De Fide,* 4; Ceva, pp. 79-80, ll. 330-336.

be shown to be contingent in one respect and necessary in another. Here he explains. The Incarnation is contingent as far as the event (*res*) is concerned, but necessary in relation to God's ordered power: "Quod si accipitur pro 'Christus incarnabitur,'[8] distinguendum est, scilicet quod duplicem habet comparationem: unam ad res, et secundum hoc habet contingentiam, alteram ad potentiam ordinatam, et secundum hoc habet necessitatem."[9] Shortly afterwards he explains this latter necessity as an "ordination according to the exigency of the event (*res*)" and quotes St. Leo to show that it refers to the fittingness of the Incarnation for man's victory over his conqueror, the devil:

> ... Loquimur de ordinatione quae est secundum exigentiam rei, de qua Leo Papa in quadam homelia circa Pascha: *Omnipotentia*[10] *Filii Dei, quae eadem est quae et Patris, potuisset genus humanum alio modo a dominatu diaboli eruere nisi negotio congrueret*[11] *ut per quod vincat vinceretur.*[12]

Thus, in summary, once the Incarnation is ordained by God, it is necessary, and although, as an event, it is in itself contingent, it has a certain necessity with respect to God's well-ordered power, that is, with respect to God's ordaining the Incarnation as the wisest means suited to man's redemption.

This last argument might be considered a kind of proof for the Incarnation. Further on within the same analysis of faith Philip raises the question of reasons (*rationes*) proving the Incarnation. The point now at issue is whether truths can be believed and also be known by reason at the same time. Did not St. Anselm, it is asked, give reasons to prove the Incarnation, so that opposition in the objects of knowledge does not suffice to distinguish reason and faith: "Item, ad probandum incarnationem[13] Filii Dei[14] ponuntur rationes, ut in libro Anselmi, *Cur Deus Homo*, et libro *De Articulis*. Ergo etiam quod sit oppositio[15] in cognitis non sufficit."[16]

---

8 incarnabatur *P.*

9 *Locis citatis.* Cf. *De Fide*, 4; Ceva, p. 80, ll. 336-339.

10 Cum potentia *T.*

11 contraheret *T*; contrahere *V*, conveniret *mg. V2.*

12 *P* 100ra; *T* 79vb; *V* 84va. Cf. *De Fide*, 4; Ceva, p. 80, ll. 353-357. Cf. St. Leo, *Sermo* 63 (*De Passione Domini*, XII), 1; PL 54, 353B: "Omnipotentia enim Filii Dei qua [quae *var.*] per eamdem essentiam aequalis est Patri, potuisset humanum genus a dominatu diaboli solo imperio suae voluntatis eruere, nisi divinis operibus maxime congruisset, ut nequitiae hostilis adversitas de eo quod vicerat vinceretur ..."

13 incarnalitatem *P.*

14 *Om. P.*

15 compositio *TV e corr. mg. V2.*

16 *P* 101va; *T* 81ra; *V* 85va. Cf. *De Fide*, 5; Ceva, p. 92, ll. 202-204. The *De Articulis* seems to be

Philip replies that in so far as one accepts a truth about God because of likenesses found in natural things, that truth is not an article of faith. But where reason sees that it fails and then adheres to the truth for its own sake rather than through anything else, that truth is an article of faith:

> Ad hoc respondeo quod unitas Dei et Trinitas, credita per similia quae inveniuntur in naturalibus, secundum quod sic credita, non est articulus, sed secundum quod ponit ratio se deficere, et in[17] lumine spirituali adhaeret ei propter se et non per aliud.[18]

Although Philip does not directly answer the question about the Incarnation, one can easily see the direction his reply would take.

In connection with Philip's investigation of the Incarnation as a mystery of faith we may examine his reply to the questions whether the Incarnation is a miracle and whether it is contrary to nature. As to the first question, Philip defines a miracle in a narrow fashion: a miracle is above nature and is not conformed to nature; it happens rarely; it is not hoped for; reason cannot grasp it. But, he says, since the Incarnation was the object of hope on the part of the ancient fathers, it was not a miracle; but it was a wondrous event:

> Hae sunt igitur conditiones miraculi, scilicet quod sit supra naturam nec naturae conforme, raro ens, et non speretur posse evenire, neque[19] sit facultas rationis ad illud. Dicendum igitur est[20] quod opus incarnationis secundum hanc rationem Augustini[21] non est miraculum quia, licet sit arduum, id est, supra naturam, tamen non est praeter spem quia speraverunt patres antiqui incarnationem. Eodem modo dicendum est de resurrectione, quam similiter speraverunt. Sunt autem haec mirabilia, licet non miracula ...[22]

Anselm's *De Incarnatione*: see its ch. 10 (Schmitt II, 25-28); most of the *Cur Deus Homo* (Schmitt II, 39-133) gives such reasons.

17 *Om. T.*

18 *Locis citatis.* Cf. *De Fide*, 5; Ceva, p. 92, ll. 205-209. Concerning God's existence as demonstrable by reason and as believed by faith, Philip says: "Sed distinguendum est quoniam duplex est credere, unum per viam rationis, secundum quod proceditur de effectu ad causam, et causae non ponuntur infinitae, et sic comprehenditur quod est prima causa, et sic cognoscentibus Deum esse non est articulus, et hoc credere non salvat. Item, est credere quo quis adhaeret ei quod est Deum esse per ipsum et non per rationes, et hoc non potest fieri nisi luce desuper [de supra V] data, et sine hoc non est salus, et sic credenti Deum esse est articulus secundum quod arctat intelligentiam ut adhaereat ei propter se" (*P* 101rb; *T* 80vb; *V* 85vb). Cf. *De Fide*, 5; Ceva, p. 90, ll. 149-158.

19 nisi ubi *T.*

20 rationis ... est] rationis. Ad id igitur dicendum est *TV.*

21 Augustine, *De Utilitate Credendi*, 16, 34; PL 42, 90: "Miraculum voco, quidquid arduum aut insolitum supra spem vel facultatem mirantis apparet."

22 *P* 73vb; *T* 61ra-rb; *V* 65ra.

Later Philip adds that the Incarnation is not a miracle for this further reason that it shows forth principally the mercy of God; this, he says, is not the principal function of miracles:

> Sciendum etiam est quod incarnatio et redemptio ostendunt principaliter misericordiam Dei, quae ad bonitatem in genere reducitur ... Miracula[23] autem non sunt ostensiva bonitatis principaliter, quare[24] non sunt hujusmodi miracula.[25]

As to the question whether the Incarnation is contrary to nature, Philip asserts that it is above nature rather than contrary to it. An event is contrary to nature, he declares, when it runs counter to the course of nature, as when a blind man receives sight. But the Incarnation does not run counter to the course of nature in this way:

> Respondeo: Quandoque accipitur "praeter" pro "contra," ut in praedictis, et secundum hoc nulla est differentia. Quandoque ita distinguuntur haec omnia quod diversa sunt, verbi gratia, opus incarnationis dicitur[26] proprie fieri[27] supra naturam sed non proprie contra, quia illud dicitur fieri contra naturam quod currit contrario cursu[28] cursui naturae, ut quod caecus visum recipiat: cursus enim naturae est ut de privatione ad habitum non fiat regressus; contra cursum naturae[29] est ut fiat. Istud autem Deum fieri hominem non est tale.[30]

Again, Philip adds, when something happens contrary to nature, it terminates in a work that is conformed to nature, as in the case of the blind man who receives natural sight. But the Incarnation terminates at something whose like cannot be found in nature, namely, that God is man. Hence it is above nature rather than contrary to it:

> Item, illud dicitur fieri contra naturam quod terminatur ad opus conforme naturae: visus enim conformis est in prius caeco et in naturaliter vidente; opus autem incarnationis terminatur ad illud cujus simile non potest reperiri in natura, verbi gratia, quod Deus sit homo. Dicuntur ergo fieri supra naturam et non contra.[31]

---

23 mirabilia *T*.
24 quasi *P*.
25 mirabilia *T*. *P* 74ra; *T* 61rb; *V* 65ra.
26 dicetur *P*.
27 *Om. P*.
28 *Om. P*.
29 *Om. P*.
30 *P* 74vb; *T* 61vb; *V* 65va.
31 *Locis citatis*.

Beyond these investigations of the Incarnation Philip has little to say about it as a mystery of faith. His expressions of the mystery are quite simple and traditional: in the Incarnation, he says, distant things are joined together, that is, the divine and human natures;[32] in this mystery the Word is incarnate, or the Son is incarnate;[33] the terminus of the work of Incarnation is that God is man.[34]

Neither in the *Summa de Bono* nor in the *Quaestiones de Incarnatione* does Philip discuss at any length heresies concerning this mystery of faith. In one text in the *Summa de Bono* he mentions certain heretics who believed that Christ was a pure creature and that he descended to hell in such a way as not to return: "... Quidam haeretici crediderunt Christum fuisse puram creaturam et ita ad inferos descendisse quod non rediisse."[35] In another passage within the study of the kind of worship owed to Christ, Philip quotes a text contained in Peter Lombard's *Collectanea* in which occurs a reference to Photinus and Paul of Samosata, who are said to have separated the man from God in Christ: "Denique si hominem separaveris a Deo, ut Photinus vel Paulus Samosathenus, illi numquam credo nec servio."[36]

Finally, in the course of distinguishing between truths that "accompany" faith and truths that "are consequent upon" faith, Philip mentions among the latter the teaching that Christ as man is *aliquid*. It has been determined with respect to this teaching, he says, that its contrary may in no way be held:

> Concomitantia autem fidem sunt ipsi articuli; consequentia vero sunt quaedam inter quae quorumdam veritas est de Deo et quorumdam non ... Item, de consequentibus articulis[37] est Christum esse aliquid secundum

---

32 *P* 77rb; *T* 63vb; *V* 67vb. "... aut fit secundum distantiam naturarum seu qualitatum quae licet distantes sibi conjunguntur, ut divina natura et humana, et quod simul Virgo et Mater."

33 *P* 39ra; *T* 33rb; *V* 34ra: "... Quod autem imago referatur ad Verbum incarnatum sive Filium aperit Augustinus ..." Cf. *P* 13va; *T* 11vb; *V* 12rb: "... et de operibus summae misericordiae quae facta sunt vel [*add.* in *T*] futura erant [erunt *T*], sicut quod Verbum Dei est incarnatum, et quae consequuntur."

34 See the text *supra* ("Item"): on the preceding page.

35 *P* 103rb; *T* 82rb; *V* 87ra. Cf. *De Fide*, 6; Ceva, p. 106, ll. 385-387.

36 *P* 180ra; *T* 127rb; *V* 134rb. Philip himself indicates that Lombard's work is his source, and he gives the scriptural passage being glossed. For the full text see Lombard, *Coll in Gal* 4, 8; PL 192, 140B. The original text quoted by Lombard is found among the sermons ascribed to St. Augustine (*Sermo* 246, 5; PL 39, 2200); the editor notes that this section "est incerti auctoris" (col. 2198, n. *b*). P. Glorieux, *Pour revaloriser Migne*, Cahier Supplémentaire to the *Mélanges de Science Religieuse* 9 (1951), p. 27, says that it is from Pelagius, but the reference he gives pertains only to *Sermo* 236 and not also, as he indicates, to *Sermo* 246. Another reference to such a heresy is found in *DeIncarn*, 2, 11; p. 172.

37 articulos *TV*.

quod homo, de quo determinatum est ut contrarium ejus nullo modo dicatur.[38]

These are the only references to heresies or doctrinal decisions that we have found in either the *Summa de Bono* or in the *Quaestiones de Incarnatione*. Philip certainly knew of others because he was quite conversant with St. John Damascene's *De Fide Orthodoxa*, which refers to many heresies and gives many statements of the Catholic doctrine on the Hypostatic Union. It must be remembered, however, that the *Summa de Bono* may well be incomplete; further, the questions of Philip on the Incarnation that we possess cover only certain aspects of the Hypostatic Union. We shall see, moreover, that Philip takes it for granted that there can be neither a union in one nature nor an accidental union of the two natures;[39] these are undoubtedly implicit references to the Church's teaching on the Hypostatic Union.

3. COMPARISON OF ANGELIC AND HUMAN NATURE AS TO SUITABILITY FOR UNION

Except for an argument taken from St. Leo, to which we have already referred, Philip, at least in the material that has come to us, presents no arguments of fittingness similar to those found in Alexander of Hales.[1] At certain points in his *Quaestiones de Incarnatione* Philip has to defend the rational possibility of the Hypostatic Union against particular arguments, but since these discussions involve his theology of the mode of union, we shall leave them for later investigation.[2]

Philip gives considerable attention to the relative suitability of angelic and human nature for being assumed.[3] The greater part of one of the *Quaestiones* also studies this problem.[4] Although at first sight this topic appears strictly hypothetical, it gives Philip the opportunity to make his most penetrating and original developments concerning personal distinction.

In general Philip sees three reasons why human nature is more suited for assumption than angelic nature: first, man is in several respects

---

38 *P* 101ra; *T* 80va; *V* 85rb. Cf. *De Fide*, 5; Ceva, p. 88, II, 78-80, 85-87.

39 See *infra*, pp. 89-92.

1 For St. Leo's argument see *supra*, p. 73 ("Loquimur"). Cf. *HypUnion* II, 82-86, for Alexander's arguments.

2 See *infra*, pp. 90-92.

3 See Philip, *DeDiscrPers*, pp. 155-157.

4 That is, *DeIncarn*, 1-i & 1-ii, 1-15a; pp. 158-166.

more like God than an angel is; second, the coming into being of a human nature does not of itself entail personal discretion (and so human nature is assumable), whereas an angel's nature, by its very realization as a nature, is at the same time a person (and so angelic nature cannot be assumed); third, man can be redeemed but an angel cannot, so that an angel is unsuited for an assumption aiming at redemption.

Concerning the first of these reasons, man's greater likeness to God, Philip recognizes that there are two sides to the argument. Thus he first lists proofs pointing to the angel's greater likeness to God. One says that angelic nature, like God's nature, is separate, that is, it does not operate through a body.[5] Another states that angelic nature is more like the divine nature in its "reason,"[6] or, again, in its intellect, which is "deiform."[7] This greater likeness of the angelic intellect consists in its receiving knowledge only from its Creator, whereas the human intellect receives knowledge from things both above and below it.[8] In a phrase that points out why this makes the angel more like God, Philip says that the divine intelligence is passive before nothing;[9] that is, since God has no source of knowledge outside himself, the angel, who has fewer sources of knowledge than man, and none below himself, is more like God.

In reply to these arguments Philip, although conceding that "in certain things" angelic nature is more like God than human nature is, points out other ways in which man is more like God: these ways, he maintains, make man more able than an angel to be united to God. One greater likeness in man is that all the members of the human race derive from one man, just as all things in creation derive from God as from their one principle; angels, however, do not derive from one angel and so do not imitate God in this way. Thus, Philip adds, in Scripture man is called the image of God, but the angel is not given this title.[10]

---

5 *Ibid.*, 1-i, 1 (p. 158), and 1-ii, 2 (p. 158).

6 *Ibid.*, 1-ii, 4; p. 161.

7 *Ibid.*, 1-i, 1 (p. 158), & 4 (p. 161); *ibid.*, 1-ii, 3 (p. 158).

8 *Ibid.*, 1-i & 1-ii, 9; p. 162. There is a slight variation in the terminology of the two parallel texts; whereas the first redaction speaks of the intellect as *passibilis*, the second says it is *possibilis*; in one place, however, the second redaction's *possibilis* is changed by the scribe or a corrector to read *passibilis* (p. 162). Both readings make sense: undoubtedly they show that here we are dealing with the *reportatio* of an oral lecture, in which the difference between *passibilis* and *possibilis* would be hard to detect.

9 *Ibid.*; p. 162.

10 *Ibid.*; pp. 161-162. The same reason for man's greater likeness seems to be implied *ibid.*, 1-i, 2 (p. 159), where Philip says that man's soul and body agree with the divine nature, "which is communicable." The communicability of the divine nature points to God's sharing his being through

There is a second way, Philip says, in which man is more like God than is an angel: just as the being of all things, both corporeal and spiritual, is in God as in their exemplar, so every [kind of] being [*omne esse*], that is, spiritual and corporeal being, is in man; the angel, on the other hand, has only spiritual being; therefore, man's greater likeness in this respect makes him more able to be united than is an angel.[11] A similar argument is developed at greater length in the *Summa de Bono*.[12] We shall see in the comparison of personal discretion in angels and men that this presence of matter in man has an added contribution to make to his greater assumability.[13]

creation and within the Divinity by the processions of divine persons. On this general argument cf. *QuaestAlex*, 15, 34; I, 203.

11 Philip, *DeIncarn*, 1-i & 1-ii, 10; p. 162. A similar argument is found in *QuaestAlex*, 15, 34; I, 203.

12 *P* 38rb; *T* 32vb; *V* 33va. "Item, si quaeritur: 'Dignior est intellectus; ergo, cum secundum dignius imitetur angelus, potius imago dici debet,' respondeo: Verum est quod angelus magis est imago secundum rationem intellectus in simplicitate [simplicitatem *T*], non tamen omnino imago quo modo homo. Primo [post *P*], quia licet intellectus sit dignior ratione, non tamen in tot habet convenientiam, nec habet cum omnibus convenientiam ut Deus; sed convenientiam habet homo ad omnem creaturam quia [*om. P*, which puts a paragraph sign here] creato angelo, nondum deductum est de exemplari omne [esse *P*] esse in [etiam *P*] spirituale, quare angelus non erit [erat *TV*] imago quia imago continet totum quod est in exemplari. Facto autem homine, totum est deductum, et spirituale et corporale et conjunctum, quare homo potius imago Dei dicitur [*om. P*] quam angelus quia non est respicienda solum esse-simplicitas [simplicitas *TV*], sed totalitas."

In the following paragraph (*locis citatis*) Philip adds that reason is more like the Trinity in that it has an order of beginning, middle (term), and final (conclusion), whereas intellect does not: "Secundo, quia non [ratio *TV*] tenet imaginem quoad rationem intellectus, et praeter hoc quia ratio est intellectus cum ordinatione. Ratione [fractione *T*] ordinationis quae consistit in principio et medio et ultimo habet imaginem primae Trinitatis et in hoc est Trinitatis expressior convenientia [et ... conv.) *post* ultimo *et ante* habet *P*]."

In the next paragraph (*locis citatis*) Philip inverts the argument of the *Quaestiones*, saying that the angel is not an image as completely as man is because the angel is not able to be united to the Divinity: "Tertio, quia angelus non habet rationem unibilem cum divinitate quam homo habet. Imago ergo, secundum quod propriissime convenit homini, posset definiri sic: Imago est maxima convenientia rei ad rem, immediate expressa de altero."

Later in the *Summa de Bono* Philip repeats his argument about man's having all degrees of being and thereby being more like God than an angel is; he teaches, however, that with respect to the angel's function of guardianship, which involves a nobler mode of understanding and moving than man has, the angel is more like the divine reason in intellect and movement than the human soul is: "Respondendum autem est ad objecta quod licet homo secundum animam gerat expressam similitudinem Dei in Trinitate et expressiorem quoad quid quam angelus, scilicet in communicantia cum omnibus rebus, ut quemadmodum Deus est causa omnium entium et moventium et sentientium et intelligentium et viventium, ita anima est principium cognitionis per intellectum, et sensus per vim sentiendi, et vitae per vegetationem, et motus quorumdam et esse quorumdam, quod non contingit in angelo reperire, nihilominus quoad illud secundum quod debetur custoditio, expressiorem gerit similitudinem angelus quam anima: est enim suus modus intelligendi nobilior et movendi rationi divinae intellectu et motu similior" (*P* 7obis ra; *T* 58ra; *V* 62ra).

13 See *infra*, pp. 81-85.

The second of Philip's three approaches to this question, that is, the difference in personal discretion between an angel and man, is the one that he most emphasizes in proving the greater assumability of human nature. For Philip this difference proves, moreover, that angelic nature is not only less suited for assumption than is human nature, but is even unable to be assumed without the destruction of the angel's perfection. This is stated rather cryptically in a preliminary solution:

> Neither a man nor an angel was able to be united to God because of its absolute and personal being; the soul and body, however, were able to be united because they come into the composition of a hypostasis or person. An angel, however, would lose its perfection if it were united, which would be against the goodness of God.[14]

The force of the argument is clarified by an argument against it, especially one that, before replying to it, summarizes it by saying:

> Again, there seems to be no validity to the argument given above that human nature has a soul and body which are especially able to be united because from them one thing, namely man, comes to be, and therefore human nature is more able to be united.[15]

In other words, the argument favoring the greater unitability of human nature stresses the fact that the parts of human nature have already been united to form one unity, man, and argues therefrom that their very union in human nature or in their hypostasis makes human nature more apt for a further union.

The objections to this argument lead at once to the discussion, central to Philip's position, about the comparison of personal discretion in men and angels.[16] Invoking the doctrine on personal discretion in God, angels, and men that has already been seen above,[17] an objection found

---

14 *DeIncarn*, 1-i, 1; p. 159.

15 *Ibid.*, 1-i, 5 (p. 160); the parallel passage (*ibid.*, 1-ii, 5; p. 160) concludes the same argument by saying: "... and so *because of that conjoining* human nature is able to be united." Emphasis mine.

16 Two objections to this argument, to which Philip makes no direct reply, take a different turn. The first (*ibid.*, 1-i & 1-ii, 6; p. 160) argues that the union of body and soul produces a person, so that a person would be united to a person, which is impossible. If they were not united to each other, there would be no composition and the argument would be null. Indirectly, Philip's position on personal discretion among men will show that body and soul can be united without there being present a human person.

The second objection (*ibid.*, 1-i & 1-ii, 7; pp. 160-161)argues that the angel, like the human soul, has a union of memory, intelligence, and will, and that the union in both is greater than the union of body and soul in man; hence the argument for the greater unitability of human nature based on the union of body and soul is not convincing.

17 *Supra*, pp. 62, 68.

in both the *Summa de Bono* and the *Quaestiones* argues as follows: Because man has greater personal discretion than an angel, and because personal discretion impedes union, therefore man is less able to be united than angelic nature. Why is man said to have greater personal discretion? Because, these objections assert, man's personal discretion arises not from one source, as do God's or the angel's, but from two: one of man's sources of personal discretion is similar to the principle of personal discretion in God, and the other is similar to the principle of personal discretion in an angel. That is, just as in God personal distinction is by origin of one person from another, so one man is distinct from another by his origin from another man; and just as one angel is distinct from another by reason of his distinct essence or "quality," so each man has his own proper and singular substance or "quality" that contributes, along with his origin, to his personal distinction.[18]

Philip's reply to this objection may be summarized as follows: In simple beings like an angel, *posse* and *esse* are identical, that is, as soon as the angelic *posse* (the nature or form) is realized, at once the angel is, and in the same instant and by its very achieving its being it achieves personal being. But because a person cannot be united to another person, an angel, whose nature is immediately a person, cannot be united to the divine person. In man, however, because the material part of his nature precludes simplicity and so an identity of *posse* and *esse*, human nature, the *posse*, can be realized without its being immediately and by that very fact a complete being and therefore a person. This gradual coming into being of human nature, which Philip seems to equate with a generation actualizing the potency of matter, makes it possible for the divine person to unite a human nature to himself before a human person exists. Hence man can be united to a divine person, but an angel, unless his personality is destroyed, cannot be so united. Let us examine his own statements on these points.

18 *DeIncarn*, 1-i & 1-ii, 8 (p. 161); cf. *DeDiscrPers*, 3-4 (pp. 155-156). In the first of these the distinction of angels is said to be according to "diverse essences"; in the second it is said to be according to quality," which may arise from either an absolute or relative property. The absolute property giving rise to a qualitative difference seems to be equivalent to the essence. In *DeDiscrPers*, 4 (p. 156), Philip adds a further qualification: among angels, personal distinction does not arise solely from a quality; rather, each hypostasis differs *per se* from every other, even without a quality being understood. Philip adds to this statement the following words: "... and because in a simple being of this kind *posse* and *esse* are identical, angelic nature is never without personal distinction." It is uncertain whether these words are meant to be an explanation of how each hypostasis differs *per se*; if they are so meant, then Philip appears to be thinking of the actually-existing hypostasis and to be saying that through the act of creation an angelic hypostasis is *per se* by the mere fact that it comes into concrete existence as an angelic nature.

The statement about the identity of *posse* and *esse* in simple beings like angels is derived from a text of Aristotle, who says in his *Physics* that "in eternal things to be possible and to be in no way differ."[19] Like many authors of this period, Philip does not differentiate between possibility and potency; thus we have already met an important text in the *Summa de Bono* that goes through the whole order of potency-act relationships in a manner parallel to the order of *posse-esse* relationships given in the present analysis.[20] In that text Philip stated that things subject to generation and corruption have potency prior to act, whereas incorporeal substances are said to have act without potency; among the latter, the intelligences that are separate substances are said to be act without potency and in addition to be the act of no other potency.[21] In another text of the *Summa de Bono* Philip contrasts "incorruptibles" with "corruptibles" by saying that in the former "the potency is never without its particular act, nor is there in them an alteration of act in matter and it is never without act," whereas "in corruptible things the act is destroyed, but not every [act], for the potency remains in relation to another act."[22]

19 *Physics* III, 4, 9; 203b 30. Firmin-Didot II, 278, give the Latin as follows: "Posse et esse, in sempiternis nihil differunt." Cf. *GlossaAlex* I, 7, 12c; p. 97. William of Auxerre applies the idea to the question of the soul and its faculties in *Summa Aurea* (Paris: Pigouchet, 1500) fol. 59vb.

20 See *supra*, p. 54 ("Sed subdividitur"). On the interchange of possibility and potency in this period see D. Callus, "Robert Grosseteste as Scholar," in *Robert Grosseteste: Scholar and Bishop*, ed. D. Callus (Oxford 1955) p. 24. For the same interchange in the twelfth century see M.-D. Chenu, *La théologie au douzième siècle* (Paris 1957) pp. 313-314.

21 See *loc. cit.* If they are without potency, they are still not God because they have a composition of *quod est* and *quo est*: cf. *supra*, p. 54.

22 The distinction occurs within a discussion of the presence of evil in living things that die but not in others. Since the text of *T* and *V* varies considerably from that of *P* at certain points, especially by certain long additions that add nothing to the argument, only the text of *P* is given here: "Respondeo: Cum malum sit ex privatione actus, non est in omnibus accipere malum oppositum secundum naturam, et [hoc] propter indivisionem potentiae ab actu. — Sed quaeres: Si hujusmodi habent indivisionem potentiae ab actu, et ita habet Primum, in quo ergo differunt? — Respondeo quod in hujusmodi, licet sit indivisio, non tamen potentia est actus nec e converso. In summo autem bono idem est potentia quod actus simpliciter; in aliis autem, etsi numquam sit potentia sine actu aut forma, nihilominus potentia quae est materia potest esse sine hac forma vel illa, et ideo in his potest cognosci malum. Sed in quibusdam cognoscitur simpliciter et est simpliciter, in quibusdam non: corpus enim quod est susceptibile vitae per mortem dicitur privari vita, et hoc malum, licet non malum in eo quod est corpus; non sic autem in materia elementorum in qua forma transmutatur. Patet ergo quod non in omnibus evenit malum. In Summo enim idem est potentia cum actu: ibi locum non habet; in incorruptibilibus potentia numquam sine suo particulari actu, nec ibi in materia alteratur, et numquam sine actu; et in corruptibilibus actus destruitur, sed non omnis, sed potentia remanet secundum alium actum: quare ibi malum secundum quid et non simpliciter" (*P* 5va; cf. *T* 5rb, *V* 5va).

This distinction between incorruptibles or simple beings on the one hand and corruptibles or material composites on the other is the basis for Philip's comparison of angelic and human nature with respect to assumability. When dealing with this problem in both the *Summa* and the *Quaestiones*, Philip distinguishes a threefold *potestas* or *posse*. The first is a possibility coming from the agent (*potestas ab agente; posse ab agente*), for example, the world's possibility of being created by God from eternity: this possibility, he says, does not "posit" or "immediately attain to" *esse* either *simpliciter* or *secundum quid*.[23] Let us listen to Philip himself describing in the *Summa de Bono* the second and third possibilities:

> ... There is also a possibility[24] from matter, according to which it can be in act, but according to this [possibility] the angel could not be because he is immaterial; and there is a possibility from form, for example, the possibility by which a triangle can be a triangle is triangulation: when that possibility is, the triangle is; likewise in an angel. According to the possibility from matter the thing is in a certain respect; according to the possibility from form it is simply. In this way, therefore, the form of the thing is that possibility which attains *esse*, because when the form is, that possibility is, and then the thing is. But in material things this is not the case because their possibility is had not only according to form, but according to matter, whereas in simple things it is had only according to form. This, then, is the reason why it is said that in an angel and in simple beings *to be and to be possible are identical*.[25]

In other words, Philip teaches that in spiritual beings, which are forms without matter, the form or essence is a possible that attains being as soon as it is a possible: this is the meaning of the dictum that *posse* and *esse* are identical in simple beings. In the *Quaestiones* Philip states the same doctrine, except that there he says that the *posse a forma* in an angel attains being "immediately" (*statim*);[26] this addition emphasizes the difference between an angel and man, in whom the material element and its possibility prevent the identity of *posse* and *esse*.

This doctrine, which may be influenced by the Avicennian notion of essence as a possible, but which also has roots in Boethius,[27] has im-

---

23 *DeDiscrPers*, 5 (p. 156), ll. 36-37), and *DeIncarn*, 1-i & 1-ii, 11 (p. 163, ll. 170-176). The former uses the terms *potestas* and *ponit esse*, the latter the terms *posse* and *statim consequitur esse*. As will be seen, these variations leave the meaning unchanged.

24 "Possibility" is used to translate the two terms *potestas* and *posse*; no appreciable difference in meaning is evident in the two terms.

25 *DeDiscrPers*, 5; pp. 156-157, ll. 38-48.

26 *DeIncarn*, 1-i & 1-ii, 11; p. 162, ll. 159-161.

27 For Boethius see his *DeHebdom* (Rand, p. 44, ll. 86-91), and cf. E. Gilson, *History of Christian*

mediate consequences regarding personal distinction and so regarding
the assumability of angelic and human nature. Philip declares that
because "personal distinction follows upon *esse*," and because in a simple being like an angel "*posse* and *esse* are identical, angelic nature is
never without personal distinction."[28] He states the same consequence
more fully in a later paragraph, and applies it to the problem at hand,
saying:

> There are, however, some things in which *esse* is the same as *posse*, and
> of these some have an *esse* that is unique and absolute, as is the case in
> angelic nature, and therefore it could not be united to the divine nature
> because a person cannot be united to a person that remains a person,
> because there [in angelic nature] the possible (*posse*) attains absolute *esse*,
> and as soon as it is, it is personally discrete: consequently it is not suited
> for being united.[29]

In other words, an angelic nature cannot be realized as a nature
without its being immediately a distinct and complete being, that is, a
person; hence an angelic nature cannot be united to the divine nature
in a personal unity such as is found in the Incarnation, where the
assumed nature lacks its own personality.

Human nature, however, can be united to the divine nature in a personal union, Philip holds, because in human nature, which has matter
as well as form, its *posse* is distinct from its *esse*: "Sed aliter est in humana
natura, in qua differt posse ab esse."[30] Again he says:

> ... There are some things in which *posse* and *esse* are the same, as in the
> higher beings, and some in which they are not the same, as in human
> nature; and therefore, because in human nature *posse* does not attain *esse*
> [i.e., at once or immediately], human nature was able to be united to
> divine nature in a personal unity, with the same person remaining [itself].[31]

Philosophy in the Middle Ages (New York 1955) pp. 104-105. For Avicenna's doctrine that may be influential here, see G. Smith, "Avicenna and the Possibles," *The New Scholasticism* 17 (1943) 340-357.

28 *DeDiscrPers*, 4; p. 156, ll. 33-34, 27-29.

29 *Ibid.*, 7; p. 157, ll. 57-62. Cf. *ibid.*, 4 (p. 156, ll. 30-32), where the same application is made: after
stating that angelic nature is never without personal distinction, Philip says: "But a person cannot
be united to a person that remains a person. Therefore it was not suitable that there be a union of
divine nature to angelic nature in a unity of person or of persons."

In *DeIncarn*, 1-ii, 11. (p. 163, ll. 184-186), Philip says: "And therefore because [*Posse*] is such in an
angel that it immediately attains personal *esse*, the angel cannot be united." Earlier in the same
paragraph (in both 1-i & 1-ii; p. 163, ll. 165-171) he had said that the personal discretion of an angel
impedes union more than that in man "because according to its nature [the angel] more quickly attains its discrete *esse*, because in the angel *posse* attains *esse*," that is, it attains *esse* immediately.

30 *DeDiscrPers*, 4; p. 156, ll. 32-33.

31 *Ibid.*, 7; p. 157, ll. 53-57.

This difference in man arises from the presence of matter in his nature. As has been seen, Philip says that "in material things ... their *posse* is had not only according to form, but according to matter,"[32] so that for human nature to come into being, this possibility of matter, which gives *esse* "non simpliciter sed secundum quid,"[33] must be taken into account. Philip appears to envisage the difference as that between a simple being whose essence attains being and personal distinction instantaneously, and a composite being like man, whose essence attains being and personal distinction through a gradual process of generation. In the latter, the essence could be realized as an essence, that is, a possible, without its thereby being an existent or a person; the divine person could take this possible to himself prior to the emergence of human personality.

Philip has to face one final difficulty arising from his own principles. Is not the human soul simple in being, and would it not attain *esse* immediately and so be a person?[34] Philip replies by distinguishing absolute or *per se esse* from conjoined *esse (esse in conjuncto)* or *esse* in or with another. The soul, Philip says, is by nature apt to be united to the body and is the act of an animated body;[35] it has its "first being" in the body,[36] and achieves *per se esse* only when it is separated from the body.[37] "Therefore," he concludes, "although *posse* and *esse* are identical in it, nevertheless, because it is not absolute, it could be assumed ..."[38]

In this whole discussion, then, where the objector had seen in the multiple principles of personal discretion in man a greater impediment to union with the Word than the single principle of personal discretion in an angel, Philip turns this very difference against his opponent. We may summarize his original and interesting discussion in his own words:

> We grant ... that in man there is greater personal discretion, but that does not impede union. On the contrary, the lesser discretion of an angel impedes it more, because according to its nature it attains its discrete *esse* more quickly ...[39]

---

32 *Ibid.*, 5; p. 157, ll. 45-46.
33 *DeIncarn*, 1-i & 1-ii, 11; p. 163, ll. 179-181.
34 For Philip's statement of the difficulty see *ibid.*, 1-ii, 11 (p. 163, ll. 189-192).
35 *DeDiscrPers*, 7; p. 157, ll. 62-68.
36 *DeIncarn*, 1-i & 1-ii; pp. 163-164, ll. 189-190, 199-200.
37 Cf. *DeDiscrPers*, 7; p. 157, ll. 66-67.
38 *Ibid.*; p. 157, ll. 67-69.
39 *DeIncarn*, 1-i & 1-ii, 11; p. 163, ll. 162-170. On all this cf. *SummaAlex* III, 16; IV, 33 (no. 5) & 35 (no. 5).

Philip's third reason why human nature is more suited for assumption than angelic nature has to do with the sin and repentance of man and the angels. Philip quotes an argument from St. Gregory contrasting the sin of the devil and of man: Since the devil was not led into sin by another, but fell by himself, he cannot be repaired by another; man, who is weaker and who fell through being deceived by another, could be repaired or cured through another.[40]

A second argument relating to the redemption has to do with the structure of angelic and human nature. Philip affirms several times that the angel does not or cannot repent;[41] he sees the source of this inability in the simplicity and incorporeity of the angel. Man, on the other hand, is able to repent because his weak corporeal nature leaves room for repentance. In only one passage is the explanation of the angel's inability to repent brought out in detail; in it Philip says: "The angel is unable to be healed because he cannot repent, since he does not have two elements in himself, in one of which he may be sorry for his sin and according to the other rejoice over his sorrow ..."[42] Philip apparently means that repentance requires a corporeal nature that can experience sorrow, no doubt as a result of bodily punishments inflicted by God because of sin; man, by his joyful acceptance of this chastened sorrow, can repent. Here the Chancellor seems to be expressing more obscurely what Alexander of Hales says more simply and clearly, namely, that satisfaction for sin requires a subjection to penal suffering, which is impossible for an angel.[43] Philip does add, however, that the angel could be repaired by the absolute power of God.[44]

---

40 *Ibid.*; p. 165. For the sources of the argument see *infra*, p. 165, n. to l. 231.

41 A quotation from Damascene (given in *DeIncarn*, 14; p. 165) states that an angel's fall is like man's death: there is no repentance after either. Philip links the inability of the angel to repent with his incorporeal nature: see *ibid.*, 1-i, 14 (pp. 164-165) and 1-ii, 15 (pp. 165-166) and cf. *ibid.*, 1-i, 15 (p. 165). Cf. also the following statement from the *Summa de Bono*: "Ad aliud respondeo quod ideo natura angelica non fuit unibilis quia non fuit reparabilis" (*P* 70*bis* ra; *T* 58va; *V* 62ra).

42 *DeIncarn*, 1-i, 14; pp. 164-165.

43 Cf. *QuaestAlex*, 15, 36; I, 204.

44 *DeIncarn*, 1-ii, 15a; p. 166. These arguments about the inability of an angel to repent as contrasted with man's ability to repent because of his corporeal nature are part of Philip's rebuttal of an objection that had claimed that man was more completely corrupted by sin, which affected his body as well as his soul, than the angel was; hence, the objection argued, man was less easily curable than an angel, who is by nature incorruptible; see *ibid.*, 1-i & 1-ii, 13; p. 164. Besides his reply that man's corporeal nature is the reason man cannot repent, Philip answers the objection by pointing out that man's soul was no more corrupted by sin than was the angel's essence. Original sin, Philip holds, affected the natural dispositions (*habitudines*) of man, but not his nature itself, just as the sin of the angel affected his natural dispositions, but not his nature itself. For this argument see *ibid.*, 1-i & 1-ii, 15; p. 165.

In the *Summa de Bono* Philip states an interesting consequence of his teaching about the relative unitability of human and angelic nature. Because the divine nature could be united to human nature and to no other, he says, everything is in a certain sense for the sake of man; one consequence of this is that the number of guardian angels created by God is proportioned to the number of men to be guarded: "Item, cum omnia sint quodammodo propter hominem in quantum erat ei unibilis divina natura et nulli alteri, videtur quod secundum numerum hominum custodiendorum sit numerus custodientium."[45]

In summary, then, we see that Philip, by the combination of three different approaches to the question of relative unitability, judges that human nature is more suited for assumption by a divine person than is an angel. There are two sides, he realizes, to the argument from likeness to God, but beyond this he maintains that the assumption of an angel is either impossible, angelic personality being so intimately and immediately linked with the realization of angelic nature, or it is at least useless because an angel cannot repent of his sin.

45 *P* 65va; *T* 54rb; *V* 57va.

CHAPTER III

THE MODE OF UNION

1. PHILIP THE CHANCELLOR'S PRESENTATION OF THE THREE OPINIONS

One remarkable feature about Philip the Chancellor's investigations of the Hypostatic Union is that he refers only indirectly to the famous three opinions so frequently discussed in the schools. As a consequence of this silence, his analyses of the *aliquid*-question and the unity-duality problem are quite restricted; for others, we have seen, these two topics were considered the very substance of the three opinions and crucial points in the theology of the Hypostatic Union. Perhaps Philip devoted a separate question, not extant today, to a detailed study of these matters; or it may be that the question-form he used made discussions of the opinions less imperative than would have necessarily been the case had he written a gloss or commentary on the *Sentences* of Peter Lombard.

The only clear allusion to the opinions occurs in passing references to the *aliquid*-question. Twice Philip indicates that the unity found in Christ cannot be accidental because it would follow from an accidental union that Christ as man would not be *aliquid*.[1] We have already seen that for Philip this teaching that Christ as man is *aliquid* is a truth "consequent upon" the articles of faith.[2]

The positions taken by Philip on the problems concerning the Hypostatic Union indicate where he would stand with respect to the opinions. He supports the concept of *hypostasis composita* and rejects terminology that would signify the existence of a man prior to his union to the Word;[3] on these and other points he aligns himself with the positions characteristic of supporters of the second opinion.

---

1 See *DeIncarn*, 2, 1 (p. 169), and 2, 3 (p. 169, ll. 22-23). An objection against the grace of union as the cause of the Hypostatic Union takes as its starting-point Christ as man being *aliquid*. Grace, it says, makes its subject to be of a particular quality but not a substance ("gratia facit qualem, non quid"), so that if grace caused the union, the Son of God as man would not be *aliquid*. See *ibid.*, 2, 18; p. 174. Philip does not reply directly to this objection. He would, however, maintain the substantiality of Christ's human nature as vigorously as the objector.

2 See *supra*, pp. 76-77.

3 See *infra*, pp. 97-105 and 123-124.

2. THE MODE OF UNION: NOT IN ONE NATURE

If the union is not accidental, neither is it, according to Philip, a union in one common nature arising from the divine and human natures. Thus in the investigation of the kind of unity resulting from the union, when an objector quotes St. John Damascene to support his own rejection of a specific unity together with a "universal nature that might be said of Christ,"[1] Philip agrees that the union in Christ does not terminate in a specific or generic unity; indeed, he adds, we should not speak of a unity of individual in Christ, because "individual" looks to a species that is a common nature, and any such common nature must be eliminated from this union.[2]

A second argument and reply within this same discussion recalls a similar exchange that has been seen in the second redaction of Alexander of Hales' *Glossa*.[3] The objector tries to prove the impossibility of the union by showing that it leads to the following alternatives, both impossible: There is something common in that union, or else there is an agreement in something common. What is that common element, he asks? One answer might be that because the union took place in time rather than from eternity, the common element would be some created nature. But, replies the objector, this would mean that the two natures come together in something common. Further, where does that created thing arise from? It could not be from the two natures, he says, for then some common nature would arise from the divine and human natures, and this is impossible; besides, he adds, nothing can be common to the created and the uncreated.[4]

In reply Philip agrees that the union cannot be in some created or temporal nature. First he distinguishes unity from union. Unity follows upon union; the former regards nature, as when we speak of the *unity* in essence or nature of the Trinity; the latter regards the hypostasis or person, as when we say that in the *union* of the Incarnation three substances are one person. Applying this distinction, Philip says that the *union* in something common will refer to the union in hypostasis or per-

1 *DeIncarn*, 2, 1; p. 169. The text of Damascene is the frequently-quoted passage, "Non est communem speciem, etc."

2 See *ibid*., 2, 3; p. 170, ll. 28-36.

3 Cf. *HypUnion* II, 113-114.

4 *DeIncarn*, 2, 2; p. 169. Cf. the argument from the *GlossaAlex* quoted in *HypUnion* II, 113 ("Praeterea").

son; but the hypostasis or person is not, as the objector suggested it was, something temporal or created. Hence it does not follow that because the union took place in time the natures came together in some nature or in something temporal; instead, they were united in the eternal person.[5]

Philip further explains why the temporal character of the union does not mean the union is something created or in some created nature. Although some things are creatures, he says, others, such as the perpetuity of the soul or the mobility of a body are not creatures but con-creatures, that is, created along with the creature. God, he adds, has no proper idea for these con-creatures; instead, they are reduced to the ideas of the creatures they follow upon. Applying this distinction to the problem at hand, Philip asserts that although the union took place in time, this union is properly not a creature but rather is "consequent"; hence the coming-together (of the natures) through that union does not take place in some (common) nature or in something temporal.[6] Philip, it will be noted, fails to state just what the union is consequent upon; his argument would seem to require some creature that has the union as its "con-creature." The point of his argument, however, is that the union is not some creature, some thing originating in time; the example of con-creatures simply shows that there can be realities that are not creatures. This suffices to prove his point that the newness in time of the Incarnation does not involve the coming-together of the natures in some new creature, that is, a new nature. In this way he agrees with the objector that the union cannot be in one nature, but at the same time maintains against him that the natures can truly come together in a union.

The objector, who had already used one argument given in Alexander of Hales' *Glossa*, draws upon it again for a second alternative. Still referring to the union as necessarily taking place in something common, he asks:

> ... What is that common element? If you say that it is the union, then those two natures of God and man come together in the union. But this is the same as if you were to say: "They come together in the coming-together (*convenientia*)," [which is] the same or another. If another, you go on to infinity.[7]

5 *DeIncarn*, 2, 4; p. 170, ll. 41-47.

6 *Ibid.*; pp. 170-171, ll. 47-59.

7 *Ibid.*, 2, 2; p. 169, ll. 14-17. Cf. *GlossaAlex* III, 2, 14c (L) (p. 28), quoted in *HypUnion* II, 113. In Philip's question the objection uses in part the reply of the author of the second redaction of the

Philip, following the *Glossa* of Alexander of Hales, replies that the natures "do not come together in the union because the union itself is the coming-together."[8] The objector's position, he implies, would involve a meaningless multiplication of entities. Rather, Philip declares, the natures "come together in the hypostasis that is constituted and composed from those two natures. But no nature is constituted from them ..."[9] In other words, no new created entity, no nature common to the divine and human nature, is necessary to explain the union of the two natures. The unity of hypostasis, in which the two natures come together and whose coming-together is itself the union, suffices both to unravel the dialectical difficulties of the objector and to show that the union involves no destruction of the divine simplicity and immutability. Philip concludes this discussion with two quotations from St. John Damascene that vigorously affirm the perfection and distinction of the divine and human natures after the union is accomplished. Christ, the first text declares, is not the name of one composite nature like that of man, a composite from body and soul, or like that of a body, a composite from the four elements, because Christ's Deity and humanity make the same one to be perfect God and perfect man from two natures and in two natures. Further, the second text continues, the heretical doctrine that Christ's nature was composite would mean that the simple divine nature was changed into a composite one; that Christ would not be consubstantial with the Father, simple in nature; that Christ could not be called man or God, but only Christ; that this name would designate (the new) nature, but not the person.[10]

Thus by both reason and authority Philip strongly defends the distinction of the two natures in Christ, even while he maintains their close unity in hypostasis or person by speaking of the *hypostasis composita*.

GlossaAlex (III, 2, 14-l; p. 30, quoted in *HypUnion* II, 114) to the other alternative that this same objection in Philip considers. The objection, however, fails to complete the argument as the redactor of the *GlossaAlex* gives it; it is Philip who gives the complete argument in reply.

8 *DeIncarn*, 2, 5; p. 171, ll. 60-66. Cf. *GlossaAlex* III, 2, 14-I (L) (p. 30), quoted in *HypUnion* II, 114. On the importance of this connection between Philip and Redaction L of the *GlossaAlex*, see *supra*, p. 67, n. 9.

9 *Ibid.*, p. 171, ll. 61-62.

10 *Ibid.*, p. 171.

3. THE MODE OF UNION: IN ONE PERSON

Philip the Chancellor denies that the union in Christ was accidental: thus, we have seen, he rejects the teaching of Photinus and Paul of Samosata because they separated the man from God.[1] Again, he says that the union is not terminated at something accidentally one, for then it would follow that Christ as man is not *aliquid*.[2] And his frequent assertions, in his comparison of the assumability of angels and man, that a person cannot be united to a person have the force at least of excluding an accidental union.[3]

Having thus denied an accidental union and having shown, in the passages examined in the previous section, that the union is not in one nature, Philip goes on to assert that the union takes place in the hypostasis or person. This, we have seen, was his reply to objections that tried to force him to say the union was in some created nature or in something temporal.[4] But now these assertions are challenged, at least if they are understood to mean that the person or hypostasis is the medium by which the union takes place. If, says an objection, "the divine nature is united to human nature in one hypostasis or person, the extreme in that union and the medium in which the uniting takes place are the same. But this cannot be true according to one and the same reason."[5]

In reply Philip indicates that the hypostasis or person is medium in one respect and extreme in another. In so far as the extremes are the two natures, the hypostasis or the person is the medium uniting these extremes. But in so far as the uniting takes place in the person through his uniting human nature to himself, the person has the notion of an extreme that is united to the human nature. Philip states this as follows:

> Solution: The extremes are the two natures, the medium uniting them is the hypostasis, and the person has the notion of that which unites and of that which is united and of that in which the uniting takes place. That person is the medium because he unites each nature; and he is that in which the uniting takes place because he united human nature to himself; and

1 See *supra*, p. 76.

2 *DeIncarn*, 2, 3; p. 170, ll. 26-28. Cf. *supra*, p. 89.

3 See *DeIncarn*, 1-i (p. 159, ll. 29-31); 1-i & 1-ii, 6 (p. 160); 1-i & 1-ii, 11 (p. 162-163); *DeDiscrPers*, 4 (p. 156, ll. 30-31) & 7 (p. 157, ll. 59-60).

4 See *supra*, pp. 90-92. Cf. *DeIncarn*, 2, 3 (pp. 169-170); 2, 4 (pp. 170-171); 2, 5 (p. 171).

5 *Ibid.*, 2, 7; p. 171. Another argument (*ibid.*, 2, 6; p. 171) rejects the composition involved if the person is medium; this argument will be seen in the following section.

because he united it to himself, he is its extreme and so has the notion of
that which is united to human nature.[6]

Thus Philip replies to the objection by showing that the person is not
medium and extreme in the same respect: he is extreme in so far as the
union is considered to be that of the human nature precisely to the person. In both cases, Philip indicates in passing, the person is the one
responsible for these two aspects of the union.

The Chancellor repeats the same idea in the next paragraph; this time
he stresses the viewpoint of the divine nature. As that which is able to
be united, the divine nature is an extreme; as that which unites, it is a
medium:

> I say, therefore, that the divine nature, in so far as it is unitable, has
> the notion of nature; in so far as it is uniting, it has the notion of the per-
> son that united human nature to itself: not that the divine essence stands
> for the person (this never happens), but it is said to have the notion of per-
> son in this respect that it united human nature to itself, and so it is ex-
> treme and medium under different notions ...[7]

A union in person requires that the person be only one, namely, the
divine person. Therefore, in defending the union in person Philip must
show why there is no human person in Christ. He does so by replying to
a number of arguments, some familiar, some new.[8]

The first of these quotes a text from St. John Damascene saying that
the nature assumed by the Word was not the nature such as it is conceived by the mind, nor was it the nature considered as species, but
rather the concrete nature (*quae est in atomo*). But, asks the objector, is
not this kind of nature a person?[9]

Philip agrees that it was not the nature as abstracted from accidents
and properties that the Word assumed, but rather the individual nature
with its properties. He adds, however, that this individual nature did
not first exist in the concrete, but was assumed as existing in its
hypostasis. He explains this last statement according to his doctrine of

---

6 *Ibid.*, 2, 9; pp. 171-172.

7 *Ibid.*, 2, 10; p. 172, ll. 106-111. Philip says that this argument answers the second objection, and
so it does; but the previous paragraph seems to answer it just as well and more directly. The first
part of par. 10 (p. 172) is devoted to a refutation of the first objection.

8 It may be noted here that the substance and even the order of most of these arguments and
replies reappear in the *SummaAlex* III, 35 (IV, 54-55). The arguments and replies are developed at
greater length in the *SummaAlex*, but the similarities are so striking that one is inclined to regard
Philip's question as a source of the *SummaAlex* at this point unless, of course, both are following an
unknown common source.

9 *DeIncarn*, 3, 21; p. 181.

twofold individuation, rejecting in this case of Christ the first individuation, which is through "particular *esse* alone without properties," and accepting the second, which is by the collection of individual properties. That is, for Philip it is not nature as individuated by particular *esse* that the Word assumes, but rather nature as individuated by the collection of properties distinguishing it from all others.[10] The first type of individuation would seem, in Philip's mind, to give either a distinct subject or even a person, at least if "particular *esse*" means independent being. This, it appears, is why Philip insists that it is the individual nature as an aggregate of properties that is assumed.

In general, it is because Christ's human nature lacks this "particular" or "absolute" *esse*, because it is not *per se unum* and is deprived of the "excellence of dignity" that, according to Philip, it is not a human person. The Chancellor, we have seen, distinguishes person from hypostasis by the property of dignity;[11] he also holds that personal *esse*, when present, so completes the nature with an *esse absolutum* that the nature is unable to be united to another person.[12] For the most part, it is this same distinction that Philip uses to answer arguments trying to show that the Word assumed a person. Thus when it is asked what is lacking to this individual (*huic*) that it should not be a person,[13] or when it is argued that, "person" being a name of dignity or excellence, and the Deity having destroyed no dignity or excellence by assuming the nature, there is therefore a human person,[14] Philip replies:

> ... Divine nature destroyed nothing in human nature, but because "person" is said, as it were, *per se sonans*, that is, one *per se* and having absolute being and the excellence of dignity, as is clear in its definition, *Person is an individual substance of rational nature*[15] — "individual substance" denotes the "what" (*quid*), "rational nature" the "who" (*quis*), and human nature united to divine nature does not have the latter — therefore it is not called a person.[16]

For the same reason, Philip says, the soul separated from the body does not acquire personality, that is, "because its *esse* is not absolute, but dependent on the body, to which it seeks by nature to be united."[17]

10 See *ibid.*, 3, 29; p. 182.
11 *Supra*, pp. 66-67.
12 *Supra*, pp. 80-85.
13 *DeIncarn*, 3, 23; p. 182.
14 *Ibid.*, 3, 24; p. 182.
15 Boethius, *ContraEut*, 3 & 4; Rand, pp. 84 & 92.
16 *DeIncarn*, 3, 32; p. 182. The *quid* is doubtless the individual or hypostasis; cf. *supra*, p. 67.
17 *DeIncarn*, 3, 34; p. 183.

And when the divine nature is united to human nature, "its *esse*, that is, of human nature, is not one *per se* and absolute, nor does it have the dignity of excellence; and therefore it is not a person, and yet nothing is taken from it because it never had that."[18]

Another objection considers the sources of personal distinction recognized by Philip himself, namely, origin, essential property, and property of origin. In the Incarnation, the objection argues, because a property of origin was assumed, a person was assumed.[19] The property of origin spoken of here would be the human nature's property of nativity from the Blessed Virgin, by which it comes into physical *esse*.

Of Philip's two replies to this argument, the first is quite obscure;[20] in the second he simply says that the Word "did not assume nativity, but the nature following upon nativity,"[21] that is, he assumed not the property of origin that might appear to constitute a human person, but the human nature resulting from the birth.

A final objection is as follows: The act of assuming begins only when the act of creation is completed. But since at the terminus of the act of creation there is a complete man and therefore a person, a person assumed a person.[22] Philip replies that the logic of the argument is fallacious "because the terminus of creation does not indicate personal *esse* that is conjoined or that can be conjoined, but it indicates an *esse* that, both actually and potentially, is not conjoined and cannot be conjoined."[23] Once again it is the absolute or complete character of personal *esse*, making the person independent and unable to be united to another person, that distinguishes person from concrete nature. It should be recalled at this point that according to Philip this distinction between person and concrete nature applies only to natures containing matter or, among spiritual substances, only to the human soul, and this only by reason of the soul's natural orientation to union with a material body.[24]

---

18 *Loc. cit.*

19 *Ibid.*, 3, 22; p. 181.

20 See *ibid.*, 3, 30; p. 182. "... He did not assume personal discretion according to origin, but he assumed [it?] according to the property of essence that is in the one who has it; this property, however, is not the nature." The "property of essence" may mean "humanity," which is in the distinct individual man but is not the concrete nature. This interpretation, however, would contradict the text of Damascene quoted *ibid.*, 3, 21 (p. 181) and accepted by Philip *ibid.*, 3, 29 (p. 182); it would also contradict Philip's reply *ibid.*, 3, 31 (p. 182).

21 *Ibid.*, 3, 31; p. 182.

22 *Ibid.*, 3, 28; p. 182.

23 *Ibid.*, 3, 33; p. 182. An analogous objection is found *ibid.*, 1-i & 1-ii, 6; p. 160.

24 See *supra*, pp. 80-85, and *DeIncarn*, 3, 34 (p. 183).

In all this Philip's position is basically the same as that of the other authors we have studied. For him, however, the property of dignity appears to be not so much an additional form as the concrete independent existence and separate unity of the person. In other words, he seems to look at the person more in its existential reality and less in its logico-metaphysical structure where it is a meeting-place for a number of essences or forms. Certainly for Philip personality is a more positive perfection than it is for Hugh of Saint-Cher. Besides this particular emphasis on Philip's part, his treatment of this problem also introduces arguments and replies that are new to the extant theological literature of this period.

4. THE HYPOSTASIS COMPOSITA

In the course of his investigation of the role of the person as medium for the union, Philip, who had been interchanging the words "hypostasis" and "person," raises the question whether it is more proper to say that the natures are united "in hypostasis" or "in person."[1] His answer to this question leads to his most fundamental exposition of the union, an exposition emphasizing the concept of *hypostasis composita*. In reply to the foregoing question Philip states that the union is more properly said to be in hypostasis than in person. If the union is sometimes said to take place in a unity of person, this expression is used, he explains, "because of heretics who posited in Christ a plurality of persons as well as a diversity of nature."[2] Philip prefers to say that the union is in hypostasis because his philosophy of hypostasis gives him in the "composed hypostasis" his best positive explanation of the union.

As has been mentioned previously and as Philip says at this point, the hypostasis "holds the middle place between the person and the individual"; the person adds to the notion of hypostasis that of an excellent property, whereas the individual is individual by its principles of individuation.[3] Philip's point is that because in Christ there is a union between a divine person and an individual of human nature, and because the hypostasis can be, from different points of view, both a per-

---

1 *Ibid.*, 2, 11; p. 172. Cf. *supra*, pp. 93-94.

2 *DeIncarn*, 2, 11; p. 172, ll. 114-116.

3 *Ibid.*, p. 172, ll. 116-121. Cf. *supra*, pp. 66-67. In *DeIncarn*, 3, 44 (p. 185), the same doctrine is presented: there Philip indicates that the hypostasis as individual looks only to the second type of individuation, that by reason of a collection of properties. Cf. *infra*, p. 98, n. 7.

son and an individual, the union of the divine person and the individual
of human nature is properly said to be in the hypostasis. Thus he continues:

> When the union of the Word to human nature was accomplished, in
> that union the hypostasis was a person with respect to the excellent
> property, and it was an individual, for Jesus is an individual, and that in-
> dividual has its foundation in the hypostasis of the Son of God...[4]

In the last phrase the expression "hypostasis of the Son of God" refers
to the divine person, whereas the hypostasis that is said to stand between the person and the individual and in which the union is said to
take place, is the familiar "composed hypostasis". This is shown from
the quotation of St. John Damascene appended to this analysis, in which
Damascene says that the natures "are united in his hypostasis (that is,
person), having one composed hypostasis..."[5] In Damascene's statement
the first use of "hypostasis" refers to the divine person in himself, the
second to the divine person in the union.

It is evident, again, from a parallel discussion in another of the
Quaestiones that when Philip speaks of the union in hypostasis as opposed to the union in person, he is referring to the *hypostasis composita*.
Thus after defining hypostasis as an incommunicable existence distinct
according to a collection of properties, and person as an incommunicable existence distinct according to a property of dignity, he
says:

> According to this definition the hypostasis is a medium between person
> and individual: however, the latter, understood properly, is not found in
> God;[6] yet the hypostasis is a person in so far as it is Son of God, but not in
> so far as it is Son of the Virgin. But since the hypostasis is an individual in
> so far as it is Son of the Virgin and not in so far as it is Son of God, for this
> reason the hypostasis is, as it were, a medium, and is called an individual,
> composed from two natures and in two natures since, as is evident, in one
> respect it looks to the person and in the other it looks to the individual ...[7]

---

4 *DeIncarn*, 2, 11; p. 172, ll. 121-124.

5 *Ibid.*, p. 173. The words "that is, the person," are added by the Latin translator to explain
Damascene's term "hypostasis."

6 This is explained *ibid.*, 2, 3; p. 170, ll. 32-38.

7 *Ibid.*, 3, 44; p. 185, ll. 225-232. Philip adds: "... I mean the individual *in atomo*, of which I have
spoken above," that is, *ibid.*, 3, 29 (p. 182), where he indicates that the individual *in atomo* is the individual constituted by the collection of properties, in opposition to the first type of individuation.
Cf. *supra*, p. 66. A similar doctrine passes into the *SummaAlex* III, 52 (IV, 76); its presentation may
have been influenced by Philip.

What exactly is composed in the *hypostasis composita?* In answering this question Philip differs from his contemporary, Hugh of Saint-Cher, who held that the composition of the hypostasis referred to the composition of the human nature that is united to the person of the Word.[8] For Philip, as for Alexander of Hales, the composition of the hypostasis refers to the "composition" of the hypostasis itself from the divine and human nature — in a way, to be sure, that does not endanger the divine simplicity.[9] In addition to the statement of the foregoing text, Philip clearly presents this same teaching elsewhere. Thus, for example, he says that the two natures of God and man "come together in the hypostasis that is constituted and is composed from these two natures."[10]

Another such statement occurs in a discussion whether the hypostasis or person is the medium of the union. An objector uses the comparison of a point joining two lines as medium: the point, he says, is not composed from the two lines, but composes them while remaining simple in itself. If the hypostasis of Christ were the medium as a point is, it would not, he concludes, be said to be composed from these two natures, but to unite and conjoin them.[11] Philip answers that in so far as the point joins the two lines as terminus of one and beginning of the other, it is composed in a certain sense (*quasi compositus*). "So," he continues, "that personal hypostasis is composed from diverse natures, which two natures come together in one hypostasis..."[12] He then quotes a passage from St. John Damascene that speaks of the two natures as "really united to each other unto the one composed hypostasis of the Son of God..."[13]

Philip the Chancellor's central exposition of the theology of the mode of union is found within a fairly lengthy discussion directly concerned with the "composed hypostasis." This discussion begins from several texts of St. John Damascene that speak of Christ as generated "from two perfect natures" or as having "one composed hypostasis from two perfect natures" or "from each."[14] "... When we name Christ and God

---

8 See *HypUnion* III, 73-75.

9 For Alexander see *HypUnion* II, 126-133.

10 *DeIncarn*, 2, 5; p. 171. Cf. *ibid*., 2, 1 (p. 169, ll. 11-12), where the objection speaks in the same way: "... Christ is a hypostasis composed from a duality, human nature and divine nature."

11 *Ibid*., 2, 6; p. 171.

12 See *ibid*., 2, 10; p. 172, ll. 93-98.

13 *Ibid*.; p. 172, l. 102.

14 *Ibid*., 3, 35; p. 183.

from each," Philip declares, "the question arises what genus of composition and what kind of parts there are ..."[15]

Philip elaborates his teaching on Christ as a "composed hypostasis" by looking at the mode of union from three slightly different viewpoints, each complementary to the other. The first has already been seen: for Philip the hypostasis is composed in that it stands midway between the person and the individual, and is identical with each under different aspects.[16]

According to Philip's second viewpoint, the hypostasis is composed in that it "stands under" or "contains" or "is placed under" each nature, thus becoming an individual of human nature, a "thing" of human nature, or a man. Philip derives this note of "standing under" from the etymology of "hypostasis": "hypo," he says, is the same as the Latin *sub*. "Yet," he adds, "I do not say that by any of these modes [the hypostasis] is, properly, composed, but [it is composed] because it is under them ..."[17] Philip adds a quotation from St. John Damascene stating that no new hypostasis is generated when the flesh of the Word comes into being, but that the flesh is in the hypostasis of the Word and not separate from him.[18]

The third viewpoint regarding the composed hypostasis extends the second viewpoint to include the manner in which the hypostasis is a person of divine and human nature, and to indicate the relationships between the two natures with respect to the one person. Although the text has some obscurities, possibly owing to scribal errors, the doctrine is manifest: the hypostasis stands under each nature; it is an eternal person according to divine nature; it becomes a person of human nature *secundum quid* or in a qualified sense. In that the eternal person becomes a person of human nature, it is said to be a "composed hypostasis." Philip explains it as follows:

> Therefore, [the hypostasis] stands under each nature, and according to divine nature it does not begin to be someone (*quis*), but according to human nature it begins to be someone (*quis*) and something (*quid*),

15 *Ibid.*, p. 183, ll. 181-182. The question raised here about parts will be examined towards the end of this section 4.

16 See the texts quoted *supra*, pp. 90-92.

17 See *DeIncarn*, 3, 45 (p. 185), for the whole argument. Cf. also *ibid.*, 3, 51 (p. 187): "Therefore the hypostasis is said to be composed from two natures and in two natures in so far as it is divine nature and [is] a thing of human nature, as has been said. Cf. also *ibid.*, 3, 53; p. 187.

18 *Ibid.*, 3, 45; p. 185.

although not without qualification, because it is the divine person, who was eternally, that begins to be.[19]

He then illustrates the qualified role of Christ's human nature by the example of man's soul; it, too, does not cause a person *simpliciter*, that is, without qualification:

> Human nature in Peter makes him someone (*quis vel quem*), simply speaking: but it is not so in Christ, because even if the soul is an incommunicable existence,[20] nevertheless it does not make someone (*quis vel quem*) without qualification because it depends on its [body],[21] since it finds complete being in its union [with the body].[22]

Philip seems to be making the point that although the soul is already individuated, it is not by that fact a person, but finds personality only when it achieves complete being in its union with the body. This seems to be what he has in mind when he moves from this example to the case of Christ, saying:

> Consequently, since the first individuation is present there,[23] the second by coming does not make a person (*quis vel quem*), because it finds complete being, but it makes [it] such (*facit ... quale*). Nevertheless it makes a person and a substance (*quis et quid*) in so far as [it makes the person to be] Son of the Virgin: makes, I say, not simply but in a certain respect: for human nature comes to the hypostasis of the Son of God according to the second individuation, which does not make a person (*quem*), but affects[24] the individuation already there, which was according to the first mode of individuation and had complete being; nevertheless it makes the one who before was an eternal person (*quis*) to be a person (*quem*) of this nature, and in so far as he begins to be a person (*quis*) of this nature, to that extent he is called a "composed hypostasis."[25]

---

19 *Ibid.*, 3, 46; p. 185. I have interpreted the last phrase to mean that since it is a divine person who begins to be, the hypostasis does not become someone or something in human nature *simpliciter*. There may, however, be a *non* missing before *incipit* in the phrase "quoniam incipit esse divina persona quae fuit ab aeterno"; in that case the qualification would be introduced by the fact that, simply speaking, a divine and eternal person does not begin to be anything.

20 In this text the word *communicabilis* seems to need correction to give meaning to the passage. The translation of the phrase in question might also be "incommunicable by existence."

21 The word *corporis*, missing in the text, seems necessary for the meaning.

22 *DeIncarn*, 3, 46; p. 185, ll. 248-251.

23 That is, in Christ, as is clear from all that follows.

24 Literally, "makes" (*facit*). A *non* may be missing before *facit*: in that case the phrase would read: "... but it does not cause the individuation already there," etc. In our interpretation, "affect" means that the nature "makes" the person who is already there to be a person of human nature: this is stated more clearly in the following sentence: "Nevertheless it makes," etc.

25 *DeIncarn*, 3, 46; pp. 185-186, ll. 252-260.

Thus, according to Philip, in the union the eternal divine person, perfectly individuated by his complete being, is not constituted a person by the individual human nature's coming to it, but it becomes a person of human nature: the divine person is made *quale*, that is, a person qualified now by human nature; thus he is a person *secundum quid*, that is, according to human nature. Because he becomes a person now qualified by human nature, he is called a "composed hypostasis." From Philip's very insistence on the identity of the person it is evident that when he uses the terms *quale* and *secundum quid* of the person as united to human nature, he is not thinking of this union as accidental. In some respects Philip's doctrine at this point resembles that of William of Auxerre, who declares that "although the humanity is substantial to that man who is the Son of God, it is nevertheless accidental to the Son of God as Son of God."[26] Philip, like William, wishes to stress the adventitious character of the human nature's union to the divine person; he also indicates that the human nature contributes nothing to the essential constitution of the divine person, for the divine person is eternal and unchangeable in himself. The composition of hypostasis thus expresses the identity of the person in two natures along with the new qualification received by the divine person in that he begins to be a person of human nature.

Philip closes this analysis with another long quotation in which St. John Damascene speaks of the simple hypostasis of the Word that is also composed of the two natures of Divinity and humanity in such a way that, along with the personal property of filiation that is his as a divine person, he also receives the "characteristic and determinative properties of the flesh, according to which he differs from his mother and other men."[27]

Like those who wrote before him, Philip must meet objections to the doctrine of the "composed hypostasis." One of these raises the question whether the hypostasis is composed in the manner that man is composed of body and soul: this comparison, it says, is made by the [Pseudo-Athanasian] Creed.[28] Other objections, refusing both this comparison and the whole idea of composition implied by the *hypostasis composita*, argue as follows: Composition implies the union of parts, but the divine nature is a whole and so cannot enter a composition as a part;[29]

---

26 William of Auxerre, *DeInc*, introitus, 3; Principe, p. 251. Cf. *HypUnion* I, 74 and 94.
27 *DeIncarn*, 3, 47; p. 186.
28 *Ibid.*, 3, 36; p. 183.
29 *Ibid.*, 3, 37-39; pp. 183-184.

again, the parts of a composite are potential rather than actual, so that if the divine nature enters into a composition, it would not be in act, which is impossible;[30] composition of this sort is opposed to the distinction of natures in Christ;[31] if the composition "from" the two natures means that the hypostasis is "in" the two natures, it would be better to say that the hypostasis is "juxtaposed" rather than "composed";[32] finally, since no mode of composition can be found that will serve to classify such a composition, the hypostasis cannot be said to be composed in any way or mode.[33]

Philip, together with these last objectors, also refuses the comparison of the body and soul in man: in their union, he says, the body cannot be said to be the soul nor the soul the body — they do not "come into one reason" — whereas in Christ it is said that "God is man" and "Man is God."[34] Again, both the body and soul are potential parts, whereas the divine nature is only in act; it is the human nature that is passible and that is changed for the better by the union: the divine nature remains unchanged.[35] Further, the divine nature is not a simple form but at best a "quasi-form" in so far as it draws the human nature to the person or hypostasis;[36] here Philip contrasts the role of the soul as an intrinsic form of man with the role of the divine nature, which is not intrinsic in the union.

As for the other objections, Philip feels that the doctrine he presents in his main solutions concerning the "composed hypostasis" eliminates the problems they raise. After stating that in his view the "composed hypostasis" refers to the eternal person's becoming a person of human nature without its becoming anything *simpliciter*, and after confirming his position with a quotation from St. John Damascene,[37] he adds: "From this it is clear that the composition is on the side of the human nature; hence, since the divine nature is totally active and in no way in potency, and since every part as such has potential being, it will not be a part."[38] In other words, for Philip composition in the sense of composition from physical and potential parts is found only in the human

30 *Ibid.*, 3, 40; p. 184.
31 *Ibid.*, 3, 41; p. 184.
32 *Ibid.*, 3, 42; p. 184.
33 *Ibid.*, 3, 43 & 53; pp. 184 & 187.
34 *Ibid.*, 3, 49; p. 186.
35 *Ibid.*, 3, 50; p. 186.
36 *Ibid.*, 3, 51; p. 187.
37 *Ibid.*, 3, 46-47; pp. 185-186.
38 *Ibid.*, 3, 48; p. 186.

nature: the composition of the hypostasis to which he refers is not a composition from potential parts and therefore implies neither that the divine nature is potential nor that it is a part rather than a whole.[39]

Philip qualifies this statement slightly in a manner that shows that the composition he rejects is that from potential parts in the physical order; thus he adds that we could say the divine and human nature are parts of the hypostasis if we think of them as logical parts entering into the definition of a thing:

> Nevertheless, we can in some way assign parts in this composition by means of parts that enter into the definition of a genus: for those parts do not number the thing that is defined. Likewise the divine nature and the human are said to be parts of the hypostasis according as Christ is said to be God and man, and yet Christ is not numbered along with God and man.[40]

Philip's reply "to the second objection" does not correspond exactly to any of the arguments that he presents as objections;[41] his reply presumes an objection arguing that the composition of the Son means that the Father is composed as well as the Son. Philip answers this implied argument by asserting that the Son is composed precisely in that in which he differs from the Father, namely in hypostasis; hence the Son's composition in no way implies that of the Father.[42]

As to the objections that the composition of the hypostasis taught by Philip does not fit any mode of composition,[43] he replies that the hypostasis is composed in the sense that it is an individual (hoc) of each nature. Therefore, he concludes, this composition differs in kind from those mentioned by the objectors: theirs were concerned with the composition of natural things.[44] As we have seen, Philip thinks that this composition of the hypostasis has some of the characteristics of a logical, as opposed to physical, composition;[45] for him this is at most an analogy, because he certainly intends the union implied by the doctrine of the "composed hypostasis" to be real and substantial. What he is

---

39 This answers the objections contained *ibid.*, 3, 37-40; pp. 183-184.

40 *Ibid.*, 3, 48; p. 186, ll. 274-278. For the interpretation of the number-aspect of this text, see *infra*, pp. 106-107.

41 Philip may oppose his reply to the objection (*DeIncarn*, 3, 41; p. 184) arguing that a "composed hypostasis" would, like the "composed nature" spoken of by Damascene, destroy the distinction of natures in Christ.

42 *Ibid.*, 3, 52; p. 187. Cf. *infra*, p. 130.

43 *Ibid.*, 3, 43 & 53; pp. 184 & 187.

44 *Ibid.*, 3, 53; p. 187, ll. 299-301.

45 See *DeIncarn*, 3, 48; p. 186.

concerned to eliminate from Christ is the potentiality and imperfection involved in composition of physical wholes from potential parts.[46]

Thus for Philip the Chancellor the "composed hypostasis" stands forth as his most basic approach to the mode of union in Christ. It expresses for him the twofold aspect of the divine hypostasis of the Word, for it considers him as "standing under" the two natures, that is, now as a person of divine nature, now as a person of human nature, the former from eternity, the latter in time and in a qualified, adventitious sense. The composition of the hypostasis means, therefore, not that the two natures are potential and imperfect parts of a union such as those found in the world of nature, but rather that the divine nature remains totally in act and a whole, whereas the human nature is perfected by being united and by having the divine person in it as its hypostasis.

5. THE UNITY OR PLURALITY OF CHRIST

Although the other authors studied in our series investigate in considerable detail the question of the unity or plurality of Christ, seeing in it one of the central problems in the theology of the Hypostatic Union, Philip the Chancellor, at least in the material that has come to us, devotes but a few paragraphs to this topic.

Philip's examination of this problem arises out of his study of the "composed hypostasis." At the end of his replies to the main objections against this concept, he presents two new arguments that reason against the "composed hypostasis" from the viewpoint of number. The first states that because in natural things "diverse perfections of diverse things make diverse perfect things," and because the same principle will apply in God, "therefore Christ will be two, understanding 'two' in the neuter gender."[1] In other words, the perfections of human nature give

---

46 The same viewpoint is expressed in Philip's explanation of the phrase "composita ex his," which is challenged in different ways *ibid.*, 3, 39 (p. 184), and 3, 42 (p. 184). In reply Philip says: "To the other: 'In what way from these,' etc., I reply that it is not unfitting for the hypostasis to be composed, since it *is of* that nature and this, and since it *is* this nature and that" (*ibid.*, 3, 54; p. 187: emphasis mine). This statement appears to refer to the argument *ibid.*, 3, 42 (p. 184), which says that ultimately the phrase *ex his* implies juxtaposition rather than composition of the hypostasis. Philip insists on the person's being really and substantially a person of each nature, not merely someone juxtaposed in a kind of local union. The statement in the preceding paragraph (*ibid.*, 3, 53; p. 187): "I reply that in this composition [the hypostasis] becomes an individual (*hoc*) of this nature and an individual (*hoc*) of that," also seems, to judge from the words preceding it, to be directed against the argument of par. 42 as well as that of par. 41 based on the text of Damascene and otherwise left unanswered by Philip.

1 *DeIncarn,* 3, 55; p. 188.

rise to a human supposit or hypostasis in addition to the divine supposit or hypostasis; hence, although there is but one person in Christ, there are two supposits or hypostases. This statement reflects the viewpoint of the first opinion. It implies that if there are two hypostases in Christ, it is incorrect to speak of one "composed hypostasis." The second objection states this conclusion more explicitly: "Again, the natures," it argues, "are diverse and remain diverse. Therefore the two natures effect diverse compositions rather than one 'composed hypostasis'."[2]

As his solution Philip simply quotes a passage from St. John Damascene that states certain principles about number in general and about number in Christ in particular. Number, this passage says, does not arise from division or union themselves, but rather from the quantity of the things to be numbered, whether these be united or divided: thus whether fifty stones are united in one wall or are lying apart from each other in a field, they are counted as fifty. So, the text concludes, although Christ is one, perfect in Divinity and humanity, his natures are numbered as two and cannot be said to be one.[3]

At first sight this text might appear to be beside the point in that its concern is to maintain a duality of natures in Christ. However, by pointing to nature as the source of number and so of duality in Christ, and by indicating in passing that "Christ is one, perfect in Deity and in humanity" and that number does not derive from union, the text in fact gives Philip his principles for the solution of the objections. These had argued from the duality of natural perfections and natural compositions to a duality of hypostases; Philip, by showing with Damascene that this duality remains on the side of nature and that "the two natures of Christ ... are united according to hypostasis,"[4] from which union no principle of enumeration can be had, proves that the unity of Christ according to hypostasis is maintained, and that thereby a "composed hypostasis" is both possible and a fact.

The principle that plurality derives from the natures in Christ rather than from the union explains another text already examined above; Philip, after saying that the divine and human natures in Christ may be likened to the logical parts of a definition, which do not number the thing defined, adds: "Likewise the divine nature and the human are said to be parts of the hypostasis according as Christ is said to be God and

2 *Ibid.*, 3, 56; p. 188.
3 *Ibid.*, 3, 57; p. 188.
4 See *ibid.*; p. 188, ll. 330-331.

man, and yet Christ is not numbered together with God and man."[5]
That is, although the "parts" of Christ may be several, no plurality is introduced in Christ himself.

In a comparison of the Trinity's unity in one nature with Christ's unity in one person, Philip expressly states the same principles. He agrees with one argument on its position that the Son of God and the Son of the Virgin, that is, the divine person and the individual human nature (or the individual according to the collection of properties) are one in subject.[6] Then in his own analysis of the problem at hand he says that "the personal unity of the Son of God is according to unity in number ... Those things are one in hypostasis that do not number the hypostasis, such as the two natures in Christ and the two in man, that is, soul and body."[7]

From these texts we can conclude that for Philip Christ is one in number by reason of the union of the divine and human natures in his person or divine hypostasis. Because the two natures are united in the one person of the Son, there is only one hypostasis, the divine hypostasis now called a "composed hypostasis," or, again, there is only one subject. Because the two natures, by their union in one hypostasis, do not give rise to two hypostases, and because hypostasis rather than nature is the basis of enumeration, Christ, who has one hypostasis "composed of" two natures, is numerically one.

6. The Relationship of the Natures in the Union

The preceding analyses have already considered several aspects of the relationship of the divine and human natures in the union. We have seen that Philip thinks of the two natures as two extremes united in the person as medium, and that for him the geometric image of a point uniting two lines is an apt illustration of this relationship.[1] Again, Philip's explanation of the *hypostasis composita* shows that he allows for neither potentiality nor change in the divine nature; only the human nature changes, and that for the better.[2] If there is any beginning on the divine side, it is a qualified beginning of the divine person, who is a

5 *Ibid.*, 3, 48; p. 186, ll. 276-278. Cf. *supra*, p. 164.
6 *Ibid.*, 2, 27; p. 177. Cf. *ibid.*, 2, 29; p. 177.
7 *Ibid.*, 2, 28; p. 177, ll. 257-261.
1 See *supra*, pp. 93-94; the texts are from *DeIncarn*, 2, 9-10 (pp. 171-172).
2 Cf. *supra*, pp. 103-105. The arguments about the union's not being in one nature also imply that there is no change in the divine nature; cf. *supra*, pp. 90-92.

divine person *simpliciter* and "becomes" a person *secundum quid*, that is, a person of human nature.[3]

When Philip discusses the problem whether it is the nature, the person, or the whole Trinity that assumes, he defines the act of assuming as a taking "in oneself" or "to oneself" or "to something."[4] These terms suggest that he thinks of the union of Christ's human nature to the divine nature as a relation of the human nature to something divine, whether this be to the person of the Son ("in oneself") or to the divine nature ("to oneself") or "to something" (when done by the whole Trinity). The same idea lies behind his explanation of the phrases "The divine nature is united to flesh" and "The human nature is united to divine nature." In these phrases, he says, the term "is united" is understood diversely, because in the first it signifies something uncreated, in the second something created.[5] That is, when the human nature is said to be united, the union signifies the created relation of union in the human nature, but when the divine nature is said to be united, although the divine being is thought of and signified as united, no created relation or union is really present in God or is affirmed in judgment.

These suggestions become more explicit when Philip has to deal with an argument maintaining that the union is impossible because it implies a relation in God which, because correlative to the relation in human nature, is likewise created:

> ... If [says the objector] the union of human nature to the divine [nature is] something created and correlative, there should correspond to the correlative something created, namely, the union of divine nature to the human. On the contrary: There is nothing created in the divine nature.[6]

In other words, because a union establishes a mutual relationship between the things that are united and because the union of human nature to divine nature is something created, the union of divine nature to human nature is likewise created.

Philip does not reject the notion of relationship altogether, but only that aspect of it which would posit a created relationship on God's part; beyond that, he appears to grant that the union relates the human nature to the divine. Among creatures, he teaches, a union of two sub-

3 Cf. *supra*, pp. 100-102.
4 *DeIncarn*, 3, 6-8; pp. 178-179.
5 *Ibid*., 3, 13; p. 179, ll. 57-60.
6 *Ibid*., 2, 8; p. 171.

jects in some accident or likeness puts each in potency with respect to the other, so that each is changed by the other. An example is the union of body and soul, in which the body receives many dispositions of the soul and the soul is limited by the body. But in the Creator, he continues, this potency or possibility cannot be found: as the "Athanasian Creed" says, the Deity was not changed into flesh. Hence, Philip replies to the objection, "on the part of human nature the union is something created, but on the other part it has no correlation corresponding to the creature, and this is because one extreme is a nature and the other [extreme is] above nature ..."[7]

This reply indicates that although Philip rejects a relation of the divine nature to the human according to which the divine nature would be in potency and would be changed, he does think of the union as something created in the creature and as a relating of the creature to the divine nature.

7. CLASSIFICATION OF THE UNION AND COMPARISON WITH OTHER UNIONS

A problem that was raised in the *Glossa* of Alexander of Hales and in his *Quaestiones* concerned the classification of the Hypostatic Union among the categories of unity.[1] Philip presents the same problem in an objection whose terms resemble a text of the *Glossa* of Alexander. First, accidental unity is eliminated; the only alternative becomes unity *per se*: "... Every union is terminated at something one. Therefore the union in Christ was terminated at something one: not at something accidentally one, because in that case Christ as man would not be something; therefore at something one *per se*."[2] If, among the kinds of *per se* unity, unity in number is chosen, this involves a unity in species. But a unity in species implies a universal nature predicated of Christ, and this is erroneous. Therefore unity in number must also be eliminated:

> But one *per se* is threefold: [one in] number, species, genus. If you say "one in number," on the contrary: One in number is followed by one in genus and species, and Damascene says: *There is no common species to be found* or even *spoken of in the Lord Jesus.* "Species" indicates a universal nature. But there is not some universal nature that is said of Christ according as Christ is a hypostasis composed of something twofold, the human nature

7 *Ibid.*, 2, 12; p. 173.

1 See *HypUnion* II, 145-148.

2 *DeIncarn*, 2, 1; p. 171. Cf. *GlossaAlex* III, 2, 14b (L); p. 28.

and the divine nature. Therefore [the union] is not one in species and so
neither [is it one] in number.[3]

In solving this problem Philip agrees with the philosophical analysis
made by the objector thus far, but he maintains that although the
division of one into one *per se* and *per accidens* holds in things of nature,
it does not apply to the Hypostatic Union; hence, in spite of the objector's argument, this union can terminate at something one:

> Solution: That union is terminated at something one, but that one
> thing is neither one *per se* nor one *per accidens*: for this division has its place
> in things of nature. One *per se* is found properly when it is divided into one
> in number, which is properly and strictly the individual; again, into one in
> species and one in genus, [each of] which follows on one in number. The
> aforesaid union is not terminated at something one of that kind, nor at
> one *per accidens* for the aforesaid reason, because according to this Christ
> as man would not be something.[4]

What kind of unity is there, then, in the union in Christ? Philip says
that one in number can be taken in a broad sense to include one in
hypostasis. A oneness in species or genus, he maintains, does not follow
upon such a "one in hypostasis"; neither is this an individual, which
would involve a universal nature, the species, that would be found en-
tire in each individual of that species:

> But "one in number" is taken in a broad sense for one in hypostasis: on
> such a oneness there does not follow one in species or one in genus, nor is
> it an individual because an individual looks to a universal nature, namely,
> the species, which is whole in each individual.[5]

Philip insists that the "one in number" he is talking about is not an individual because, he says, the divine essence cannot be held to be a
species with respect to an individual: this would be implied, he indicates, if the "one in number" here meant an individual. After
eliminating this possibility, Philip concludes that because the two
natures come together in the hypostasis, the union is terminated at "one
in hypostasis":

> But the divine essence, although it is common to the three persons, is
> not to be called a universal nature like a species: for nothing can be un-
> derstood to come to the divine nature by which it might be said to be

3 *Loc. cit.* Cf. *GlossaAlex*, *loc. cit.*
4 *DeIncarn*, 2, 3; pp. 169-170, ll. 22-28.
5 *Ibid.*, p. 170, ll. 28-32.

drawn to one particular thing. Therefore there is not there[6] something one in number or an individual, because an individual is that in which the whole being of the species is preserved ... In this way, therefore, that union is terminated at one in hypostasis: for those two natures come together in hypostasis.[7]

Philip thus gives the same general type of solution as Alexander of Hales' *Glossa* and *Quaestiones*, with this slight difference that where Alexander simply rejects the attempt to classify the Hypostatic Union in any philosophical division of the one, Philip associates the oneness of the union with the category of things "one in number" by understanding the latter in a broad or extended sense.[8]

Philip returns to these classifications of oneness or unity when he investigates the question which unity is greater, that of the three persons of the Trinity in the one divine nature or that of the two natures in the one hypostasis of the Word. The discussion opens with arguments favoring the unity of the Trinity in one nature. The unity of the Trinitarian persons in one nature, says the first, is the greater unity, for in the personal unity of Christ there is a union of uncreated and created being (*ens non ab alio et ens ab alio*), and since these are most different, their coming-together will be the least unity;[9] further, another argument runs, since the least difference is found among the Trinitarian persons, they will have the greatest coming-together, and since this coming-together takes place in the divine nature, the greatest unity is in the divine nature and not in the person of Christ.[10]

An opposed argument holds that the greater unity is that of Christ's natures in his one hypostasis; it insists on the unity of subject in Christ. The Son of God, it says, and the Son of the Virgin are one subject, and each of these names has the same supposition. Hence whereas in Christ

---

6 That is, in Christ, if our interpretation is correct.

7 *Ibid.*; p. 171, ll. 32-40.

8 For Alexander's doctrine see *HypUnion* II, 145-148.

9 *DeIncarn*, 2, 24; p. 176. Cf. *GlossaAlex* III, 2, 14a (L) (p. 28), and *HypUnion* II, 149.

10 *DeIncarn*, 2, 26; pp. 176-177. Elsewhere (*ibid.*, 2, 25; p. 176) an argument opposed to the one in par. 24 (p. 176) uses the same principles as this second argument in par. 26: it says that the "least difference" found in the Trinity refers not to the one nature, as par. 26 says, but to the persons and to their minimal personal discretion. Two interpretations of this obscure passage may be suggested. This argument may simply be objecting to the conclusion of the first argument by maintaining that one personal union, that of the Trinitarian persons, is the greatest; or it may intend to argue more generally that because the greatest union is found on the level of persons in the Trinity, the personal union of the two natures in Christ must be thought to be greater than any union in nature. Neither interpretation, it must be admitted, is entirely satisfactory; it may be that at this place the text is defective.

what is said of one of these is said of the other because of the unity of
subject and supposition, in the Trinity the one nature comprises three
supposits, so that "the unity that is produced by the union of natures in
a unity of person is greater than the unity in the Trinity."[11] In other
words, what is said of the Father may not be said of the Son or Holy
Spirit because they are three distinct supposits; but this indicates a
lesser unity in the Trinity than in Christ, where such distinct supposition does not obtain.

In a sense Philip accepts both lines of argument. His solution takes
account of two ways of looking at the question, namely, the viewpoint
of nature and the viewpoint of person. If we look at a union in nature,
he says, the Trinity is the greater unity; if we look at personal unity, the
oneness in hypostasis is greater. Philip prefaces his solution with a list of
unities: unity may be generic, specific, or numerical. Among these,
unity in the divine nature is a specific unity, while the unity of person in
Christ is a numerical unity:

> Solution: Unity is multiple, namely, in genus, which is said according to
> the [same] figure of the predicate; further, unity in species; further, [unity]
> in number, which is according to form; a proper accident and the dif-
> ference are not numbered with that with which they come together. Unity
> in the divine nature is according to unity in species; the personal unity of
> the Son of God is according to unity in number.[12]

Next Philip shows how these unities affect number:

> The Father is one in nature with the Son, because paternity and
> filiation do not number the nature, since they are properties. Those things
> are one in hypostasis that do not number the hypostasis, such as the two
> natures in Christ and the two in man, that is, soul and body. What is one
> by nature numbers the persons, which is contrary to one in hypostasis.[13]

Having stated these rules concerning oneness and plurality of number,
Philip applies them to the question at hand. According to the particular
aspect considered, he shows, one of the two unions can claim a greater
unity than the other:

> Therefore I say that with respect to person, the unity in hypostasis is
> greater, but with respect to nature it is less. — Again, according as one
> looks to person, the coming-together in hypostasis is greatest, but with

11 *Ibid.*, 2, 27; p. 177.
12 *Ibid.*, 2, 28; p. 177, ll. 253-258.
13 *Ibid.*, p. 177, ll. 258-262. The last phrase obviously refers to the Trinity, where the one nature
is in three persons.

respect to nature it is least. Conversely, with respect to nature, the coming-together in three persons is greatest, but with respect to hypostasis it is least.[14]

Since the objections argue from either the viewpoint of nature or of hypostasis, Philip, by such a reply, is able to agree with all of them; each is right, he would say, from its own point of view.[15] This harmonization of viewpoints, however, leaves Philip's reader somewhat dissatisfied, and he seems to be aware that it would. Hence he goes on to say:

> Nevertheless, if one were to ask which unity, simply speaking, is greater, my answer is the unity of nature. Yet unity in person is more complete as to degree, as is clear in this way: Being is threefold: the being of nature, of the individual, and personal being. The being of nature is concerned with the subject, the being of the individual with the hypostasis; the being of the person is moral and is concerned with dignity, so that according to these three degrees the person is more complete.[16]

This reply presents some difficulties. At first sight Philip seems to be saying that, simply speaking, Trinitarian unity is greater than the personal union in Christ, but that the latter includes the union of more elements. Philip, however, can hardly mean that the union in person in Christ includes all the degrees of being that he mentions, particularly the being of nature.[17] At this point Philip appears to be copying the *Glossa* of Alexander of Hales; it, however, expressly excludes the union in Christ from the greater completion found in a union in person: the union in Christ, it says, "is not a coming-together in a subject," that is, in nature.[18] When Philip makes such a statement, either he must be speaking about personal unity in general and be making this remark as an afterthought, or he has failed to see the contradiction implied in his statements. The former alternative is more plausible.

Thus Philip the Chancellor classifies the union in Christ among numerical unities by extending this notion to include a oneness in hypostasis. In this way he eliminates the objection that a numerical unity of itself involves a unity in species or genus, which would be impossible in Christ in view of the distinction of his two natures. By comparison with the union in one nature of the three persons of the Trinity,

14 *Ibid.*; p. 177, ll. 262-267.
15 See *ibid.*; 2, 29; p. 177.
16 *Ibid.*, 2, 30; p. 177.
17 Cf. *supra*, pp. 90-92.
18 See *GlossaAlex* III, 2, 14i (L): p. 30. Cf. *HypUnion* II, 150.

the Hypostatic Union is, simply speaking, a lesser union. From the viewpoint of personal unity, however, the Hypostatic Union is a greater union than that of the Trinity, for in the Trinity the three persons remain distinct, but in Christ there is in the two natures an identity of person.

8. THE GRACE OF UNION

In imitation of his immediate predecessors, Philip the Chancellor uses the concept of the grace of union when he speaks of the Hypostatic Union. He quotes such commonly-used texts as that of St. Augustine: "For thus each man from the first moment that he has faith is made a Christian by grace just as that man from the first moment was made Christ by grace,"[1] and the statement: "Whatever belongs to the Son of God by nature belongs to the Son of Man by grace."[2] While investigating the role of the soul as medium of the union he introduces in an objection a text from St. Augustine that says: "Among things happening in time there is no greater grace than that God willed to be united to our weakness."[3]

Twice in the *Summa de Bono* Philip, without actually using the term "grace of union," links the Hypostatic Union with grace. In the first of these, within a discussion of the division of prophecy known as the "prophecy of predestination," he identifies predestination to the Incarnation with "the good of a grace" and distinguishes this from the good that is the predestination of ordinary men to glory. Among God's works, he says, some are done apart from our free will and some with our free will's cooperation. The prophecy of predestination is concerned with the good that God does apart from man's free will. Among these goods is the grace pertaining to Christ's Incarnation; with this good the prophecy of predestination is primarily concerned. Another such good is the grace in Christ's members ordaining them to glory; with this good the prophecy of predestination is concerned secondarily:

---

1 *Summa de Bono:* P 82va-vb; T 67va; V 72ra. In Philip's quotation the text reads: "Ita enim ab initio fidei suae homo quicumque gratiâ fit Christianus sicut gratiâ homo ille ab initio factus es Christus." With slight variations it is the text of St. Augustine, *De Praedestinatione Sanctorum*, 15, 31 (PL 44, 982), which is quoted in Lombard, *Sent* III, 6, 2 (p. 575), and in Lombard, *Coll in Rom* 1, 4 (PL 191, 1309C).

2 *DeIncarn.* 3, 18; p. 180. Cf. *HypUnion* I, 280, n. 56, for the background of this text, and cf. St. Augustine, *Contra Sermonem Arianorum*, 8; PL 42, 688.

3 *DeIncarn*, 1-i, 17; p. 167. The objection adds to this quotation the words: "Therefore that union is from grace."

Opus autem Dei aut est sine nostro libero arbitrio aut cum. Si sine, aut est bonum aut malum. Si bonum, tunc pertinet ad prophetiam praedestinationis, ut est bonum gratiae quod pertinet ad Christi incarnationem, de quo est prophetia praedestinationis principaliter, de bono vero gratiae in membris ordinato ad gloriam secundario.[4]

Thus the Incarnation is depicted as a good in the order of grace coming from God's predestination apart from man's merits.

In the second passage Philip contrasts sonship through adoption with the sonship of grace; he connects this sonship through grace with Christ's being the proper rather than adopted Son of God. Thus, referring to an objection based on a text of St. Jerome,[5] he says:

Respondeo quod illud potest intelligi non de filiatione secundum naturam divinam vel humanam, neque secundum filiationem adoptionis, sed secundum filiationem gratiae: non enim dicendus est Christus filius adoptivus, ut dicitur ad Rom. 1, super illud: *Quem*[6] *promisit*[7] *per prophetas suos in Scripturis sanctis de Filio suo*[8], *Glossa: Non adoptivo, sed*[9] *Filio, scilicet*[10] *proprio et sibi consubstantiali, coaeterno, et coaequali.*[11]

One of Philip's most original investigations of the Hypostatic Union asks whether the union of the human nature to the divine takes place

---

4 *P* 82vb; *T* 67vb; *V* 72ra. In these same places Philip gives a long quotation from St. Augustine that lies behind his statements in the present passage. The quotation, based on St. Augustine, *De Praedestinatione Sanctorum*, 15, 30-31 (PL 44, 981-983), follows Lombard's summary of this text in his *Coll in Rom* 1, 4 (PL 191, 1309B-D). Philip then adds the following commentary: "... Ergo et principaliter praedestinatio secundum quod dicitur prophetia praedestinationis accipitur de bono gratiae quod pertinet ad caput, id est, de praedestinatione Christi secundum quod homo, et non de gratia corporis nisi secundario. Bonum quidem praedestinationis ordinatum est ad gloriam tam in capite quam in membris, primo in capite, demum in membris. Unde secundum quod large accipitur, ad utrumque se extendit secundum prius et posterius" (*P* 82vb; *T* 67va; *V* 72ra).

5 The objection (in *P* 103rb; *T* 82rb; *V* 87ra) reads as follows: "Sed iterum quaeritur de hoc quod dicitur Is. 11; super illud: *Et requiescet super eum spiritus Domini* [Is 11, 2], *Glossa: In evangelio Nazaraeorum ita habetur: 'Super eum descendit* [om. P] *Spiritus Sanctus et requievit* [requiescit P] *super eum, et dixit illi: "Expectabam* [expectavi P] *te, Fili, in omnibus prophetis, ut venires et requiescerem in te. Tu es requies mea; tu es Filius meus primogenitus."* ' [cf. St. Jerome, *In Is*, Book IV (cap. XI); PL 24, 148B-D]." I have been unable to identify the *Glossa* using this text of St. Jerome; it is not found in the *GlossaOrdinaria* on the Gospels or on Isaias, nor in Lombard, *Coll in Rom* 1, 3-4 (PL 191, 1305C-1315A), a likely place because many patristic texts concerning Christ's predestination and non-adoptive sonship are gathered there. For the same text cf. *De Fide*, 6; Ceva, p. 105, ll. 353-358.

6 Quod autem *Vulgate*.

7 promiserat *Vulgate*.

8 Rom 1, 2-3.

9 *Add.* de *mg. V2*.

10 *Om. TV*.

11 *P* 103rb; *T* 82rb; *V* 87ra. Cf. *De Fide*, 6; Ceva, p. 105, ll. 359-365. For the text of the *Glossa* see Lombard, *Coll in Rom* 1, 3; PL 191, 1305C: "De Filio dico non adoptivo, sed, 'suo,' scilicet proprio et sibi consubstantiali, coaeterno, coaequali."

through "aliquid circa animam,"[12] that is, through some created
disposition in the soul that is likened to a force or mediating virtue or
grace.[13] A series of objections pose the problem: If one nature is united
in preference to another that is its equal in nature and grace, there
must be something in the one united on account of which God, in his
well-ordered wisdom, prefers it to the other;[14] again, because the union
is consequent upon something natural, there should be some nature or
something in the one united that is not in another;[15] further, since the
different grades of likeness in creatures culminate in the likeness according to grace, the union, which seems to be according to an excellent grace, is reducible in fact to the similitude according to grace;[16]
finally, since this grace cannot be a power or passion or habit of
knowledge, it must be a virtue, so that the union takes place with a virtue as medium.[17]

Philip resolutely rejects such notions of a created quality, force, virtue, or grace that would be a medium for the union of human nature
with the Word. He distinguishes two types of grace, one naturally
preceding the union, which he calls the grace of pre-election, and
another naturally following upon the union, which is the fullness of all
good things and charismatic gifts. The grace of pre-election is ordained
to the becoming and assumption of the soul, that is, to its being as opposed to its well-being; the well-being of the soul is assured by the
grace that is consequent upon the union:

> Solution: The soul, created to the image and likeness of God, and being
> an incorporeal substance, was able to be united to God ..., but not any
> soul, but rather that one which had the grace of pre-election, the one
> chosen by God from eternity before others ... So therefore there is a grace
> naturally preceding the union, which is ordained to becoming and to
> assuming: for it is ordained to the being of the soul, that it may be
> assumed. There is also another that follows upon the union naturally and
> is ordained to well-being; it is the fullness of all good things and
> charismatic gifts ...[18]

---

12 *DeIncarn*, 2, 13; p. 173.

13 Cf. *ibid*., 2, 14-16; p. 174. The *GlossaAlex* touched briefly on the question whether the grace of
union is a medium between the two natures in the union; see *HypUnion* II, 172-173.

14 *DeIncarn*, 2, 13; pp. 173-174.

15 *Ibid*., 2, 14; p. 174. Damascene is quoted regarding the giving of generative power to Mary's
flesh: so, too, argues the objector, the soul should be given some power by which it would be
united to the Word of God.

16 *Ibid*., 2, 15; p. 174.

17 *Ibid*., 2, 16; p. 174.

18 *Ibid*., 2, 19; pp. 174-175, ll. 184-187, 190-193.

This "grace of pre-election" corresponds to the "bonum gratiae quod pertinet ad Christi incarnationem" spoken of by Philip in the *Summa de Bono* and there called a "predestination."[19] It is not, however, simply the gratuitous will of God choosing one nature in preference to others; it implies the conferring of certain privileges upon the soul of Christ:

> *Blessed is he whom thou hast chosen and assumed*: this is the choice of the Lord God that has prepared this soul, in which there were previous natural endowments that were better and that surpassed all the other natural endowments of any soul ... Therefore since that soul had powers and forces in its nature transcending other creatures, as well as a surpassing natural goodness, it was rightly chosen by preference and united to the Deity ...[20]

Thus the preferential choice of the soul of Christ by God means that God endowed his soul with qualities in the order of being that raised it above other souls and meant it was fittingly chosen and united to God in preference to the others. Philip, then, simultaneously maintains the gratuitousness of the choice, shows its efficacy as to the being and endowments of Christ's soul, and eliminates the idea of a force, virtue, or grace that would be a medium interposed between the soul and God in order to effect the union. The "grace of pre-election" does have effects in the nature, but these effects ennoble the nature in itself and make it worthy to be united immediately.

Are these ennobling effects, which we may think of as dispositions of the human nature similar to those mentioned in the *Glossa* of Alexander of Hales, effects in the order of nature only or in the order of grace as well?[21] The text quoted above, which speaks of "powers and forces in its nature transcending other creatures, as well as a surpassing natural goodness," gives no indication of anything beyond natural endowments. In a second argument, however, Philip seems to indicate that at least some of the ennobling effects coming from the grace of pre-election are graces that make the soul worthily prepared for the union. Philip's argument follows a theme used by Alexander of Hales, according to which God is present in all things in three ways: "The same conclusion is also reached by the fact that God is said to be in things in three modes: in the first mode by essence, presence, and power; in the second mode by grace; in the third mode by union."[22] According to Philip, in

19 See *supra*, p. 115.
20 *DeIncarn*, 2, 19; p. 175, ll. 187-190, 197-199.
21 See *GlossaAlex* III, 7, 27 (L) (p. 99), and *HypUnion* II, 172-173.
22 *DeIncarn*, 2, 20; p. 175, ll. 201-203. Cf. *GlossaAlex* I, 37, 1 (p. 363); III, 4, 10 (A) (p. 51); III, 4, 23 (L) (p. 54). Cf. also *HypUnion* II, 157-158.

order to move fittingly from the presence by nature to the presence by
the Hypostatic Union, the second mode of presence, that by grace,
should intervene to prepare the soul of Christ for the union:

> Therefore, in order that there be a fitting transition from the first
> mode to the last, it will come about by way of the middle mode, namely,
> through grace. So, therefore, that soul, worthily prepared through grace
> of this kind, was united to the Word ...[23]

To this argument Philip adds a text, supposedly from St. Augustine,
that speaks of the anointing of the soul of Christ with the oil of glad-
ness.[24] Because this grace is said to have a role of preparing the nature
for the union, it must be a disposition inhering in the nature and
distinct from the will of God effecting this preparation and choosing the
soul for union.

For Philip the grace effecting the union, whether it be the grace
disposing the soul or the actual choice made by God's will, is quite
distinct from habitual grace and the virtues. An objection using a
phrase attributed to Julian the Apostate had implied that if the union is
according to grace, any human being, because of his (habitual) grace,
could be united to the Son of God: "Moreover," argues the objection,
"if grace is cause of the union, what kind of error does he fall into who
says: 'I do not envy Christ the Lord, because I can become the Son of
God?' "[25] In answer Philip distinguishes, as he had in his main solution,
between the grace ordained to being and that ordained to well-being:

> To the objection that if the union is according to grace, therefore [it is]
> also according to the likeness of grace, [and] therefore we too can be
> united, I reply: As I have said, the union is caused by the grace that is or-
> dained to being, and you are objecting with respect to the grace that is or-
> dained to well-being, and therefore the argumentation is not valid.[26]

---

23 *DeIncarn*, 2, 20; p. 175, ll. 203-206.

24 *Ibid.*, p. 175. See *infra*, p. 175, n. to l. 214, concerning the work that is quoted.

25 *Ibid.*, 2, 17; p. 174.

26 *Ibid.*, 2, 22; p. 176. This reply seems to suppose that the original objection incorporated some
of the elements of one of the earlier objections (*ibid.*, 2, 15; p. 174), which reduces the union
through grace to the union through habitual grace making one like God.

This reply of Philip helps to correct what seems to be a misinterpretation of his doctrine by A.
Vugts, *La grâce d'union d'après S. Thomas d'Aquin* (Tilburg 1946) p. 119, repeated by J. Rohof, *La sainteté substantielle du Christ dans la théologie scolastique* (Fribourg, Suisse 1952) p. 27. For them, Philip
teaches that the grace disposing for union is habitual grace. Vugts relies solely on the passage in
DeIncarn, 2, 20 (p. 175), without taking into account Philip's distinction (made *ibid.*, 2, 22; p. 176: cf.
ibid., 2, 19; p. 175) between the "gratia quae est ad esse" or "ad fieri et ad assumere" and the
"gratia quae est ad bene esse." That the "gratia quae est ad esse" is not only the "gratia praeelectionis," that is, God's will freely bestowing the union, is clear from the movement of the argument

Thus for Philip grace appears to intervene in the union from two points of view: there is a grace of pre-election or predestination on God's part, that is, his gratuitous choice of one particular soul for the union; there is also, as an effect of the choice, a grace in the soul so chosen ennobling it beyond other creatures for the union. This dispositive grace, however, is not a medium between the soul and God; it makes it a worthy being, which is then united immediately. This dispositive grace, preparing for being, is distinct from the graces that follow upon being and make both that soul and ordinary men good once they already exist. In this question, then, Philip goes beyond the sparse indications given by the second redaction of Alexander of Hales' *Glossa*; it too, we have seen, appeared to think of the grace of union as a disposition inhering in the assumed nature, but rejected the notion of this grace as a medium.[27]

Before closing this section, we may note certain remarks of Philip, all in the *Summa de Bono*, concerning some of the more immediate consequences of the grace of union, or of the union of the human nature to the divine nature in the person of the Son. While rejecting a *summum malum* supposed to be at the source of material things, Philip points to the case of Christ: the union in Christ, he says, meant that the supreme good was united to the body of Christ; hence his body could not come from the principle of darkness: "Item, de Christo objicitur: Secundum corpus esset a principio tenebrarum quia in eo erat malum poenae. Sed quomodo, cum summum[28] bonum esset ei unitum?"[29]

In discussing the article of the Creed professing belief in Christ's ascension, Philip affirms one limit of the effect of the Hypostatic Union:

reported by Philip: "...Si secundum gratiam est unio, ergo et secundum *assimilationem* gratiae" (emphasis mine). The "assimilation by grace" refers to habitual grace (cf. *ibid.*, 2, 15; p. 174), but Philip rejects it as a disposition towards the union.

27 In the *Summa de Bono* an argument against Christ's having a guardian angel reasons from the immediacy of the union of the Divinity to all the parts of Christ's human nature: "Item, ille cui unitur omnis virtus custodiae non indiget particulari custodia. Sed divinitas unita fuit immediate non solum rationi sed etiam sensualitati et corpori. Ergo non indiget quoad sensualitatem vel corpus particulari custodia. Sed unusquisque angelus custos est particularis. Non ergo indiget custodia angelica: inconvenientia enim esset inter superius et inferius, scilicet deitatem et carnem unitam, ponere medium separatum" (*P* 70*bis* vb; *T* 59ra; *V* 62va). Philip does not accept the conclusion, but his explanation seems to indicate that he agrees with the principles about the immediacy of the union. He says: "Ad quod dicendum quod non habuit anima Christi angelum ad custodiendum proprie sed ad ministerium, et si prohiberet [prohibet *T*] a vexatione corporali, non tamen custodiret nisi ministerio" (*P* 70*bis* vb; *T* 59ra; *V* 62va-vb).

28 summe *T*.

29 *P* 6va; *T* 6ra; *V* 6rb.

as man Christ did not ascend to equality with God; the Ascension served
rather to *manifest* his equality as God:

> *Ascendit ad caelos*: Secundum quod homo ... Item, *Glossa* dicit quod ascen-
> dit[30] ad aequalitatem.[31] Sed contra: Nec secundum quod homo ascendit ad
> aequalitatem,[32] quia numquam aequalis ei secundum quod homo, nec
> ascendit ad aequalitatem secundum quod Deus, et ita non ascendit ad
> aequalitatem.
>
> Solutio: Non ascendit in re, sed in notitia, id est, innotuit. Simile
> habetur[33] Matth. ult.: *Data est mihi potestas*,[34] id est, apparet mihi data.[35]

The union of Christ's human nature to the divine nature places it
above the highest angel, Philip declares, because in his human nature
the fullness of the Godhead dwelt bodily:

> Ad aliud vero dicendum quod optimum in genere hominum dicitur
> melius optimo in genere angelorum non unde est homo, sed unde unitur
> naturae divinae. In ea enim natura sive in eo homine *plenitudo divinitatis
> corporaliter inhabitavit*, sicut dicitur ad Col. 2 ...[36]

Hence Christ did not need a guardian angel to counsel him to do good
or to turn him from evil. Philip gives two different reasons for this lack
of need. The first, given in a preliminary counter-objection, links it with
Christ's confirmation in good arising from the union itself:

> Praeterea, quae necessitas esset ut Christus haberet angelum ad sui
> custodiam? Non enim necessaria est custodia quantum ad consilium
> faciendi bonum vel declinandi a malo, cum confirmatus sit secundum
> quod est homo ex ipsa unione divinae naturae ad ipsum facere bonum et
> declinare a malo. Consilium autem non requiritur in necessariis.[37]

---

30 descendit *TV e corr. V2*.

31 aequitatem *T* (and thus throughout the passage). I have been unable to identify this text.

32 *Om*. Sed... aequalitatem *T*.

33 *Om. T*.

34 Mt 28, 18: "Data est mihi omnis potestas in caelo et in terra."

35 *Om. P*; *P* 103vb-104ra; *T* 82vb; *V* 87va.

36 *P* 70bis ra; *T* 58va; *V* 62ra. See Col 2, 9: "... Quia in ipso inhabitat omnis plenitudo divinitatis corporaliter."
In another text Philip quotes Lombard's scriptural commentary concerning the exaltation of human nature in Christ above all creatures through the Incarnation: "Glossa: Ante Christi ... adventum permittebant se angeli ab hominibus adorari, etc... Sed non post incarnationem ... ut intelligant humanam naturam in Christo super omnem creaturam exaltatam ..." (*P* 69rb; *T* 57rb; *V* 6ovb). Cf. Lombard, *In Ps* 23, 8; PL 191, 250C. Cf. Gregory, *XL Homiliae in Evangelia*, Lib. I, Hom. 8, 2; PL 76, 1105A.

37 *P* 70bis va-vb; *T* 58vb; *V* 62va.

In his main solution, on the other hand, Philip connects Christ's lack of need for a guardian angel with the presence of the Holy Spirit in Christ from the beginning:

> Differenter autem est de anima Christi et de aliis, nam aliae in-digentiam habent naturaliter custodiae angelicae in consulendo ad declinandum a malo et ad faciendum bonum. Anima autem ejus a prin-cipio habuit Spiritum Sanctum requiescentem in ea, sicut dicitur Is. 7.[38]

This second text thus seems to link Christ's confirmation in good more directly with the presence of the Holy Spirit and, undoubtedly, with the resulting gifts of created grace than immediately with the union; probably for Philip both the union and the created graces were equal or ordered sources of this confirmation in good.

Elsewhere Christ's confirmation in good is put in terms of his fullness of created grace resulting from the union of his human nature with the Divinity. Operating grace in Christ, he says, had only one effect, that is, to do good, not to remit fault. Nor in Christ is it properly called "prevenient" grace because with the divine being that was his through the union there came a fullness of grace such that his will was good simultaneously with the influx of grace; grace is properly called "prevenient" in those who are adoptive sons. This grace was a "cooperating" grace only with respect to temptations from without:

> In Domino nostro Jesu Christo erat gratia operans, sed non nisi ad unum effectum qui est facere bonum, non quantum ad remissionem culpae. Neque in eo dicitur proprie "praeveniens," quia cum esse-divinitas per unionem erat gratiae plenitudo: plenitudo ita quod simul erat bona voluntas cum gratia; proprie autem dicitur "praeveniens" in illis qui sunt filii adoptionis. "Cooperans" vero non erat nisi respectu exteriorum temp-tationum.[39]

As for original sin, Philip teaches that it was not present in Christ; no doubt this was so because of the Hypostatic Union. Thus, speaking of the death of Christ, he says that although mortal flesh was assumed in the union, Christ's flesh was not obliged to die because it was not born with sin, that is, with original sin:

> Ad secundum dicendum quod sola illa caro obligata est morti quae originaliter nascitur cum peccato: sic autem non est in Christo, nec est

---

38 *P* 7obis vb; *T* 59ra; *V* 62vb. Cf. Is 11, 2: "Et requiescet super eum spiritus Domini ..." For another text of Philip on Christ's guardian angel, see *supra*, p. 119, n. 27.

39 *P* 57vb; *T* 48va; *V* 5ovb.

concedendum quod licet caro Christi fuit assumpta mortalis, quod propter
hoc fuerit morti obligata. Non enim necessitate meriti sed voluntate
redimendi fuit assumpta ..."[40]

Hence, as in Adam, and even more so, Christ's sense-movements were
ordered according to reason: "... Unde in Adam motus sensuales erant
ordinati primo secundum rationis imperium ..., et similiter in Domino
nostro Jesu Christo, et multo amplius."[41]

In his human nature Christ enjoyed the highest liberty to be found in
a changeable nature; this perfection of liberty came not from an immutability of his nature, but through the union of this nature with the
highest liberty, that is, God: "... Nec intendimus hic de Christo secundum quod homo, cujus libertas fuit summa in natura mutabili. Sed hoc
non fuit ex immutabilitate[42] naturae, sed per unionem summae liber-
tatis."[43]

Two further consequences of the grace of union are the adoration to
be paid to the humanity of Christ and the unique type of predication to
be used concerning Christ. Since, according to Philip's presentation,
these two consequences are closely linked with one another, they will be
examined subsequently in the section devoted to the second of these
consequences, the communication of properties or idioms.[44]

40 P 154rb; T 109rb; V 115ra.

41 P 33ra; T 28vb; V 29rb. This is stated elsewhere in different ways, e.g., if Christ's body were
from a principle of evil, "secundum hoc esset continua pugna, cum maxima pax fuerit in eo"
(P 6va; T 6ra; V 6rb). An objection whose statement seems acceptable to Philip says: "... Ex toto
potest fomes per gratiae amplitudinem exstingui, ut in Beata Virgine et Christo" (P 31rb; T 27rb;
V 27vb).

42 immutabilis PT.

43 P 15ra; T 12vb; V 13ra.

44 See *infra*, p. 138-140.

CHAPTER IV

THE DIVINE PARTICIPANT IN THE UNION

1. The Divine Nature and the Son of God as Incarnate and United

Philip the Chancellor's attention is briefly engaged by several questions about the union looked at from the viewpoint of the divine participant. The first of these that we shall examine asks about the expressions "The divine nature is incarnate," "The divine nature is united to flesh," and "The divine nature is man." Philip shows no hesitation in using each of these expressions so long as they are understood correctly.

As for the divine nature's being incarnate, Philip quotes two apparently opposed statements of St. John Damascene. The first says: "We have never heard that the Deity was born a man or was incarnate or became human ...";[1] the second, quoted by Philip with evident approval, explains the divine nature's becoming incarnate as its being united to flesh.[2] Philip says, however, that there is a difference between the signification of "becoming incarnate" and "being united":

> This is true: "The divine essence is incarnate," because ["incarnate"] indicates that its subject is related to the terminus or end; but "united" indicates the terminus of the Incarnation; that is, to speak plainly, "incarnate" signifies its subject without the pre-existence of a man, whereas "united" [signifies it] with the pre-existence of a man, as Damascene says.[3]

In this text Philip explicitly accepts the validity of the expression and even distinguishes it from the expression "The divine nature is united to flesh." He seems to refer the term "incarnate" to the very process of becoming man; this appears to be his reason for saying that it "signifies its subject without the pre-existence of a man." In this view the human

---

1 *DeIncarn*, 3, 18; p. 181. For the reference see *infra*, p. 181, n. to l. 102.

2 *Ibid.*, 3, 19; p. 181.

3 *Loc. cit.* Cf. Damascene, *DeFideOrth* III, 11; PG 94, 1024B-C; Buytaert, p. 205: "Igitur aliud quidem est unitio, et aliud incarnatio. Nam unitio quidem solum demonstrat copulationem; ad quid autem facta est copulatio, non adhuc. Incarnatio autem, idem autem dicere et inhumanatio, eam quae ad carnem, scilicet ad hominem copulationem demonstrat, quemadmodum et ignitio eam quae ad ignem unitionem."

nature of Christ is not presupposed to the action of becoming incarnate, but comes into being as the terminus or end of the process.
The expression "united," however, signifies for Philip the completed
process; it presupposes that the human nature of Christ is already in
existence as one of the extremes or termini that enters into union with
the other:[4] we have already seen other passages in which Philip speaks
of the two natures as extremes in the union.[5]

Philip expresses the same viewpoint regarding the term "united"
when he defends the second expression, "The divine nature is united to
flesh," against those who would interpret it of the divine nature's efficient activity in causing the union. In this phrase, he says, "united"
designates not the act of uniting, but the accomplished fact:

> To the other objection I reply that the divine nature is united to flesh,
> but "united" (*unita*) in that phrase does not express an action, but shows
> what is done (*factum*), and this itself expresses the person of the Son; but
> "united" (*univit*) expresses an action, and therefore it expresses the
> nature.[6]

Once again, then, Philip appears to interpret the divine nature's union
to flesh to mean the completed process of union and, in a sense, the
very person of the Son who, as Philip says here and elsewhere,[7] is the
medium of the union. But why does Philip maintain that the completed
union expresses the person of the Son? It is because of the objector's
argument that to say the divine nature is united would indicate that the
union took place in the divine nature common to the three persons
rather than, as it really did, in the one person of the Son. We shall see
more of this point shortly.

Can it be said that the divine nature is man? This, the third of the
above-mentioned expressions, is denied by an objection using the
familiar argument that if the divine nature is man, then it was born, it
suffered, and it died;[8] in other words, human qualities would inhere in
or at least be predicable not only of the Son, but even of the divine

---

4 Philip's explanation seems to differ somewhat from Damascene's as given in the previous note.
For Damascene the difference is not that "incarnate" fails to signify the pre-existence of the human
nature whereas "united" does signify it, but rather that "incarnate" signifies the terminus to which
the divine nature is joined, whereas "united" signifies only the joining itself, without clearly indicating that it is a joining to flesh or human nature. Perhaps Philip's statement means the same
thing, but it is difficult to find this meaning in his words.

5 See *DeIncarn*, 2, 9-11 (pp. 171-172), and *supra*, pp. 93-94, 97-98.

6 *DeIncarn*, 3, 17; p. 180.

7 E.g., *ibid.*, 2, 10-11; p. 179.

8 *Ibid.*, 3, 15; p. 180.

nature. Philip's reply is brief: "As for that [dictum] 'The divine nature is man,' I reply that it is true, because 'whatever belongs to the Son of God by nature belongs to the Son of Man by grace'; nevertheless, terms that stand for the divine nature do not stand for the Son of God."[9] In other words, Philip refers the expression to the union of the divine and human natures through the grace of union: when it is understood in this way, he sees nothing wrong with it. However, because he must meet the problem raised in the objection, he concludes by saying that terms cannot be transferred indiscriminately from the divine person to the divine nature and vice versa. That is, although birth, suffering, and death may be predicated of the Son, it does not follow that in such predication we may understand the divine nature. Philip's position recalls that rejected by William of Auxerre: Philip grants that if such expressions are predicated "substantively" (that is, if it were meant that the divine essence is the *one who* was born, suffered, and died), they are true;[10] but, he adds, if they are understood "adjectivally" (that is, as directly modifying the divine essence as their subject), they are false. Hence, he says, some hold that these expressions are false without any qualification; St. John Damascene, he indicates, is one of these.[11]

In the following paragraph Philip restates his view and notes the reason for it: such expressions are incorrect in so far as they imply a limitation of the divine being: "Likewise, as often as some predication is made about the divine substance that denotes a limitation [of it], it is false, such as this: 'The divine essence is born.' "[12] To judge from his manner of speaking in this text and in the previous one, Philip does not seem to reject such expressions categorically, but only when they are used to refer directly to the divine essence as the subject of inherence for created, finite properties.

From these various discussions one gathers the impression that Philip the Chancellor is not so greatly concerned as others about the validity of such expressions: so long as they are rightly understood, Philip seems less inclined than his predecessors to eliminate one or the other. This attitude itself appears to reflect his generally greater concern with the realities involved than with the subtleties of speculative grammar.

9 *Ibid.*, 3, 18; p. 180, ll. 87-89.
10 Cf. William of Auxerre, *DeInc*, 9, 1-3; Principe, pp. 278-280.
11 *DeIncarn*, 3, 18; p. 180.
12 *Ibid.*, 3, 19; p. 181.

2. The Divine Nature and the Son of God as Assuming or Uniting
Human Nature

In both the *Summa de Bono* and in the *Quaestiones* Philip the Chancellor
asserts the common efficient causality of the three persons of the
Trinity. One text in the *Summa de Bono* is especially interesting because
in it Philip, even while asserting this community of works *ad extra*, indicates that by reason of the Incarnation appropriation of human attributes to the Son differs from the ordinary manner of appropriating
divine attributes to the Trinitarian persons. To suffer and to die, he
says, are predicated of the Son differently from the way power is appropriated to the Father: to suffer and to die belong to the Son alone;
power, although appropriated to the Father, is really common to all
three persons:

> ... Alio modo est appropriatio de Filio quam de Patre vel de Spiritu
> Sancto, nam quaedam dicuntur quae sunt propria Filii, sicut passum et
> mortuum; quae vero dicuntur de Patre, ut potentia et hujusmodi, licet ap-
> propriata sint Patri, tamen conveniunt Filio et Spiritui Sancto: indivisa
> enim sunt opera Trinitatis ...[1]

In the *Quaestiones de Incarnatione* this same principle of the three persons' common efficient activity is used in an inquiry whether the act of
assuming belongs to the divine nature or to the divine person. One
argument uses the principle as follows: Since to create and to unite
belong to the same entity, to create and to assume also belong to the
same entity. But because the divine nature is common to the three persons and because the whole Trinity creates, the act of creation belongs
to the divine nature; therefore the act of assuming will also belong not
to the divine person, but to the divine nature.[2] A second argument
restates the same principle and conclusion in slightly different form: To
assume means to effect an assumption; but since all efficient activity
belongs to the whole Trinity and so to the divine nature, to assume also
belongs to the divine nature.[3] Against this position comes the obvious

---

1 *P* 101vb; *T* 81ra; *V* 85vb. Cf. *De Fide*, 6; Ceva, p. 95, ll. 48-53. The principles of appropriation
are discussed earlier in the *Summa de Bono* (*P* 19rb; *T* 17ra; *V* 17va) with respect to *potentia* and
sapientia. At one point in the discussion Philip says in passing: "... licet inseparabilia opera
Trinitatis."

2 *DeIncarn*, 3, 3; p. 178.

3 *Ibid.*, 3, 4; p. 178. Cf. also *ibid.*, 3, 1-2 (p. 178), where the arguments in favour of the nature's
assuming rely on the identity of nature and substance in God and on an authoritative text from St.
Augustine.

objection: If the divine nature assumes rather than a divine person, and if all three persons share the activity of the divine nature, then all three persons of the Trinity assume human nature, which is false.[4]

Philip's solution follows the general lines of his predecessors, but is more systematic than theirs. Although most properly only the Son assumes human nature, he teaches, it is correct to say that, properly, the divine nature assumes human nature, and even that in a less proper sense the whole Trinity assumes human nature. Philip distinguishes three meanings of "to assume": to take into oneself, to take to oneself, and to take something. The first is an act belonging to the Son alone, the second to the divine nature, the third to the whole Trinity:

> Solution: "To assume" is sometimes used for "to take into oneself": in this way this act belongs only to the Son; sometimes it is used for "to take to oneself"; in this way it belongs to the divine nature; sometimes it is used for "to take to something": in this way it belongs to the whole Trinity.[5]

Philip then interprets the different propositions in line with these distinctions:

> According to the first meaning this is false: "The divine nature assumed human nature," and this is true: "The person assumed human nature." According to the second meaning this is true: "The divine nature assumed human nature." According to the third this is true: "The whole Trinity assumed human nature." And "to assume" is taken most properly in the first way, properly in the second, and less properly in the third.[6]

According to Philip, then, the divine person, the Son, most properly assumes human nature since he fulfils the most proper meaning of assuming by taking human nature *into* himself. The divine nature, however, can be properly said to assume human nature because it takes human nature *to* itself. In a less proper sense the whole Trinity assumes human nature by effecting the taking of the human nature to a terminus, that is, to the nature and even more properly to the person of the Son. Philip, therefore, accepts the proposition that the divine nature assumes human nature, but he holds it to be even more correct to say that it is the divine person who assumes human nature.

In replying to the objections that argued for the prior claims of nature over person in the assumption Philip simply applies the three

---

4 *Ibid.*, 3, 5; p. 178.
5 *Ibid.*, 3, 6; p. 178.
6 *Loc. cit.*

meanings of the term "to assume": unlike the verbs "to create" and "to unite," the verb "to assume" implies something additional, that is, the terminus to which the thing in question is assumed and the manner in which the thing is united to it. Hence between acts such as creating and uniting, which are common to the three persons, and the act of assuming there is no exact parallelism, except in the third and less proper meaning of the term "assume."'

This raises a new question: What of the act of *uniting* human nature as distinct from the act of assuming it? Does this belong more properly to the divine nature or person? Philip puts the question as follows: "Whose is the act of uniting when it expresses only an act (*actum pure*)?"⁸ That is, if we consider "to unite" simply as an act,⁹ is it more proper to say that the divine nature unites human nature or that the divine person does so? Philip's position is that the act of uniting is more properly the work of the divine nature than of the divine person or sub-stance. Although at first he seems to admit the argument of a counter-objection that this act is properly an act of the person or substance possessing the nature, as in created natures,¹⁰ he goes on to say that because in God the person (or substance) is identical with the nature, "frequently an act that properly belongs to the substance is attributed to the nature, such as to create and to unite."¹¹

From the foregoing passage it might appear that for Philip the act of uniting belongs properly to the person and less properly to the nature; further on, however, he agrees with an argument which, by dif-ferentiating between the act of assuming (*sumendi*) as corporeal in its primary signification and the act of uniting as a purely spiritual act, reaches the conclusion that the two acts cannot be attributed according to the same reason.¹² Philip says of this conclusion: "I grant this, and I say that the act of assuming is properly said according to substance, but

7 See *ibid.*, 7-8; pp. 178-179.

8 *Ibid.*, 3, 9; p. 179.

9 By the phrase *actus pure* Philip appears to wish to exclude a passive use of the term such as it has in phrases like "Divina natura est unita carni." Cf. *ibid.*, 13 & 16 (pp. 179 & 180). In the second of these texts he clearly states that a verb signifying the union must be distinguished according to its active and passive use: when used actively, he says, it signifies the uncreated; when used passively, it signifies the created.

10 For this counter-objection see *ibid.*, 3, 9; p. 179. In lower natures, the argument runs, the one having nature acts, not the nature itself. This should also be the case in God, it is argued, so that to unite is the act of the person or substance. not of the nature. But if this is true, the divine nature did not unite the human nature to itself.

11 *Ibid.*, 3, 10; p. 179, ll. 45-47.

12 *Ibid.*, 3, 12; p. 179.

that the act of uniting is properly said of the nature."[13] From this statement it is clear that Philip thinks it more proper to say that the divine nature rather than the divine person unites the human nature. In all that he says in this question about assuming and uniting Philip's starting-point seems to be that because the act of uniting, like the act of creating, is an act common to the three persons of the Trinity rather than proper to one of them, it is therefore an activity proceeding from the nature rather than from a particular person. However, Philip fails to prove convincingly that the act of uniting is more proper to the divine nature than to the three persons acting in common.

Having stated that the act of uniting is said properly of the divine nature, Philip encounters further objections based precisely on the sharing of this act by the three persons of the Trinity. Is it not wrong, one objection asks, to say simply that the divine nature united flesh or human nature?: the union took place in person, but such a statement gives no indication of the person in whom the union took place.[14] Further, a second objection argues, even the expression "The divine nature united human nature to itself" is false because the divine nature is common to the three persons and the union was to only one person.[15]

Philip agrees with the first of these objections: "But when one says: 'The divine nature united human nature,' in that phrase there is not a true and express reciprocation; but when 'to itself' is added, the reciprocation is more express and the divine nature is joined ..."[16] Thus Philip feels that the reflexive pronoun designating the terminus of the union should be included.

But what of the second objection? Is not even the expression "The divine nature united human nature to itself" insufficient? Philip disagrees: Because the Son is identical with the divine nature, the reflexive pronoun *sibi* refers to the person of the Son, at least in its connotation.[17] Thus Philip would say that the expression "The divine nature unites human nature to itself" means that the divine nature causes the union of the human nature to itself in the person of the Son, who is identical with the divine nature.

Philip's positions on these questions may be summarized as follows: Because of the signification of the terms in question it is most proper to

13 *Loc. cit.*
14 *Ibid.*, 3, 13; p. 179.
15 *Ibid.*, 3, 14; p. 180.
16 *Ibid.*, 3, 17; p. 180, ll. 81-84.
17 *Ibid.*; p. 180, ll. 83-86. Cf. *ibid.*, 3, 16; p. 180.

say that the Son assumes human nature, that is, takes it into himself; however, one may say properly that the divine nature assumes human nature, and less properly that the whole Trinity assumes human nature. As to the act of uniting, this is proper to the divine nature rather than to the person: the terminus of the act, however, should always be indicated, at least by saying that the divine nature unites human nature "to itself," understanding by the reflexive pronoun the person of the Son.

3. THE UNION OF HUMAN NATURE TO ONLY ONE DIVINE PERSON

The principles established by Philip in the foregoing texts serve as his basis for solving the question how the union in the Incarnation can take place in one person of the Trinity to the exclusion of the others. As Philip makes clear, even though the activity of uniting to itself or even of assuming to itself proceeds from the divine nature, common to all three persons, only the Son assumes human nature in the sense of taking it into himself.[1] The Son's taking of human nature "into himself," which is different from the divine nature's taking it "to itself" or the Trinity's taking it "to something,"[2] is likely the same reality as is expressed by the term "composed hypostasis"; the latter concept, we have seen, is fundamental to Philip's theology of the Incarnation.[3] Thus when an objection argues against the concept of "composed hypostasis" that if the Son is composed, the Father is likewise composed, Philip replies that the Son's composition takes place precisely in that which differentiates him from the Father, namely, in hypostasis. Hence, Philip concludes, the Son can be a "composed hypostasis" without the Father's being composed: "To the second objection I say that the Son is said to be composed in that which differs from the Father, namely in hypostasis; hence it does not follow from this that the Father is composed if the Son is composed."[4]

As was seen in the section on the *hypostasis composita*, no efficient activity proper to the Son is signified by the Son's being a "composed hypostasis." The same can undoubtedly be said of the Son's taking human nature "into himself": hence neither expression need be predicated of the divine nature or of the three persons in common. If,

---

1 Cf. *supra*, pp. 126-128.
2 Cf. the text *supra*, p. 127.
3 Cf. *supra*, pp. 97-105.
4 *DeIncarn*, 3, 52; p. 187.

therefore, the divine nature or the three persons, acting in common, unite the human nature, no composition of the divine nature results for the Father or Holy Spirit in the way it does for the Son; neither do the divine nature or the Father and Holy Spirit take the human nature "into" itself or "into" themselves. Thus the Son alone can assume human nature without the other two persons' doing so, and without the divine nature's doing so in the same way.

CHAPTER V

THE HUMAN NATURE ASSUMED IN THE UNION

1. CHRIST AS MAN

Philip the Chancellor has few references to Christ considered precisely in his humanity. Although these references have already been seen, we shall recall them briefly here in order to complete the analysis of Philip's doctrine from the viewpoint of the human nature assumed in the union.

When Philip discusses the lack of human personality in Christ, he is careful to assert that "The divine nature destroyed nothing in human nature,"[1] and to say that although human nature is not a human person, "yet nothing is taken from it since it never had that."[2]

How are we to think of Christ precisely as man, or in his human nature? Philip indicates several times that Christ as man is something, *aliquid*.[3] Most frequently, however, he speaks of Christ in his humanity as an individual. In one text he calls this individual "Jesus," saying: "When the union of the Word to human nature was accomplished, in that union the hypostasis ... was an individual, for Jesus is an individual ..."[4] In another text the individual man is referred to as "Son of the Virgin" by contrast with the divine person as "Son of God."[5] Perhaps the fullest description of Christ as man is given when Philip says that the hypostasis of the Word "is placed under each nature, and is the divine nature and is a reality (*res*) of human nature or a man."[6]

In every case Christ's individuality as a man refers to the individuation of his human nature by the second type of individuation distinguished by Philip, that is, "the collection of properties individuating it from every other thing."[7] This individuation, Philip says, comes to the hypostasis of the Son of God and qualifies it, making it a

---

1 *DeIncarn*, 3, 32; p. 182, ll. 153-155.

2 *Ibid.*, 3, 34; p. 183, ll. 165-166.

3 Cf. *supra*, pp. 76-77, 89. Cf. also *supra*, p. 95 ("Divine nature").

4 *DeIncarn*, 2, 11; p. 172, ll. 121-123. See *supra*, p. 98, for the full text and commentary.

5 *DeIncarn*, 3, 44; p. 185, ll. 227-228. See *supra*, p. 98, for the full text. For another reference to Christ as man under the title "Son of the Virgin," see *DeIncarn*, 2, 27; p. 177.

6 See *ibid.*, 3, 45; p. 185, ll. 237-238. Cf. *ibid.*, 3, 46 (pp. 185-186), and see *supra*, pp. 100-102.

7 *DeIncarn*, 3, 29; p. 182, ll. 145-147.

quis or *quid* according as it is Son of the Virgin; it does so, however, only *secundum quid*, not *simpliciter*.[8]

Thus, although Philip does not raise the question whether Christ is man in exactly the same sense as other men,[9] these texts seem to imply that he would reply affirmatively to such a question.

2. THE UNION OF CHRIST'S BODY AND SOUL TO THE DIVINITY AND TO EACH OTHER

In several different passages Philip the Chancellor asserts that both the body and soul of Christ were united to the Divinity or to the Word, and that they were united to each other as well. We have already seen a text from the *Summa de Bono* speaking of the Divinity's immediate union not only to Christ's reason, but also to his sensitive appetite and to his body.[1] In the *Quaestiones* Philip quotes a text from St. John Damascene speaking of the union of the Word of God to the flesh with the intellect as medium.[2] Shortly afterwards he examines in some detail the unions of the body and of the soul to the Divinity and compares these unions with the union of the body and soul to each other. Even though the latter union ceased during the triduum of Christ's death, the Word, Philip says, was not separated from the flesh and soul, and both soul and flesh remained united to God.[3]

In these texts from the *Quaestiones* Philip mentions such different unions while studying the order in which body and soul were united to the Divinity and also the role of the soul as medium. Hence we leave the examination of these texts for the analysis immediately following.

3. THE ORDER OF THE UNIONS OF BODY AND SOUL

Several authoritative texts mentioning the role of the soul as medium for the union of divine and human nature are either quoted or referred to by Philip the Chancellor in his *Quaestiones de Incarnatione*. The text of St. John Damascene already mentioned is undoubtedly among those

---

8 *Ibid.*, 3, 46; p. 185, ll. 252-255.

9 See *HypUnion* I, 121-122; II, 189-191; III, 125-126. In *DeIncarn*, 2, 1 (p. 169), Philip quotes the text of Damascene that gave rise to this question in other authors, but he uses it in connection with the problem of a nature common to the divine and human natures.

1 See *supra*, pp. 119, n. 27.

2 *DeIncarn*, 2, 19; p. 175, ll. 194-197.

3 See *ibid.*, 2, 21; p. 176. Elsewhere (*ibid.*, 1-i, 20; p. 168, ll. 318-320) it is taken for granted that the body is not separated from the Divinity in the triduum.

"authorities in the *Sentences*" that Philip refers to,[1] and to which he joins the pseudo-Augustinian *De Spiritu et Anima* as well as a passage from Peter Lombard himself.[2] A lengthy passage from what Philip calls St. Augustine's *De Divinitate et Humanitate Christi* also speaks of the soul as medium.[3]

In approaching this problem of the soul as medium Philip first compares the natural order of the different unions in Christ. Although everything took place simultaneously, he says, nevertheless according to the order of nature the union of Christ's soul to his body was prior to the union of either his soul or flesh to the Deity:

> Again, the soul of Christ was simultaneously created, infused, joined to the body, and united to the Deity; nevertheless, if we consider the order of nature, the union of the soul to the body was prior to [the union] of the soul and flesh to the Deity...[4]

Philip then turns to the problem of the soul as medium for the union of the flesh to divine nature. It was not, he maintains, the soul's union to the body that gave it this role primarily, but rather the dispositions put into the soul by the Son of God: because of them the soul was the principal medium for the union of the flesh to divine nature. Speaking of the soul as united to the body, he says:

> ... The soul thus considered did not have [the capacity] to be united to divine nature, nor did the flesh with the soul as medium, but [the soul] received dignity and fittingness from the Son of God so that, having become of such a quality and so noble, it should be united, and the soul itself was the principal medium of the union of the flesh to the divine nature, that is, because it was so great and so noble.[5]

For Philip, then, the soul, in so far as it was disposed for the union by the grace of union (in the sense explained previously),[6] was principal medium for the union of the flesh; but in so far as the soul was united

---

1 See *DeIncarn*, 1-i, 16; p. 166, ll. 265-267. For Damascene's text see *ibid.*, 2, 19 (p. 175), mentioned *supra*, p. 133. It is quoted in Lombard, *Sent* III, 2, 2; p. 555.

2 For the allusion to the *De Spiritu et Anima* and for the quotation from Lombard see *DeIncarn*, 1-i & 1-ii, 16; p. 166. Lombard's text is given under the name of St. Gregory in q. 1-i and under that of St. Augustine in q. 1-ii; cf. *infra*, p. 166, n. to l. 276.

3 *DeIncarn*, 2, 20; p. 175. Cf. *infra*, p. 138. On this work, made up of excerpts from Origen, see *infra*, p. 175, n. to l. 214.

4 *DeIncarn*, 2, 21; p. 176, ll. 215-217.

5 *Ibid.*; p. 176, ll. 217-221.

6 See *supra*, pp. 115-119.

to the body it was, he says, only an incidental or accessory medium (*medium ex incidenti*).[7]

The importance of this last distinction becomes evident when Philip considers the standard objection to the role of the soul as medium: If the soul is medium of union for the flesh, then in the triduum, when the soul is separated from the body, will not the body's union to the Divinity be broken? Philip solves this difficulty by saying that although the incidental medium ceased in the triduum, the principal medium remained, that is, the soul in so far as it was ennobled by the dispositions it received. "... Therefore," he concludes, "the Word was not separated from the flesh and soul, but the union of the soul to God and [the union] of the flesh to the Deity remained."[8]

By this argument Philip shows that he regards the role of the soul as medium to be not in the order of physical causality, but in the order of the soul's fittingness for union. He states this view more clearly in another of the *Quaestiones*, one section of which is entirely devoted to the problem whether in its role in the union the soul is a necessary medium. Philip's reply is categorical: The soul is "a medium not of connection, but of fittingness ..."[9] Or, again, it is "a medium not of necessity, but of fittingness and principality."[10] One of the very reasons he gives this position is to maintain the physical union of the body to the Divinity in the triduum of Christ's death.[11] And in the *Summa de Bono* Philip, as we have seen, appears to accept the statement of a counter-argument saying that the union of the Divinity to the flesh was immediate.[12]

Thus Philip teaches that the soul is not a physical link uniting the body to the Divinity: it is the soul's fittingness for union that makes it function as medium for the body. That is, because this soul is made fitted for union, it is in fact united, and along with it the body; hence the soul's fittingness, which leads to its own union, makes it a medium for the body's union.

In addition to the special endowments conferred on the soul by the Son of God, there are other reasons, according to Philip, why it is a fitting medium for the body. The soul also has this role of fittingness, he

---

7 *DeIncarn*, 2, 21; p. 176, ll. 221-222.
8 *Ibid.*; p. 176, ll. 222-226, where the implicit objection and the full solution are given.
9 *Ibid.*, 1-i, 20; p. 168, ll. 316-318.
10 *Ibid.*, pp. 167-168, ll. 312-314.
11 See *ibid.*; p. 168, ll. 318-320.
12 See *supra*, p. 119, n. 27.

indicates, because the union was effected more principally for the sake of the soul.[13] Again, by interpreting the authoritative texts in this matter as referring to a medium of fittingness, Philip shows that for him the subtlety and spirituality of the soul emphasized in these texts also make the soul a fitting medium.[14]

Elsewhere in the same question Philip changes his terminology slightly, but not his doctrine. From God's viewpoint, he says, no medium is necessary for the union. The ability of divine nature to be united refers to the uncreated active power of God; since his power can effect things beyond what the creature can do, for him no medium is necessary:

> ... On the part of the one uniting no medium is necessary. For when I say: "The divine nature could be united to human nature," by this word "could" I express an active power and I express something uncreated. Nothing created could do this, and therefore no medium is required on the part of the one uniting: I mean a necessary medium, because on the other side there can be posited a medium of fittingness.[15]

But from the viewpoint of human nature, Philip adds, a medium is necessary not absolutely, but in a certain respect. A medium is not absolutely necessary because of the agent who acts above nature; if he were not so powerful, a medium would be absolutely necessary:

> On the part of the unitable human nature there is a medium of necessity not absolutely (*simpliciter*), but in a certain respect (*secundum quid*), and this happens because of the one acting. For the work is above nature; hence a medium would be absolutely necessary unless there were the highest agent itself that acts above nature.[16]

In this text the "medium of fittingness or principality" has become a "medium of necessity *secundum quid*," but because this is opposed to a "medium *simpliciter*," Philip's teaching remains consistent.

Thus, in summary, the soul is medium for the body or for human nature in its union with the divine nature not by connecting the body or nature with the divine nature in a physical way, and so not principally by reason of its own union to the body, but because its qualities, especially the endowments coming to it from the Son of God, made it fitted to be united to divine nature. Of course, if the soul is fitted for

13 *DeIncarn*, 1-i, 20; p. 168, ll. 314-318.
14 See *ibid.*, 1-ii, 20; p. 167, esp. ll. 304-307.
15 *Ibid.*, 1-ii, 20; pp. 167-168, ll. 308-319.
16 *Ibid.*, 1-ii, 22; p. 168. Cf. *ibid.*, 1-i, 22; p. 168.

union and in fact is united, its body will be drawn along with it into the union, so that it is the soul's fittingness for union that makes it medium for the body's union. The soul's union to the body is incidental or accessory: by this Philip probably means that the union of the soul to this particular body determines that it is this body rather than another that is united; but it is primarily because the soul is fitted for union that the body is united in the first place. Finally, because the soul is not a physical link for the body in its union, the separation of the soul from the body in Christ's death does not entail the separation of the body from the Divinity.

CHAPTER VI

THE COMMUNICATION OF PROPERTIES OR IDIOMS

In Philip's *Quaestiones de Incarnatione* there are only a few references to the communication of properties; the *Summa de Bono*, however, treats this topic more extensively.

The first reference in the *Quaestiones* occurs in a quotation that Philip gives from a pseudo-Augustinian work which he calls *De Divinitate et Humanitate Christi*.[1] This text quotes a verse from the Psalms speaking of the anointing of the king with oil; it applies this verse to Christ, interpreting the anointing as the union of his soul to the Son of God through the Incarnation. The result of this anointing or union is that the soul of Christ is both one with the Son of God and is called by his names; further, because of the soul's union to the Word, it performs all its actions as God:

> So therefore, that soul, worthily prepared through grace of this kind, was united to the Word. Hence Augustine [says] in his book *De Divinitate et Humanitate Christi: The Son of God was not in the soul of Christ as in the soul of another man. For it was "anointed with the oil of gladness above" its "fellows" and was incapable of sin; and therefore it is one with him and is called by his names ... Without a medium it was impossible that that soul of Christ should be anointed which, being always in the Word as iron is in the fire, felt, did, and understood as God everything that it did, felt, and understood.*[2]

Since Philip quotes this text with approval, we may conclude that he accepts its teaching that names of the Son of God may be attributed to the soul of Christ and that the soul performs its activities "as God." These are evident statements of the doctrine of the communication of properties or idioms.

Elsewhere in the *Quaestiones* Philip quotes a passage from St. John Damascene in which that authority, speaking of the "composed hypostasis" of the Incarnate Word, declares that it "bears ... the characteristic and determinative idioms" of both the divine sonship of the Word and of the flesh.[3] Again, Philip asserts that the union in Christ

---

1 On this work see *infra*, p. 175, n. to l. 214.
2 *DeIncarn*, 2, 20; p. 175, ll. 205-214.
3 *Ibid*., 3, 47; p. 186, ll. 265-270. On the reading of the text see *infra*, p. 186, n. to l. 269.

results in our being able to say "God is man" and "Man is God."[4]

A final reference in the *Quaestiones* to this doctrine occurs in an objection whose teaching Philip accepts.[5] It argues from the unity of subject in the Son of God to the unity of supposit and to the sharing of predicates: "The Son of God and the Son of the Virgin are one in subject, and when the Son of God is understood (*supposito*), the Son of the Virgin is understood, and whatever is said of the Son of God is said of the Son of the Virgin."[6] This is an argument characteristic of the second opinion on the Hypostatic Union.

In the *Summa de Bono* Philip introduces the doctrine of the communication of properties within his study of the kind of veneration to be offered to Christ's body or to Christ as man.[7] After explaining how the flesh of Christ may properly be adored,[8] Philip examines what is meant by saying that Christ the man is adored, or that the human nature united to the divine nature is adored in the same way as God. The reason for this, he says, is the very union of the divine nature to the human nature; it is so great a union that whatever is said of Christ is said of him both as man and as God: "Quod autem dicitur Christus homo adorari vel humana natura unita divinae quemadmodum dicitur Deus adorari, ratio est ipsa unio divinae naturae ad humanam, quae tanta est quod[9] quicquid dicitur de Christo, de[10] homine dicitur et de Deo."[11] Here the adoration of Christ as man, or of his humanity, or, at least, the predication of such adoration is based by Philip on the communication of properties, which in turn he explicitly derives from the union of the two natures in Christ. Examples of the communication of properties now follow: "The Son of God suffers," "Christ the man created the stars," "Christ the man is adored by latria": "Unde istae_ conceduntur: 'Christus homo patitur,' 'Filius Dei patitur,' et sicut dicitur 'Filius Dei creavit stellas,' ita et haec: 'Christus[12] homo creavit stellas.' Eodem modo: 'Filius Dei adorandus est latria,' 'Christus homo adorandus est latria.'"[13]

---

4 *Ibid.*, 3, 49; p. 186.

5 See *ibid.*, 2, 27; p. 177. Cf. *ibid.*, 2, 29; p. 177. The question at issue is the comparison of unity as between the Trinity and the Incarnation; see *supra*, pp. 111-114.

6 *Ibid.*, 2, 27; p. 177.

7 Philip's teaching on this topic has been amply examined by Landgraf, *Dogmengeschichte* II/2, 162-165.

8 For the text see *ibid.*, p. 162.

9 quia *TV*.

10 *Om. P:* this variant changes the meaning of the sentence slightly.

11 *P* 179vb; *T* 127ra; *V* 134ra.

12 iste *P*.

13 *Locis citatis.* Cf. Landgraf, p. 163, n. 12.

Philip then adds a rule about supposition that helps to clarify procedure in the communication of properties: A term standing for the human nature does not stand for this man (*iste homo*), but a term standing for this man stands for the Son of God, and vice versa:

> Tamen posset fieri differentia inter hanc: "Caro Christi unita deitati adoratur latria," et hanc: "Christus homo adoratur latria," quia supposítâ[14] naturâ humanâ, non supponitur iste homo, sed supposito illo homine, supponitur Filius Dei, et e converso.[15]

In saying that terms standing for human nature do not stand for "this man," Philip seems to be teaching that such terms do not denote the supposit or unique subject in Christ and that therefore terms referring exclusively to the human nature of Christ should not be predicated of the Son of God. In saying that terms standing for "that man" stand for the Son of God, and vice versa, he seems to be teaching that concrete terms denote the supposit or unique subject and that therefore concrete terms referring to either the divine or human in Christ may be predicated of the Son of God and of each other. If this interpretation is correct — and it seems to be what Philip has in mind — this statement marks an advance in the clarification of the rules of procedure in the communication of properties or idioms.[16]

Thus in both the *Summa de Bono* and in the *Quaestiones* Philip the Chancellor accepts the communication of properties or idioms, basing this practice on the Hypostatic Union itself in that this union makes the Son of God and the Son of the Virgin an identical subject of predication. Further, Philip appears to refine the procedure by pointing to the difference between predication of abstract and concrete terms: although he does not explicitly reject abstract terms from the communication of properties, it is a legitimate inference from his statements to conclude that he meant to do so and thereby to reserve such communication of properties to concrete terms denoting the single supposit or subject in Christ.[17]

14 supponitur *P*.

15 *Locis citatis.* Cf. Landgraf, *loc. cit.*

16 Although Philip uses the example of *caro Christi*, he may have abstract terms in mind, for it is this type of term that ordinarily signifies the nature but not the supposit or subject. It may be noted, too, that later on in the century Thomas Aquinas will maintain that *caro* and *anima* are signified in the abstract; the corresponding concrete term would be *carneum* (or *corporeum*) and *animatum*. See his *Summa Theologiae* III, q. 16, a. 1, ad 3m.

17 In speaking of a rejection of abstract terms from the communication of properties we mean, of course, their rejection in affirmative propositions. It would be perfectly correct to deny the communication of abstract properties, e.g., to say that Christ's rationality is not his uncreated wisdom.

Chapter VII

SUMMARY AND CONCLUSION

Although Philip the Chancellor's *Summa de Bono* treats only a few topics concerning the Hypostatic Union, his separate disputed questions, edited here, examine most of the issues discussed by contemporary theologians regarding this mystery. In addition to their inherent value as theological analyses, these questions furnish a new touchstone of Philip's originality as a thinker, a topic whose discussion has been reopened with the discovery of his frequent copying from Alexander of Hales' *Glossa*. If these questions definitely manifest the influence of this *Glossa*, more often they reveal Philip as an independent, forceful thinker who rarely treats any of our problems without giving to his solution the impress of his own vigorous personal thought.

The *Summa de Bono*, which, at least as a literary influence, is one of the most important theological works in this transitional period, furnishes much of the philosophical and theological background for the roughly contemporary questions on the Hypostatic Union. It combines the traditional teachings, both theological and philosophical, of the *sancti* with the new currents from the *philosophi* flowing into the West. In this respect, and in his interests and his method of approaching problems, Philip greatly resembles Alexander of Hales, whose philosophical and theological insights he often reproduces in lengthier, clearer, and better-formulated treatments.

The texts that we have quoted to illustrate Philip's basic concepts should give, better than any description, an appreciation of the growing philosophical maturity of Western theologians. Philip greatly advances the organization of the treatise on the transcendental properties of being: he discusses being, the one, the true, and the good at considerable length and intelligently. Led by Alexander of Hales, he seems to have been constantly aware of the different levels of being, of the order of priority and posteriority among these levels of being and within its divisions, and of the varieties of intellectual disciplines corresponding to these levels and divisions of being. From this awareness flows his frequent use of the concepts of analogy and proportionality, a use that is reflected by the more frequent appearance of the terms "analogy" and "analogically," together with the more usual terms "proportion" and "proportionally." Philip often introduces the potency-act relationship in his analyses of the origin of contingent beings or of the internal structure of created beings. For God, by contrast, "Everything is act," or God is "purely Act."[1] Philip follows and develops Alexander of Hales' investigations of the kinds of composition found in created things but excluded from God, who is entirely simple.

Within the Chancellor's philosophy, fresh as it is in many respects, the Augustinian-Boethian metaphysics continues to play a fundamental role. The most basic composition in creatures remains that of *quod est* and *quo est*, interpreted as subject on the one hand and form or essence on the other. Besides referring to being in general, the term *esse* is often identical with *quo est* and is essentialist in connotation. If at other times *esse* signifies existence, in these cases it refers to the concrete physical existence of a being in the order of nature: metaphysics considers not this, but the essence or the *quod est-quo est* relationship. At the same time, however, as a result of Philip's frequent recourse to the distinction between the metaphysical and the natural or physical consideration of being, he appears, in handling certain problems, to take this concrete physical *esse* into account more frequently than others had done. *Esse* in this sense intervenes in Philip's clearly-made distinction of two kinds of individuation; it intervenes, too in his analysis of personal distinction in men and angels; it influences his whole approach to the important problem of personality. At the same time individuation and personality are also analyzed according to concepts derived from Porphyry and Boethius and developed in the metaphysics of formal properties already seen in Philip's predecessors.

The question-form of both Philip's *Summa de Bono* and his *Quaestiones de Incarnatione* means that his theology of the Hypostatic Union develops independently of the *Sentences* of Peter Lombard. This at least partially accounts for his variations in method and for the differences in emphasis that he manifests within the particular topics he discusses. His main presentation of the Incarnation as a doctrine of faith occurs, for example, within his analysis of the virtue of faith rather than in explanations of patristic texts or in refutations of heresies such as were given by Alexander of Hales or Hugh of Saint-Cher, obliged as they were by their method to comment on the *Sentences* of Peter Lombard. On the other hand, his extensive use of St. John Damascene enriches his

---

1 See *supra*, pp. 54-55.

investigations; this use, however, occurs more within Philip's theological analyses of the union than in his presentation of it as a mystery of faith.

The Incarnation, Philip teaches, was in some respects contingent, in some respects necessary. Although, absolutely speaking, it did not have to happen, once God ordained the union, it had to take place. And in relation to the end of man's redemption, it was so fitting a means that it can be said to have been necessary in a certain way, that is, with respect to God's well-ordered power. It is these necessary aspects of the Incarnation to which faith adheres. The Incarnation, Philip adds, was neither a miracle nor something contrary to nature; it was nevertheless a wondrous event and one above the power of nature. In showing that the Incarnation was not a miracle, Philip says that it was the object of hope on the part of the Fathers of the Old Law and that, along with the Redemption, it manifests principally the mercy of God.

Philip's positive statements of this mystery are few in number and elementary in expression. Among heresies opposed to the Catholic teaching he mentions those that regard Christ as a creature and separate the man in him from God, or that maintain that the union results in one common nature composed of the divine and human natures as parts. He lists the teaching that Christ as man is *aliquid* among truths consequent upon faith, whose contrary may not be held.

One of the Chancellor's most original theological developments concerning the Hypostatic Union comes within his comparison of angelic and human nature as to their suitability for such a union. In some respects his investigation of this question resembles that of Alexander of Hales, particularly in the comparison of the angel and man according to their likeness to God, as well as in the view that the angel's inability to repent for sin makes him less suited for a redemptive Incarnation than is man, who can repent. But it is especially when Philip analyzes the effect of personal discretion in angels as compared with men that he shows his originality. Here, under the influence of Aristotle and perhaps also of Avicenna, he states that in simple creatures like angels the realization in being of their essence or *posse* so immediately entails their personal discretion that God could not create an angelic nature and unite it to himself without first destroying an angelic person that would be present in that nature in the first instant. In material beings like man, however, personal discretion comes only at the end of a process of natural generation, in which the essence or *posse* can be realized without the human nature's being immediately a person; hence God can intervene to assume the nature prior to the emergence of human personality. Thus the very structure of personality in men and angels makes for a difference in their ability to be united to the divine nature in a personal union. In this analysis Philip utilizes his metaphysical notions of potency and act, applying them, it appears, to the order of concrete physical existence of natures and persons.

With respect to the mode of union in Christ, Philip presents his theology independently of the usual discussions of the three opinions. He takes it for granted that Christ as man is *aliquid*; his other conclusions concerning the mode of union generally correspond to those characteristic of the second opinion; but, at least in the data that we now possess, he neither analyzes the opinions nor expressly refutes or supports any of them.

· In saying that Christ as man is *aliquid*, Philip maintains this must be held so as to exclude an accidental union in Christ. He does not argue at length against an accidental union, but takes it for granted that this kind of union is rejected by the true faith. A union in one nature, he indicates, is also rejected by faith; in this case, however, he adds to the teaching of faith particular theological arguments showing why such a union in nature is impossible. This union of the two natures, he says, does not take place in some new common element, some creature originating in time that would destroy the divine simplicity and immutability or make God the part of some new common nature; the common reality in which the two natures are united is, rather, the hypostasis or person of the Word. Hence the two natures remain distinct and retain their properties even while becoming intimately united in the one hypostasis.

Analyzing in detail the union in person or hypostasis, Philip indicates that in one respect the person or hypostasis is a medium uniting two extremes, that is, the two natures, and in another respect it is an extreme to which it unites the other extreme, human nature. A more important question concerns the lack of human personality in Christ's perfect human nature. For Philip, as for the preceding authors, nothing is lacking to the intrinsic perfection of Christ's human nature; nevertheless human personality is lacking because this human nature, individuated by the second type of individuation (the collection of properties), lacks the property of dignity. It is not one *per se*. It lacks that absolute, complete, particular *esse* which, if possessed, would render the nature incapable of union to another and thereby endowed with independent human personality. Although this doctrine is similar to that of Philip's predecessors, he stresses the concrete independent existence of the person more than the others: he seems to look at the person in its existential reality as well as and perhaps more than in its status as a concretion of essentialist forms. Certainly for Philip personality is something more than the merely negative perfection it was for Hugh of Saint-Cher.

The lack of human personality in Christ is complemented by the presence in the perfect human nature of a divine person. Philip expresses this positive aspect of the union most clearly in his analysis of the "composed hypostasis." For him this concept signifies the hypostasis or person not as to the composition of the human nature that is united to the hypostasis or person, but as composed itself, in that it is a hypostasis or person of two natures. The "composed hypostasis" is the hypostasis of Christ in so far as it is both a divine person and an individual of human nature: here Philip applies his description of the hypostasis as that which stands midway between the person and the individual. The hypostasis is also "composed" in that, as its etymology shows, it "stands under" two natures. But most profoundly the hypostasis is "composed" in a way that goes to the very heart of the Hypostatic Union: the hypostasis of the Word, that is, the divine person, becomes by reason of the union a hypostasis or person of human nature, that is, it becomes a divine person now qualified by human nature; it becomes a person *secundum quid*, that is, a person according to human nature. All this happens without the least change in the divine nature or person, and without the person's entering into a composite unity as a mere part. In all this it is evident that Philip is greatly influenced by the writings of St. John Damascene, whom he quotes at length in this analysis.

The Chancellor's teaching on the composed hypostasis gives him the principles for his reflections, unusually brief for this period, on the unity of Christ. Since there is only one hypostasis or subject in Christ, and since hypostasis or subject rather than nature is the principle of enumeration, Christ, even though he has two natures, is numerically one. In his presentation of the "composed hypostasis" and in his remarks on the unity of Christ Philip retains certain of the fundamental intuitions of William of Auxerre; he expresses them, however, with greater profundity and without recourse to the term "quasi-accidental" proposed by William but accepted by others only cautiously or not at all.

When he considers how the two natures stand towards one another in the union, Philip thinks in terms of the category of relation. He explicitly denies that in the divine nature the union is some created entity, but he seems to accept the idea that in the human nature it is a created relation of this nature to the divine nature.

As to the category of unity in which the Hypostatic Union is to be classified, Philip follows the same general lines as those of Alexander of Hales' *Glossa* and *Quaestiones*, rejecting the normal categories of unity *per se* and *a fortiori* the category of unity *per accidens*. However, by an analogical extension of the meaning of one kind of *per se* unity, that is, "one in number," to include "one in hypostasis," he is able to associate the oneness of the Hypostatic Union with the category of *per se* unity. So intimate is the union of the two natures in Christ, he says elsewhere, that it can be compared with the unity of the three persons of the Trinity: from the viewpoint of nature, he declares, their unity is the greatest; from the viewpoint of person or hypostasis, however, the unity .of natures in the one person or hypostasis of Christ is a greater unity than theirs.

When there is question of the grace of union, Philip speaks of the Incarnation in terms of grace from two points of view: first, God's predestination of the human nature of Christ for this union is a "grace of pre-election"; second, this grace has as its effect the endowment of the soul of Christ with graces ennobling it and disposing it for the union. These dispositive graces prepare this soul for *esse*, Philip says; thereby he distinguishes them from the habitual graces that follow upon being and make for the soul's *bene esse* once it already exists. At the same time, these dispositive graces are not a medium standing between the soul and the Word; they prepare the soul for union, but it is united immediately. Among the effects flowing from this choice of Christ's human nature and its union to the Word Philip lists the following: Christ's human nature is united to the highest good, although it does not equal it; it is above the highest angel; it has no need of a guardian angel; it is confirmed in good and free from sin; it enjoys the highest liberty possible to a changeable nature.

In examining the role of the divine nature in the Incarnation, Philip accepts the use of expressions indicating that the divine nature is incarnate, is united, and is man. He explains how each is to be understood so as to avoid erroneous inferences. In particular, they must not be taken in such a way that created properties could be said to inhere in the divine nature.

All three persons of the Trinity act in common to effect the Incarnation, Philip teaches. But because the Son takes the human nature *into* himself, he is said most properly to *assume* human nature. Since the divine nature properly takes the human nature *to* itself in the Incarnation, the divine nature can properly be said to assume human nature. In a less proper sense the Trinity as a whole can be said to assume human nature because the three persons concur to effect the union, not in themselves or to themselves, but "to something," that is, either to the divine nature or in the person of the Son. As for the act of *uniting*, Philip maintains that this act is more properly an act of the divine nature than of the divine person: his reason seems to be that because this is an efficient activity, it proceeds more properly from the nature than from the person. However, he adds, one should designate the personal terminus of the act of uniting by adding the reflexive pronoun: thus one should say that the divine nature unites the human nature "to itself," that is, to itself in the person of the Son. On these principles Philip is able to explain how the human nature is united to only one person of the Trinity: the hypostasis of the Son alone is "composed" with human nature in the sense that human nature is united by the divine nature only within the person of the Son, who as a person or hypostasis is distinct from the Father and the Holy Spirit.

Although the material that we have from Philip on the Hypostatic Union says little of Christ precisely as man, there are clear statements indicating that Philip views Christ as fully human, having all the perfections of human nature. If there is no human personality in Christ, this takes nothing from the perfection of his human nature as a nature; Christ as man is substantial, an *aliquid*, an individual of human nature, individuated by the second type of individuation, which is through the collection of properties belonging only to his individual human nature.

With respect to Christ's humanity Philip's most important investigations deal with the soul as medium of union for the body. Soul and body are united to each other and each is united to the Word. Of these unions that of the soul and body to each other is prior to the rest by nature, even though all unions took place simultaneously. If the soul is said by authoritative texts to be the medium of the body's union to the Word, the soul has this role principally because of the endowments it receives preparing it for the union; it is thus a medium of fittingness in the sense that, being fitted for union with the Word itself, it also carries along with it the particular body to which it is united. Hence the soul's physical union to the body plays only an accessory or "incidental" part in its function as medium for the body's union. The soul is not medium for the body as a physical link between it and the divine person without which the body could not be united; therefore, in the triduum of Christ's death, the body, though separated from the soul, could and did remain united to the divine person.

In both the *Quaestiones* and the *Summa de Bono* Philip gives principles for and examples of the communication of properties or idioms.

Because of the unique character of the Hypostatic Union, in which there is one subject or hypostasis for the two natures, what is said of the Son of God is said of the individual man and vice versa. At the same time Philip places certain limitations on this practice: predication of human attributes must be such that these refer to the individual man and not only to the human nature as such; otherwise they may not be predicated of the Son of God.

Philip the Chancellor's treatment of the Hypostatic Union displays early thirteenth-century theology, especially in the school of Alexander of Hales, moving away from a theology dominated by grammar and dialectic towards one that increasingly incorporated metaphysical concepts into its structure by applying them analogically to the divine mysteries. However, it was not only the new philosophical currents nor only the influence of Alexander that left a mark on Philip's approach to the Hypostatic Union: the speculations of St. John Damascene were more important to his work than to that of his predecessors, and all these elements were combined with the more abiding influence of the traditional theology of the Parisian schools. Perhaps the most striking evidence of this combination of influences appears in Philip's highly personal discussions of individuation, of personality and personal discretion, and of the "composed hypostasis." If our interpretation is correct, Philip frequently penetrates beyond a consideration of individuation and personality that views them only in terms of a conglomeration of abstract forms and arrives more frequently than others before him at a real, if not decisive, awareness of the concrete physical existence of the subject or person.

It lies beyond the scope of our study to trace the subsequent influence of Philip's theology of the Hypostatic Union. No doubt these isolated questions attracted less attention than the firmly-structured and massive *Summa de Bono*; however, we have been able to note in passing that the *Summa Fratris Alexandri* seems to have been influenced in a few places by these *Quaestiones* (unless, of course, there was some unknown common source for the two treatises). Beyond such possibly direct literary influence, Philip's theology of the Hypostatic Union, by reflecting the theological climate of his day, helps to understand both the problems and solutions of theologians of the following generation who came to maturity within this very climate that Philip himself helped to create.

PART TWO

TEXTS OF
PHILIP THE CHANCELLOR
ON THE
HYPOSTATIC UNION

CHAPTER I

INTRODUCTION TO THE EDITION

The following edition presents the *Quaestio de Discretione Personali* from Philip the Chancellor's *Summa de Bono* together with three of Philip's disputed questions dealing with the Hypostatic Union. These last three questions have been grouped under the general title: *Quaestiones de Incarnatione*.

Quaestio de Discretione Personali.

This question occurs early in the *Summa de Bono* within the treatise on the angels.[1] The sources used for this edition are the following:

B = Bruges, Bibliothèque de la Ville 236, fol.13rb-va.
       Thirteenth century hand.[2]

F = Florence, Biblioteca Laurenziana, Plut. 36, dext. 4, fol. 17ra-rb.
       Thirteenth century hand.

L = Paris, Bibliothèque Nationale *Latin* 3146, foll. 7vb-8ra.
       Two thirteenth century hands.[3]

M = Paris, Bibliothèque Nationale *Latin* 15,749, fol. 9va-vb.
       Late thirteenth or early fourteenth century hand.[4]

N = Paris, Bibliothèque Nationale *Latin* 16,387, foll. 15vb-16ra.
       Thirteenth century hand, corrected by a later hand (N2).[5]

P = Padua, Biblioteca Antoniana, Scaff. VIII°, Cod. 156, fol. 10ra-rb.
       Thirteenth century hand, corrected by a second hand of the thirteenth century (P2).

Q = Padua, Biblioteca Antoniana, Scaff. X°, Cod. 214, fol. 5va-vb.
       Thirteenth century hand.

---

1 On the plan of the *Summa de Bono* see Keeler, p. 7, and Ceva, p. 14. A more detailed analysis is given by P. Minges, "Philosophiegeschichtliche Bemerkungen über Philipp von Grève († 1236)," *Philosophisches Jahrbuch* 27 (1914) 22-23.

2 Description in A. de Poorter, *Catalogue des manuscrits de la Bibliothèque Publique de la Ville de Bruges* (Gembloux-Paris 1934) p. 277.

3 Description in *Bibliothèque Nationale: Catalogue général des manuscrits latins*, tome IV: *N°⁵ 3014 à 3277* (Paris 1958) pp. 235-237.

4 Description in Keeler, p. 14.

5 Description in Keeler, p. 14.

S   = Pisa, Bibliotheca Seminarii S. Catharinae 143, fol. 9ra-rb.
       Thirteenth century hand.[6]
T   = Toulouse, Bibliothèque de la Ville 192, foll.8vb-9ra.
       Thirteenth century hand. Numerous corrections by a
       second hand of the thirteenth century (T2).[7]
V   = Vatican *Latin* 7669, fol. 9rb-va.
       Thirteenth century hand, corrected by a second hand of
       the thirteenth century (V2).[8]

The interrelationships of these manuscripts, and indeed of all the extant manuscripts of the *Summa de Bono*, have presented considerable difficulties for scholars. The problems will be examined in full in the
critical edition, the first volume of which is approaching publication.[9]
For our edition we adopt the readings of *P* unless correction from the
other manuscripts is evidently required.[10]

Quaestiones de Incarnatione

Three distinct questions on the Hypostatic Union belonging to Philip
the Chancellor are found in *MS*. Douai, Bibliothèque de la Ville 434 (=
D), the only known copy of these questions. This manuscript was written between 1228 and 1236.[11] The first of these questions has two redactions in the manuscript, one in Volume I, folio 81va-vb, the other in
Volume II, folio 93rb-vb. The second and third questions are found in
Volume I, folios 81vb-82rb and 82vb-83vb respectively.

---

6 Description in Keeler, p. 15.

7 Description in *Catalogue général des manuscrits des bibliothèques publiques des départements*, Tome VII:
Toulouse-Nîmes (Paris 1885; reprint 1968) pp. 120-121.

8 Description in Keeler, p. 15.

9 Information given to me personally by the editor, Nikolaus Wicki.

10 Reviewing L. Keeler's edition of Philip the Chancellor, *De Anima*, H. Pouillon says:
"Malheureusement le P. K. n'a pas même vu *Padoue Ant. 156* qui est sans conteste le meilleur témoin
de la meilleure famille, ce qui ne signifie pas qu'il soit absolument sans fautes" (*BullThAncMéd* 3
[1937-40] 384, p. 169*).

This same manuscript was chosen by H. Meylan for his preparation of the edition of the *Summa
de Bono*: see his "Les 'Questions' de Philippe le Chancelier," p. 93. M. Meylan wrote to me that this
manuscript "me paraît de beaucoup le meilleur témoin."

11 Thus the authors of *ProlGlossaAlex* IV, 35*, using V. Doucet, "A travers le manuscrit 434 de
Douai," *Antonianum* 27 (1952) 532-550. The dates 1231-1236 are given by P. Glorieux, "Les 572
Questions du manuscrit de Douai 434," *Recherches de Théologie ancienne et médiévale* 10 (1938) 260.
These studies, together with the abrupt style of these questions, indicate that we are probably
dealing with *reportationes* rather than with a version prepared for publication by Philip.

In P. Glorieux's study of this manuscript our Question 1 is number 141 for the first redaction and number 450 for the second redaction. Our Question 2 is number 143 and our Question 3 is number 145.[12] In the manuscript only our Questions 2 and 3 are explicitly said to be "secundum Cancellarium," that is, without any doubt, Philip, who was Chancellor of Notre-Dame de Paris from 1218 to 1236, the period in which this manuscript was written.[13]

Although both redactions of our Question 1 are anonymous, it is morally certain that their author is Philip the Chancellor. O. Lottin indicates that our Question 2 refers back to Question 1: he does not say explicitly, however, that our Question 1 belongs to Philip nor does he list it among Philip's questions.[14] The reference in question, contained in the introductory remark of Question 2, "Dictum est supra de unione,"[15] could have been made by the compiler of these questions rather than by Philip the Chancellor. Thus this reference by itself gives no absolutely certain indication that Questions 2 and 1 have the same author. P. Glorieux, however, thinks that the similarity of subject-matter together with the proximity of the two questions in the manuscript give sufficient grounds for attributing our Question 1 to Philip.[16]

Further confirmation of Philip's authorship of this anonymous question can be found in another allusion to it in Question 2 that has not been previously noticed. Here it is quite evidently Philip rather than the compiler of the manuscript who, speaking of the soul, says that "unibilis Deo fuit, *ut supra dictum est* ..."[17] This teaching on the soul occurs neither earlier in Question 2 nor in any of the other Christological questions in the preceding part of the manuscript, but only in Question 1: hence Philip must be alluding to Question 1 as his own.

---

12 *Ibid.*, pp. 139, 236. Glorieux does not identify number 450 as a second redaction of number 141. Number 140 (Vol. I, fol. 81ra-va) is also concerned with the Incarnation (see Glorieux, *ibid.*, p. 139), but it deals exclusively with the need of the Incarnation for man's redemption and adds nothing to our study of the Hypostatic Union. Glorieux assigns this question to Philip (*ibid.*, pp. 256, 264).

13 As Glorieux points out (*ibid.*, p. 255), within the same sections as those containing questions "secundum Cancellarium" there are questions by Guiard de Laôn and Odo of Châteauroux, the next two chancellors after Philip; they, however, are called by their own names in the manuscript, so that the "cancellarius" in question must be Philip. Odo's chancellorship extended to 1244 (Glorieux, *Répertoire* I, 13).

14 "Quelques 'Quaestiones' de maîtres parisiens aux environs de 1225-1235," *Recherches de Théologie ancienne et médiévale* 5 (1933) 85, n. 17.

15 See Philip, *DeIncarn*, 2, 1; p. 169.

16 "Les 572 Questions," p. 256; cf. *ibid.*, p. 264.

17 See Philip, *DeIncarn*, 2, 19; p. 174, l. 174. Emphasis mine.

A final confirmation of Philip's authorship of Question 1 comes from the great similarity between certain portions of this question and the *Quaestio de Discretione Personali* in Philip's *Summa de Bono*. Although it is possible that these two questions might have distinct authors, one of whom influenced the other or both of whom were influenced by a common source, there are no positive reasons suggesting this. Taken with the foregoing indications of Philip's authorship, this parallelism of doctrine is an added reason justifying our acceptance of this anonymous question as the authentic work of Philip the Chancellor.

In the edition of this first question the two redactions, indicated as *Quaestio* 1-i and *Quaestio* 1-ii, have been put in parallel columns. To bring out the parallelism it has been necessary to change the order of several paragraphs of *Quaestio* 1-ii towards the end of the text. This change has been noted in each case.

The following abbreviations used in the footnotes of the *Quaestiones de Incarnatione* should be remarked:

D = *MS*. Douai, Bibliothèque de la Ville 434.

D1 = Corrections made in D by the original hand.

Buyt. = text of John Damascene, *De Fide Orthodoxa*, as edited by E. Buytaert.

var. Buyt. = variants in Buytaert's edition to the main text he gives; Philip's quotations of Damascene sometimes follow the variant readings.

CHAPTER II

SUMMA DE BONO: QUAESTIO DE DISCRETIONE
PERSONALI

1 Secundo quaeritur quantum ad quid attenditur discretio personalis, et in quibus rebus, et secundum quem modum in angelis. Hoc
enim valet ad quaestionem de unione divinae naturae cum humana et   5
de non-unione naturae divinae cum angelica.

2 Est autem discretio personalis in quibus est personarum multitudo,
personarum autem multitudo in quibus est persona. Persona vero est
rationalis naturae hypostasis individua. Rationalis vero natura est secundum
tres differentias: divina, angelica, et humana, quare in istis tribus est   10
distinctio personalis. Humana vero natura personam non habet nisi
cum separata fuerit a divina natura, nam persona est hypostasis individua. Erit ergo distinctio personalis hypostasis naturae rationalis
secundum has tres differentias, sed indifferenter.

3 Distinctio autem est secundum originem aut secundum qualitatem,   15
et hoc est aut secundum proprietatem absolutam aut secundum
proprietatem respectivam ex conditione originis. In Deo autem, cum sit
una essentia, idem vero sit qualitas quod est essentia, non est personarum distinctio secundum qualitatem, sed est simplicissima distinctio, quae est ex conditione originis, in hoc scilicet quod Pater non habet   20

2 De ... personali] De unione divinae naturae B; Quare natura humana potius personam [persona
F] faciat quam angelica FMS; Quare natura humana prima primam faciat quam angelica N; De
discretione personali *mg.* N2P; Quomodo attendatur discretio personalis Q; *om.* LTV   3 Secundo]
cundo LP, ecundo QV *e add.* "S" *mg.* PQV   attenditur] extenditur L   5 enim] *om.* N   6 cum]
om. humana ... cum S   7 discretio] distinctio B   personalis] *add.* est T   est²] *om.* T, *s.s.* T2
multitudo] mutitudo *e corr.* L   8 personarum] *add.* est *mg.* N2   multitudo] *om.* personarum ...
multitudo L   9 *hypostasis*] [h]ypotasis T   *individua*] Boethius, *ContraEut,* 3; Rand, p. 84: "...
Reperta personae est definitio: 'naturae rationabilis indiuidua substantia'."   10 angelica] *om.* T,
s.s. T2   et] *s.s.* P1   11 natura] *om.* T, *mg.* T2   12 natura] *om.* LP   persona] personam *e corr.* L
hypostasis] [h]ypotasis T   13 erit] erunt Q   hypostasis] *om.* M, *om.* individua ... hypostasis LNST,
mg. N2, T2   rationalis] rationabilis P   14 indifferenter] differenter L, tamen differenter Q, indifferenter V, differenter V2   15 autem] enim aut L   aut] *add.* est L   16 hoc] haec T   aut²]
et B   secundum²] *om.* FMNSV, *s.s.* N2, V2   17 proprietatem] *om.* et ... proprietatem Q   respec-
tivam] *add.* aut secundum utrumque *mg* V2   conditione] additione L   cum] non *e corr.* T
18 essentia¹] *add.* aut una natura *mg.* T2, *add.* et T *e corr.* T2, *add.* est T2   est¹] *om.* LP   19 sim-
plicissima] simplissima QT   19-20 distinctio] *mg.* P1   20 in] et FMNSV *e corr.* N2, V2, secundum

originem sed est origo, Filius vero habet originem ab uno solo. Spiritus
Sanctus a pluribus habet principium.

4 In angelis est distinctio secundum qualitatem et non secundum
originem, quia omnes ab uno. In homine est distinctio secundum
originem et qualitatem. Non autem sic intelligatur in angelis quod sola   25
differentia personalis sit penes qualitatem solam, sed per se unaquaeque
hypostasis ab alia differt, nulla etiam intellecta qualitate, et quia in
huiusmodi simplici idem est posse et esse, numquam est angelica natura
sine distinctione personali. Similiter in Deo non dividitur posse ab esse:
fuit enim ab aeterno distinctio personalis. Persona autem personae   30
manenti personae non est unibilis. Non ergo conveniebat unio divinae
naturae ad angelicam in unitate personae neque personarum. Sed aliter
est in humana natura, in qua differt posse ab esse. Distinctio autem personalis consequitur esse, propter quod poterat esse unio naturarum,
una persona permanente.   35

5 Et nota quod est potestas ab agente, ut cum dicitur quod ab
aeterno potuit esse mundus, et haec non ponit esse, nec simpliciter nec
secundum quid; et est potestas a materia, secundum quam potest esse
actu, et secundum hanc non potuit esse angelus quia immaterialis est; et
est potestas a forma, ut potestas qua triangulus potest esse triangulus   40
est triangulatio: quando illa est, triangulus est; similiter in angelo.
Secundum potestatem a materia, res est secundum quid; secundum
potestatem a forma, simpliciter. Sic ergo forma rei est illud posse quod
consequitur esse, quia tunc est illud posse cum forma est, et tunc res

Q   non] *om.* T, *s.s.* T2   21 Filius] *add.* et T   vero] huero *e corr.* L, non QT *e del.* Q1 *aut* Q2, *e*
corr. T2   originem²] *om.* BFMNQSV, *s.s.* N2   22 principium] cf. Richard of Saint-Victor, *De Trin*
IV, 13 & 15; Ribaillier, pp. 175-176, 177-178   23 angelis] angelicis T   secundum¹] *om.* N   et] *om.*
T   25 originem²] **B   qualitatem] et non ... qualitatem *mg.* P1, *om.* non secundum ... qualitatem
T, *mg.* T2; cf. Richard of Saint-Victor, *DeTrin* IV, 13-14; Ribaillier, pp. 175-177   sola] *om.* Q
26 sit] secundum Q   se] hoc B, *add.* est S, *om.* T, *mg.* T2, *add.* una *mg.* T2   se / unaquaeque] T
9ra   unaquaequae] quaequae T *e corr.* T2   27 etiam] et FN *e corr.* N2   etiam / intellecta L 8ra
et] *om.* BFNSTV, *s.s.* N2, V2   in] *om.* L   28 et] *om.* N, *mg.* N2   esse / numquam] F 17rb
30 enim / ab] M 9vb   distinctio] discreto T   autem] enim M   31 manenti] inanti T *e corr.* T2
personae] *om.* LS, *mg.* P, *add.* manenti personae F   ergo] enim L   conveniebat] conveniebat L
33 est] *om.* T   in¹] *om.* L   autem] *om.* L   33-34 personalis / consequitur] N 16ra   34 unio]
uno QT *e corr.* T2   35 permanente] manente BFLMNSV   36 nota] non T *e corr.* T2   quod¹] *om.*
Et ... quod L   est] esti L, *om.* T, *s.s.* T2 (cf. following variant)   potestas] *add.* est T   potestas / ab]
B 13va   37 haec] hoc BFLMNQSV   non] videtur L   ponit] impossibile L, potuit MS   esse²]
om. M   nec¹] modo FMNSV *e corr.* N2, neque BQTV2, *add.* secundum T   nec²] neque BFM
NQSTV   39 actu] antiChristus LQ   est] *om.* L   et²] *om.* L   40 ut] *add.* est L   triangulus¹]
triangulis L   triangulus²] *om.* potest ... triangulus² LS   41 est¹] erit L   est²] *add.* in L
triangulus] triangularis L   est³] et L, *om.* est triangulatio ... est³ BFMNQSTV   43 Sic] Si T
ergo] igitur T   44 consequitur] *add.* ad Q   est illud posse] illud posse est BFMNQSTV

est. In rebus autem materialibus non est ita quia illarum posse non at-   45
tenditur tantum secundum formam, sed secundum materiam; in simplicibus tantum secundum formam. Ideo ergo dicitur quod in angelo et
simplicibus rebus *idem est esse et posse.*

6 Item, cum natura humana distinguatur et secundum originem et
secundum essentiam, videtur quod major sit in ea distinctio et quod   50
major discretio personalis. Quare si natura angelica assumptibilis non
fuit, multo magis nec ipsa.

7 Respondeo quod quaedam sunt in quibus posse et esse idem, ut in
superioribus, quaedam autem in quibus non idem, ut est in natura
humana; et ideo, quia in natura humana posse non consequitur esse,   55
fuit natura humana unibilis divinae in unitate personali, eadem persona
manente. Quaedam autem sunt in quibus est idem esse quod posse, et
horum quaedam sunt habentia esse unicum et absolutum, ut in natura
angelica, et ideo non potuit uniri divinae eo quod persona non potest
uniri personae manenti personae, quia posse ibi consequitur esse ab-   60
solutum, et quam cito est, est in discretione personali: unde uniri non
conveniebat. Quaedam autem sunt in quibus posse consequitur esse,
sed non absolutum, ut in anima. Sicut enim in angelica intelligentia
posse consequitur esse, ita et in anima, sed in anima est considerare
duplex esse: esse in conjuncto, quod habet secundum quod est actus   65
corporis animati, et esse per se, quod praecedit naturâ, non actu, et
sequitur actu cum separatur a corpore, licet apta nata conjungi. Ideo,
licet posse et esse idem in ipsa, quia tamen non est absolutum, potuit
assumi, et distinguitur triplex posse ut supra.

45 est¹] *om.* BT, *del.* V2   materialibus] *om.* B   illarum] illorum Q   posse] *add.* esse *mg. inf.* P2
46 tantum] tamen M   46-47 simplicibus] *add.* non B   47 secundum] *om.* T, *mg.* T2   formam]
om. Sic ergo (l. 42) ... formam LP, *mg. inf.* P2   dicitur] concedimus L   et] vel T, *add.* in BLT
48 simplicibus rebus] simplicioribus L   simplicibus / rebus] P 10rb   posse] Cf. Aristotle, *Physics*
III, 4, 9; 203b 30; Firmin-Didot II, 278: "Posse et esse, in sempiternis nihil differunt."   49 Item] *om.*
L   et¹] *om.* BFLMNQSTV   secundum] *om.* L   originem] *om.* Item ... originem N, *mg.* N2   et²]
add. non BFMNST *e del.* N2, T2   50 secundum] *om.* PT, *mg.* T2   secundum / essentiam] Q 5vb
51 discretio] *om.* et q. m. discretio FMNSV, *mg.* N2, et maior discretio *mg.* V2   personalis]
sonalis N *e corr.* N2   assumptibilis] insumptibilis T, inassumptibilis BFMNQST2V   non] *om.* BFM
NQSTV   53 idem] *add.* sunt *s.s.* N2   54 superioribus] superiori B, *om.* ut in superioribus L
autem] *om.* L   55 consequitur] sequitur L   56 in] et V *e corr. s.s.* V2, *om.* F   unitate] *om.* F
personali] personae L   57 est] *om.* L   esse] posse L   quod] et BL   posse] esse L   58 sunt
habentia] habent L   unicum] unitum B, vincum T, univocum V *e corr.* V2   ut] *om.* L   59 ideo]
om. L divinae] natura angelica. De L   potest] *om.* L, *add.* potest B   60 manenti] *om.* L   personae]
om. L, *add.* et L   ibi] *mg.* P1   esse] est T *e corr. s.s.* T2   61 quam cito] quanto S   est²] *om.*
FLMNSTV *e corr. in linea* N2, *s.s.* T2, V2   unde] *om.* LP   uniri] iuniri T   62 conveniebat] con-
veniebant FT, conveiebat L   autem] *om.* S   quibus] *om.* est idem (l. 56) ... quibus Q   63 ut] in F
Sicut / enim] V 9va   enim] *om.* B   angelica] *add.* [9rb] Sicut enim in angelica S   64 et] *om.* L
considerare] *om.* V   65 conjuncto] iuncto L   secundum quod] *om.* BFMNPSTV   est] *om.*
BFLMNPSTV   66 praecedit] procedit L   et²] sed BT   67 actu] *om.* L   cum] sed L   apta] *add.*
sit *mg.* N2   nata] sit T   conjungi] *add.* et L   68 posse] per se L, posset Q   esse] *add.* sunt *s.s.* N2
ipsa] ipso LP   tamen] *om.* L   69 assumi] *om.* B   supra] par. 5.

CHAPTER III

QUAESTIONES DE INCARNATIONE

[Quaestio 1]

[Quaestio 1-i (a)]: *Utrum angelica natura sit unibilis.*

[Quaestio 1-ii (a): *Cujusmodi creatura seu natura sit unibilis divinae naturae?*]:

1 Quaeritur cujusmodi creatura seu natura sit unibilis divinae naturae, angelica scilicet vel humana; secundo, an ipsa reparatio sit necessaria; tertio, quid sit medium incarnationis, et si aliquod est, utrum sit necessitatis vel congruitatis. 5 ... 10

2 Circa primum probatur quod natura angelica magis sit unibilis per illud Eccli. 13: *Volatilia ad sibi similia convertuntur.* Sed constat quod angelica natura similior est divinae naturae quam humana quia divina natura est separata, et dico naturam separatam quae per corpus non exercet actionem, et talis est natura angelica. 15 ... 20

1 Eccli. 13: *Volatilia ad similia convertuntur.* Cum ergo angelica natura magis assimiletur divinae quam humana quia separata est substantia angelica, per corpus non exercens operationes, et habet intellectum deiformem et personalem discretionem solummodo per essentiam, homo autem secundum originem et essentiam, magis debuit divina natura uniri angelicae quam humanae. Triplex enim diversitas personalis: per originem tantum, per essentiam tantum, vel utroque modo.

3 Item, angelus intellectum habet deiformem; ergo similior est angelica natura divinae quam humana; ergo magis unibilis. 25

Quaestio 1-i: I, 81va-vb D

15 *convertuntur*] Eccli 27, 10: *Volatilia ad sibi similia conveniunt.*   28 modo] cf. Richard of Saint-Victor, *DeTrin* IV, 13-15; Ribaillier, pp. 175-178.

Quaestio 1-ii: II, 93rb-vbD

15 *convertuntur*] See note at this point in q. 1-i.
23 deiformem] diformem D

— Solutio: Nec homo nec angelus unibilis fuit Deo propter esse absolutum et personale; anima autem et corpus unibiles sunt quia veniunt in compositionem hypostasis sive personae. Perfectionem autem suam amitteret angelus si uniretur, quod esset contra Domini bonitatem. Nihil enim potest Deus quod contrarium est rationi et bonitati, quia potentia ejus conjuncta est ejus sapientiae et bonitati.

2 Ad primum dicimus quod licet angelus magis similis sit Deo quantum ad simplicitatem essentiae, tamen in aliis quae ad unibilitatem faciunt magis convenit tam anima quam corpus naturae divinae quae communicabilis est.

3 Ad aliud dicimus quod licet homo habeat duplicem discretionem personalem, non tamen anima aliqua: non est enim anima persona. Quod anima sit unibilis non concedimus, sicut nec angelus.

4 Nota: Dicunt quidam quod anima secundum superiorem partem rationis similior est Deo, et propter illam assimilationem magis unibilis, secundum quod videtur probari super Hebr., 4: *Vivus est sermo Dei et efficax*, etc., in

4 Si dicat quod anima secundum superiorem partem rationis similior est Deo et propter illam assimilationem, ea mediante, unitur Deo, secundum quod videtur per Apostolum ad Hebr., 4: *Sermo Dei vivus et efficax*,[4] in

30

35

40

45

50

55

60

42 primum] *supra*, par. 1　　50 aliud] supra, par. 1　　55 non] *s.s.* D1　　63 etc.] Heb 4, 12: *Vivus est enim sermo Dei et efficax et ... pertingens ad divisionem animae et spiritus.*

62 Apostolum] Bernardum D　　63 *efficax*] efficanx D; Heb 4, 12: see note at this point in q. 1-i.

Glossa. Sed hoc nihil est, quia angelus magis assimilatur divinae naturae secundum rationem quam habet deiformem.

5 Item, non videtur valere ratio supra posita quod humana natura habet animam et corpus quae unibilia sunt maxime eo quod ex eis fit unum, scilicet homo, et ideo humana natura magis unibilis. Contra: (Stemus in illa compositione): Necesse est quod sequatur discretio personalis propter discretionem dignitatis vel excellentiae proprietatem quae ibi invenitur. Ergo minus unibilis est.

6 Item, aut accipis unionem de illis conjunctis: sic persona uniretur personae et personam assumeret, quod esse non potest; aut de non conjunctis, et sic praedicta solutio nulla est, quia non est ibi compositio.

7 Item, anima habet memoriam, intelligentiam, et voluntatem, et haec tria magis sunt una vita, et

Glossa. Sed hoc nihil est, quia angelus magis assimilatur divinae 65 naturae secundum rationem. Ergo magis est unibilis.

5 Si dicat quod non sequitur hoc quoniam humana natura habet animam et corpus quae 70 maxime unibilia sunt eo quod ex eis fit unum, scilicet homo, et ita propter illam conjunctionem magis est humana natura unibilis, contra: (Stemus in illa compositione): 75 tione): Necesse est quod sequatur discretio personalis propter discretionem dignitatis sive propter excellentem proprietatem quae ibi invenitur. Ergo minus unibilis est. 80

6 Item, aut tu accipis unionem de illis conjunctis, et si hoc, jam erit unio personae, quod esse non potest; aut de non conjunctis, et sic praedicta solutio nulla est, quia 85 non est ibi compositio.

7 Item, anima habet memoriam, intelligentiam, et voluntatem, et haec tria sunt una vita, et 90

---

64 *Glossa*] *GlossaOrd in Heb* 4, 12; PL 114, 650D & 651A: "'Pertingens.' Tota consideratione perveniens ad separationem animae, id est sensualitatis, et spiritus, id est rationis ... 'Ac spiritus.' Pertingit sermo Dei cognitione inseparabili, quia cognoscit quomodo dividatur sensualitas a ratione, et ipsa a se, dum plus dedita infimis rebus, inferior est, vel ab his revocata dignior. Sic etiam videt quomodo spiritus a seipso dividatur, vel dum in Deum inhiat de divina visione cogitans, vel dum inferius coelestia considerat, vel inferius in terra de mundanis recte agendis pertractat, vel quomodo spiritus, id est ratio, a sensualitate secernitur, dum quod in se interius est, superat quod in illa altius est." 73 unibilis] see par. 1

64 *Glossa*] See note at this point in q. 1-i quia] quod D   73 illam / conjunctionem] II, 93va D 77 discretio] dilectio D   personalis] dilecl discretionis D, personalis *ss*. D1 80 minus] terminus D   89 intelligentiam] intellectivam D

unum magis sunt quam corpus et anima. Et praedicta tria in angelo magis sunt unum quam anima et corpus in homine, et ita praedicta ratio nulla est.

8 Item, tres sunt distinctiones sive discretiones personales. Prima est in Trinitate per modum habendi essentiam: sunt enim diversi modi in personis habendi essentiam, quia Pater a nullo, Filius a Patre, Spiritus Sanctus ab utroque, et haec est minima discretio personalis. Alia est in angelis in hoc, scilicet, quod ab uno principio sunt et habent diversas essentias, et haec distinctio plus habet discretionis personalis. Tertia est in homine, et haec maxime habet discretionem personalem, quia homines sunt a diversis principiis proximis et habent proprias et singulares substantias, et haec continet utramque illarum discretionum. Ergo, cum constet discretionem personalem impedimentum unionis esse, homo, qui majorem habet discretionem, minus unibilis est, et angelica natura magis unibilis, quae magis appropinquat divinae naturae.

9 Solutio: Licet in quibusdam angelica natura majorem habeat

magis unum sunt quam anima et corpus. Sed praedicta tria etiam in angelo magis sunt unum quam anima et corpus in homine. Ergo praedicta ratio nulla est.   95

8 Item, tres sunt distinctiones sive discretiones personales. Prima est in Trinitate per modum habendi essentiam: diversis enim 100 modis habetur divina essentia [in] tribus personis: Pater a nullo habet, Filius a Patre, Spiritus Sanctus ab utroque, et haec est minima discretio personalis. Alia 105 est in angelis, quae est in hoc quod omnes ab uno principio sunt et habent diversas essentias, et haec distinctio plus habet discretionis personalis. Tertia est in homine, et 110 haec maxime habet discretionis personalis, quoniam homines sunt a diversis principiis proximis et habent proprias et singulares substantias, et haec continet utram- 115 que illarum discretionum. Ergo cum constet discretionem personalem esse impedimentum unionis, cum homo majorem habeat discretionem, minus unibilis est 120 divinae naturae quam angelica, quae magis appropinquat divinae naturae.

9 Solutio: Concedimus in angelis majorem esse conve- 125

116 discretionum] Cf. Richard of Saint-Victor, *DeTrin* IV, 13-15; Ribaillier, pp. 175-178.

101 in] *om.* D   109 distinctio] distictionis D, distictio D1   113 a diversis] adversus D 116 discretionum] discretionem D; cf. Richard of Saint-Victor, *DeTrin* IV, 13-15; Ribaillier, pp. 175-178.   121 angelica] humanae D   122 quae] quia D

convenientiam cum Deo quam humana, quia angelus habet intellectum passibilem tantum respectu sui Creatoris, a quo solo recipit, homo vero habet intellectum passibilem et quoad suum superius et quoad inferiora se: intelligentia vero divina nullo passibilis est. Tamen homo in aliis majorem habet convenientiam, rationis cujus magis est unibilis. Habet enim convenientiam cum Deo in hoc quod, sicut omnia sunt a Deo sicut ab uno principio, ita omnes homines ab uno homine, et propter hoc dicitur vir *imago Dei* et non mulier, I Cor. 11, et hoc non est in angelo quia non omnes sunt ab uno angelo.

10 Item, sicut esse omnium rerum in Deo est quia ipse est exemplar spiritualis creaturae et corporalis, ita in homine concurrit omne esse spirituale et corporale. Unde nomine omnis creaturae homo intelligitur: habet enim aliquid commune cum omni. Sed in angelo unum est esse: spirituale, et propter hoc humana natura magis unibilis divinae.

11 Item, alia ratio, quoniam posse angeli statim consequitur esse absolutum; non sic posse

nientiam ad divinam naturam quam in hominibus, non in omnibus, sed in quibusdam, quoniam angelus habet intellectum possibilem tantum respectu sui Creatoris, a quo solo recipit, homo vero habet intellectum possibilem et quoad suum superius et quoad inferiora se: intelligentia vero divina a nullo passibilis. Sed homo in aliis majorem habet convenientiam, ratione cujus convenientiae magis est unibilis. Habet enim convenientiam cum Deo in hoc quod, sicut omnia sunt a Deo tamquam ab uno principio, ita omnes homines ab uno, et in hoc etiam dicitur vir imago Dei et non mulier, I Cor. 11: *Vir est imago Dei.* Hanc imaginem non habet angelus quoniam non sunt omnes ab uno angelo.

10 Item, est alia convenientia: sicut enim esse omnium rerum in Deo est quia ipse est exemplar spiritualis creaturae et corporalis, ita omne esse est in homine, spirituale scilicet et corporale. Sed in angelo tantum est esse spirituale, unde haec aptitudo sive haec convenientia facit quod homo magis sit unibilis quam angelus.

11 Item, alia ratio est, quoniam posse angeli statim consequitur esse, et ideo uniri non

13

13

14

14

15

15

16

---

142 11] I Cor 11, 7: *Vir quidem non debet velare caput suum, quoniam imago et gloria Dei est.*

135 passibilis] possibilis D, passibilis D1   138 est] *add.* est D   144 *Dei*] See note at this point in q. 1-i.   146 omnes] homines D   149 esse] omne D

animae, licet consequatur esse statim, et ideo ut prius. Concedimus tamen quod in homine major est discretio personalis, sed illa non impedit unionem, immo minor discretio angeli magis impedit, quoniam secundum suam naturam consequitur citius esse suae discretionis, quia in angelo posse consequitur esse. Est autem posse tripliciter: ab agente, ut Deus potuit creare mundum ab aeterno: hoc posse non statim consequitur esse, nec secundum quid nec simpliciter. Item, a materia: ibi posse consequitur esse secundum quid, non esse simpliciter; tale esse est in corpore: dat enim esse non simpliciter sed secundum quid. Item, a forma, ut in triangulo: si enim triangulus est, triangulatio est; et hoc posse statim consequitur esse. Similiter nota quod in angelo et anima posse consequitur esse statim, sed in angelo esse per se absolutum, in anima esse in altero vel cum altero, scilicet corpore, quia primum esse animae est in corpore.

potest. Concedimus tamen quod in homine major est discretio personalis, sed illa non impedit unionem, immo minor discretio angeli 165 magis impedit, quoniam secundum suam naturam consequitur esse citius suae discretionis, quia, ut dictum est, in angelo posse consequitur esse. Est autem posse tri- 170 plex: ab agente, a materia, et a forma. Posse ab agente, ut Deus potuit creare mundum ab aeterno: hoc enim posse non statim consequitur esse, nec secundum quid 175 nec simpliciter. Posse a materia consequitur esse secundum quid et non esse simpliciter; tale est in corpore: dat enim esse non simpliciter sed secundum quid. Posse 180 a forma est in triangulo: si enim triangulus est, triangulatio est: et hoc posse statim consequitur esse. Et ideo, quia sic est in angelo quod statim consequitur esse per- 185 sonale, non est angelus unibilis. Secus est in homine, in quo aliquid est possibile et materiale. — Sed contra: Id quod dictum est de angelo [idem] videtur esse quod 190 in anima, et ideo in simplici invenio statim posse consequi esse. — Ad quod dicimus quod est esse absolutum et est esse quod est in aliquo prius quam sit absolutum. 195 Esse absolutum est in angelo, sed esse quod est in aliquo prius quam sit absolutum est in anima, quoniam suum primum esse est in

12 Ex his patet solutio ad praedicta, quoniam illae assimilationes quae sunt angeli ad Deum non faciunt magis unibile.

13 Item, Damascenus: *Quod curabile est, assumptibile.* Sed natura angeli citius curabilis, cum non sit natura corruptibilis quia, sicut [dicit] Dionysius: *Nihil secundum substantiam vel naturam corrumpitur, sed secundum habitudinem ordinis, harmoniae, et commensurationis.* Homo vero, totaliter infectus in corpore et anima, minus cito curabilis; ergo minus unibilis. Et quod totaliter infectum est, minus susceptibile est curationis; ergo minus assumptibilis.

14 Solutio: Incurabilis est angelus quia non potest poenitere, cum non habeat in se duo unum in quorum altero doleat de peccato et secundum alterum gaudeat de

corpore; unde patet quod non 200 procedit illa ratio.

12 Per haec etiam quae dicta sunt patet solutio ad id quod objicitur, scilicet quod superior pars similior est divinae naturae, quo- 205 niam illa assimilatio non facit unibile.

13 Item, objicitur sic: Dionysius: *Nihil secundum substantiam vel naturam corrumpitur, sed secundum* 210 *habitudinem ordinis, harmoniae, et commensurationis.* Ergo, secundum hoc, tantum in angelo habitudo naturalis corrupta est, non natura vel essentia. Non ergo in ipso 215 totum infectum est sive corruptum. Quod enim totaliter infectum est sive corruptum non est susceptibile sanitatis. Homo autem totaliter corruptus est, quia et 220 secundum carnem et secundum animam. Ergo minus est unibilis homo quam angelus.

225

---

208 *assumptibile*] *DeFideOrth* III, 6; PG 94, 1005B; Buytaert, p. 188: "Quod enim inassumptum, incurabile."   210 corruptibilis] corrupta D, corruptabilis D1   211 dicit] *om.* D 214 *commensurationis*] See note at this point in q. 1-ii.

205 similior] sublimior D   206 quoniam] quam D   209 *corrumpitur*] corrumpuntur D   211 *commensurationis*] *DeDivNom* 4, 23; PG 3, 724D; PL 122, 1142A; *Dionysiaca* I, 274. Erigena's translation reads: "Sed neque corrumpitur quid existentium, secundum quod essentia et natura, sed defectu juxta naturam ordinis, harmoniae et commensurationis ratio infirmatur, manere similiter habens."   215-216 infectum e.s. corruptum] confectum est corrumpens D: emended according to the sense of the argument as seen from the sentence following.

dolore: et quia per se cecidit, non per alterius instinctum, cum habeat intellectum. Homo vero habet unde poenitere potest, et, infirmior, per alium peccavit et sic fuit curabilis, diabolus non. Unde Damascenus: *Oportet scire quoniam quod est hominibus mors, hoc est angelis casus. Post casum enim non est eis poenitentia quemadmodum nec post mortem hominibus.*

15 Praeterea, essentia angeli corrupta non est, sed certe nec animae, sed naturales habitudines. Malum enim non potest esse nisi in bono, unde in homine manet bonitas naturae; tamen, spiritualis sanitas non est quia "sanum" dicit aequalitatem quae non est in homine corrupto. Unde Luc. 10, de semivivo relicto, dicit *Glossa* quod in diabolo nihil sanum relictum est et ideo diabolus insusceptibilis est poenitentiae, homo vero corporeus susceptibilis.

14 Item, alibi: *Diabolus per se cecidit, quare per alium non est reparabilis. Homo, per alium deceptus, cecidit;* 230 *ideo per alium reparatus est.* Item, Damascenus: *Oportet autem scire quoniam quod hominibus est mors, hoc est angelis casus. Post casum enim non est eis poenitentia quemadmodum nec* 235 *post mortem hominibus.*

15 Solutio: Verum est quod essentia angeli non est corrupta, 240 sed certe nec animae, sed naturales habitudines. Malum autem non potest esse nisi in bono, unde in homine [manet] bonitas naturae seu bonum; sanitas tamen spiri- 245 tualis non est quia "sanum est" dicit aequalitatem quae non est in ipso. Unde Luc. 10, de semivivo relicto, ubi dicit *Glossa* quod in diabolo nihil sanum relictum est, 250 et Joannes Damascenus: *Diabolus insusceptibilis est poenitentiae quoniam*

234 *Oportet*] *add.* autem *Buyt.*   235 *hoc*] haec D   236 *casus*] calus D   237 *nec*] ut D, neque (*var* nec) *Buyt.* (cf. q. 1-ii at this point) 238 *hominibus*] *DeFideOrth* II, 4; PG 94, 877C; Buytaert, p. 77.   248 relicto] Lk 10, 30 250 est] Cf. *GlossaOrd in Luc* 10, 30; Lyranus V, 153ra. Although the robbers are interpreted as devils, no statement is made about *nihil sanum relictum*. The text of the *GlossaOrd* is based on Bede, *In Luc* III, 10, 30; CorChrSerLat 120, 222-223. Cf. Ambrose, *Exp. Ev. sec. Luc.* VII, 73 (CorChrSerLat 14, 238-239), and Augustine, *Quaest. Evang.* II, 19 (PL 35, 1340). No such statement occurs in them or in any of the commentaries on Lk in PL.   252 susceptibilis] cf. Damascene's text quoted at this point in q. 1-ii, and the note thereto.

228 14] In q. 1-ii par. 13 is followed by par. 15, after which comes par. 14. The order is inverted here to maintain the parallel with q. 1-i, whose order is followed   231 *est*]. Cf. Gregory, *Moralium* IV, 3, 8; PL 75, 642B: "Est adhuc aliud, quo et perditus homo reparari debuit, et superbiens spiritus reparari non possit, quia nimirum angelus sua malitia cecidit, hominem vero aliena prostravit." Cf. also Anselm, *Cur Deus Homo* II, 21; Schmitt II, 32. 235 *nec*] neque (*var.* nec) *Buyt.* 236 *hominibus*] See note at this point in q. 1-i. 239 15] In D par. 15 precedes par. 14   242 Malum / autem] II, 93vb D   244 manet] *om.* D; cf. the text at this point in q. 1-i   249 relicto] relecto D; Lk 10, 30 250 relictum] relectum D   est] See note at this point in q. 1-i.   252 *insusceptibilis*] insubceptibilis D

166 CHAPTER III

incorporeus; homo enim propter corporis infirmitatem poenitentiae susceptibilis est. 255

15a Ex his patet quod homo reparabilis est, angelus non; tamen, de absoluta Dei potentia fuit reparabilis.

[Quaestio 1-ii (b): *De medio unionis in Christo*.] 260

16 Circa secundum articulum quaeritur sic: Si requirat medium unio, per quod medium divina natura humanae uniatur? Et 265 videntur hoc dicere auctoritates in *Sententiis* et in libro *De Spiritu et Anima*, scilicet quod per intellectum medium. Sed si ita est, quaeritur an sit necessarium illum 270 medium, et videtur, quia dicit Augustinus: *Tantae subtilitatis et simplicitatis est divina natura ut eam non congruat uniri animae nisi per spiritum medium et per animam cor-* 275 *pori, ut corpori de limo formato eam non conveniret uniri nisi per animam.*

[Quaestio 1-i (b): *De medio unionis in Christo*.]

16 Item, quaeritur per quod medium divina natura unita fuit humanae infirmitati. Circa hoc sunt auctoritates. Videtur per intellectum medium, secundum Augustinum in libro *De Spiritu et Anima*. Si ita est, quaeritur an tale medium sit necessarium. Videtur secundum Gregorium qui dicit: *Tantae subtilitatis et simplicitatis est divina natura ut eam non congruat uniri animae nisi per spiritum medium et per animam corpori; etenim corpori de limo formato eam non conveniret uniri nisi per animam.*

264 infirmitati] infinitati D   268 *Anima*] Cf. Ps.-Augustine, *Liber de Spiritu et Anima*, 14; PL 40, 789-790: "Sicut enim supremum animae, id est, intelligentia sive mens imaginem et similitudinem gerit sui superioris, id est Dei, unde et ejus susceptiva esse potuit et ad unionem personalem etiam, quando ipse voluit, absque ulla demutatione naturae fuit assumpta: sic supremum carnis, id est, sensualitas animae gerens similitudinem ad personalem unionem ejus essentiam suscipere potest."   275 formato / eam] I, 81vb D   276 *animam*] The text quoted gives words of Lombard himself rather than of Gregory or of Augustine (q. 1-ii assigns it to the latter). Lombard says: "Tantae enim subtilitatis atque simplicitatis est divina essentia, ut corpori de limo terrae formato uniri non congruerit, nisi mediante rationali essentia" (*Sent* III, 2, 2; p. 555). Philip may have in mind a text in which Gregory says: "Carmen quippe

254 *susceptibilis*] subceptibilis D   255 *est*] *DeFideOrth* II, 3; PG 94, 868B; Buytaert, p. 70: "Insusceptibilis paenitentiae, quoniam et incorporeus. Homo enim propter corporis infirmitatem paenitentia fungitur."   256 15a] In D the words in par. 15a follow immediately on those in par. 14   269 medium] Cf. Lombard, *Sent* III, 2, 2 (pp. 555-556) for texts from Damascene and Augustine. For *De Spiritu et Anima* see the note at this point in q. 1-i.   275-276 corpori] corporis D   276 limo] ligno D   277 *animam*] See the note at this point in q. 1-i.

17 Item, Augustinus: *In rebus per tempus ortis nulla major gratia quam quod Deus infirmitati nostrae voluit uniri.* Fuit ergo illa unio ex gratia. Sed in homine nihil est susceptibile gratiae nisi anima. Ergo de necessitate anima media est.

18 Contra: In intentione unientis primum fuit finis, scilicet fruitio; medium inter Deum unientem fuit intellectus, qui primo fruitur illa fruitione. Sed id quod est ultimum in intentione primum est in operatione. Sed in ipsa unione omnia simul fuerunt, et ita in via operationis nullum medium, sed tantum medium assimilationis, quod est in via intentionis.

19 Sed contra: In unione corporis et animae medium est spiritus inter grossitiem carnis et subtilitatem animae. Ergo et hic debet esse medium, vel dic quare non.

20 Solutio: Ex parte unientis nullum fuit medium necessarium. Cum enim dico: "Divina natura potuit uniri humanae," sic dico quiddam increatum, scilicet potentiam activam: nullum enim creatum potuit hoc facere. Ex parte vero humanae naturae unitae fuit medium non necessitatis, sed congruitatis et prin-

17 Item, quod sit medium necessarium videtur, quia unio illa maxima est gratia. Sed gratiae sus- 280 ceptibilis non est in homine nisi anima. Ergo de necessitate anima media est.

18 Contra: In intentione 285 unientis primum fuit finis, scilicet fruitio; medium inter ipsum Deum unientem fuit intellectus, qui primo fruitur fruitione illa. Sed id quod est ultimum in intentione 290 primum est in via operationis. Sed constat quod in via operationis in ipsa unione omnia simul. Ergo in via operationis nullum fuit medium, sed tantum medium assimi- 295 lationis, quod est in via intentionis.

19 Sed contra: In unione corporis et animae medium est spiritus inter grossitiem carnis et subti- 300 litatem animae. Ergo et hic debet esse medium, vel dic quare non.

20 Solutio: Auctoritates loquuntur de medio congruitatis, ut 305 patet, quoniam in illis ponitur verbum congruitatis. Unde dicimus quod ex parte unientis nullum est medium necessarium. Cum enim dico: "Divina natura uniri potuit 310 humanae naturae," potentiam dico activam per hoc verbum "potuit," et quid increatum dico.

divinitas anima mediante suscepit" (*Moralium* XXXI, 23, 42; PL 76, 595C).   281 *uniri*] Cf. Augustine, *De Trinitate* XIII, 19, 24; Pl 42, 1033; CorChrSerlat 50/2, 416; "In rebus enim per tempus ortis illa summa gratia est quod homo in unitatem personae coniunctus est deo ..."

298 unione] unioe D   302 quare] quod D 304 Auctoritates] *add.* quae D   310 potuit] *add.* divinae D

cipalitatis. Principalius enim animae quam corpori unitio facta, quia principalius propter animam, quae est medium non connexionis, sed congruitatis, ut diximus. Aliter separata esset a corpore divinitas in triduo. Cum vero dico: "Humana natura potuit uniri divinae," potentiam dico passivam et creatum quid.

21   Et illa potentia est obedientia creaturae ad Creatorem, et licet obedientia sit in angelo, non tamen unibilis quia non habet aptitudinem de qua supra dictum est.

22   Sic igitur ex parte humanae naturae unibilis est medium necessitatis, non simpliciter sed secundum quid, et hoc contingit propter ipsum agentem. Opus enim supra naturam est; unde esset medium necessarium nisi esset superius agens quod agit supra naturam.

Nullum creatum potuit hoc facere, et ideo nullum medium 315 exigitur ex parte unientis: medium dico necessarium, quia ex altera parte potest poni medium congruitatis. Cum enim dico: "Humana natura potuit uniri 320 divinae naturae," potentiam dico passivam et creatum quid.

21   Si autem quaeratur quae sit illa potentia cum dicimus: "Humana natura potuit uniri divinae," respondeo quoniam obedientia est uniri ad Creatorem, quae quidem est et in angelo, sed propter hoc non sequitur quod sit unibilis 330 quoniam non habet aptitudinem de qua supra locuti sumus.

22   Et ex parte humanae naturae unibilis est medium necessitatis, non simpliciter sed secundum quid, et hoc contingit propter ipsum agentem. Opus enim supra naturam est; unde esset medium necessarium simpliciter nisi esset ipsum superius agens 340 quod agit supra naturam.

---

329 est] pars. 9-15

317 altera] illa D   324 21] In D par. 21 follows par. 22   326 uniri] unire D, uniri D1   328 uniri] unire D   332 sumus] pars. 9-15a   333 22] In D par. 22 precedes par. 21   341 agit supra] supra agit

[Quaestio 2]

Secundum Cancellarium.

[2 (a): *De termino unionis.*]

1 Dictum est supra de unione, et omnis unio terminatur ad unum. Ergo unio in Christo terminata fuit ad unum: non ad unum per accidens, quia sic Christus secundum quod homo non esset aliquid; ergo 5
ad unum per se. Sed triplex est unum per se: numero, specie, genere. Si dicas "unum numero," contra: Ad unum numero sequitur unum genere et specie, et dicit Damascenus: *Non est communem speciem invenire vel etiam dicere Domino Jesu.* "Species" dicit universalem naturam. Non est autem aliqua universalis natura quae dicatur de Christo secundum 10
quod Christus est hypostasis composita ex duplici, natura humana et natura divina. Ergo non est unum specie et ita nec numero.

2 Item, in illa unione est aliquid commune, vel convenientia in aliquo communi: quaeritur quid sit illud. Si dicat quod unio, ergo conveniunt in unione illae duae naturae Dei et hominis. Sed hoc idem est ac 15
si dicas: "Conveniunt in convenientia, vel eadem vel alia." Si alia, in infinitum ibis. Si illud commune est aliqua natura creata (quod videtur' quia unio illa fuit temporalis, non ab aeterno), ergo in creato conveniunt, et illud creatum unde surgit? Si ex duabus naturis, ergo aliqua natura communis constat ex divina et humana, quod est impossibile, et 20
praeterea nihil potest esse commune creato et increato.

3 Solutio: Illa unio terminata est ad unum, sed illud unum nec est unum per se nec unum per accidens: haec enim divisio locum habet in rebus naturalibus. Unum per se proprie sumitur cum dividitur in unum numero, quod proprie et stricte est individuum; item, in unum specie et 25

3 supra] See Philip the Chancellor, *DeIncarn*, 1-i; *supra*, pp. 158-168. Cf. our introduction to Philip's questions, *supra*, pp. 153.   5 esset] esse D   6 genere] Cf. Aristotle, *Metaphysics*, Delta, 6; passim, esp. 1016b 31-34   9 *Jesu*] *DeFideOrth* III, 3; PG 94, 993A; Buytaert, p. 176: "In Domino autem nostro Iesu Christo non est communem speciem suscipere ... Hinc non est dicere unam naturam in Domino nostro Iesu Christo."   20 constat / ex] I 82ra D   24 Unum] unde D 25 individuum] Cf. Aristotle, *Metaphysics*, Delta 6 (1016b 6-9), and *Categories*, 5 (3b 10-13).

unum genere, quod sequitur ad unum numero. Ad tale unum non terminatur dicta unio, nec ad unum per accidens ratione praedicta, quia
secundum hoc Christus in quantum homo non esset aliquid. Sed large
accipitur "unum numero" pro uno in hypostasi: ad tale unum non
sequitur unum specie vel unum genere, nec est individuum, quia in-   30
dividuum respicit naturam universalem, scilicet speciem, quae tota in
singulis individuis. Divina vero essentia, licet sit communis tribus personis, tamen non est dicenda natura universalis quemadmodum species:
non enim potest intelligi aliquid advenire divinae naturae per quod
dicatur trahi ad particulare unum. Non est igitur ibi unum numero vel   35
individuum, quia individuum est in quo salvatur totum esse speciei, et
individuatio duplex: una quantum ad proprietatem essentialem, alia
quantum ad *collectionem accidentium quam in nullo alio est reperire*. Sic igitur
ad unum in hypostasi terminatur illa unio: illae enim duae naturae conveniunt in hypostasi.   40

   4 Ad aliud dicendum quod differunt unio et unitas, licet unitas consequatur unionem. Unitas respicit naturam, unio hypostasim. In
Trinitate sunt tres personae et una natura: hic unitas in essentia sive
natura; in incarnatione sunt tres substantiae una persona: hic est unio.
Dicendum ergo quod in hypostasi est convenientia, non in aliquo tem-   45
porali vel creato, nec sequitur: "Unio temporalis est; ergo conveniunt in
aliqua natura." Et ut plenius intelligas, attende quod tria sunt
creaturarum genera: intelligentia, vita, scilicet anima, et corporalis
creatura. Quaedam autem sunt quae consequuntur ista et dicuntur
proprie [non] creaturae sed concreaturae, quia cum creaturis creatae.   50
Verbi gratiâ, anima creata est perpetua; anima proprie creatura dicitur;
perpetuitas non dicitur creatura sed quid concreatum consequens ipsam animam. Similiter corpora [creata] fuerunt mobilia et in tempore:
mobilitas non est proprie creatura sed concreatura, mobili corpori
scilicet, et illa quae taliter consequuntur naturaliter creaturas non   55
habent proprias ideas in Primo, sed reducuntur ad ideas creaturarum
quas consequuntur. Cum ergo unio proprie creatura non sit sed potius

   26 numero] Cf. Aristotle, *Metaphysics*, Delta, 6; 1016b 36-1017a 1 & 1016b 17-21.   32 individuis]
Cf. Boethius, *Commentaria in Porphyrium a Se Translatum* III, c. *De Specie*: "Species vero, et pars et
totum est, pars quidem generis, totum vero individuis" (PL 64, 115A).   36 speciei] Cf. the
preceding note   38 *reperire*] Porphyry, *Isagoge*, ch. *Peri eidous* (ed. A. Busse, *Porphyrii Isagoge et in
Aristotelis Categorias Commentarium*, Commentaria in Aristotelem Graeca, IV, 1 [Berlin 1887] p. 7);
trans. Boethius, *Porphyrii Introductio in Aristotelis Categorias a Boethio Translata* (*ibid.*, p. 33): "individua ...
dicuntur huiusmodi quoniam ex proprietatibus consistit unumquodque eorum, quarum collectio
numquam in alio eadem erit."   41 aliud] See par. 2   differunt] differt D   42 unio] immo *e*
corr. D1   50 non] *om.* D   53 creata] *om.* D

consequens, licet temporalis sit non propter hoc fit convenientia per unionem illam in aliqua natura vel aliquo temporali.

5 Item, in unione non conveniunt quia ipsa unio est convenientia, sed conveniunt in hypostasi quae constat et composita est ex illis duabus naturis. Nulla autem natura ex illis naturis constat; unde Damascenus, libro III, *De duabus naturis: Nos autem neque unius compositae naturae Christum nominamus neque ex aliis [aliud] quemadmodum ex anima et corpore hominem, vel ex quattuor elementis corpus, sed ex aliis idem. Nam deitate quidem et humanitate Deum perfectum et hominem perfectum eumdem esse et dici, et ex duabus et in duabus naturis confitemur. Et in eodem dicit: Si igitur secundum haereticos unius compositae naturae Christus post unionem existit, ex simplici natura versus est in compositam, neque Patri simplicis existentis naturae est consubstantialis ... nec homo nec Deus vocabitur, sed Christus solus, et erit nomen naturae, non personae.*

[2 (b): *De medio unionis.*]

6 Consequenter videndum est qualiter fiat illa unio, unde quaeritur quo medio et quid sit medium. Si hypostasis vel persona, contra in simili: Idem punctus medius est inter duas lineas, uniens illas, nec dicitur compositus punctus ex duabus lineis sed componens illas, et est simplex; si sic esset in hypostasi Christi, tunc non diceretur composita ex illis duabus naturis, sed uniens et conjungens illas.

7 Item, cum natura divina unitur humanae in una hypostasi vel persona, idem est extremum in illa unione et medium in quo fit unitio. Sed hoc non potest esse secundum unam et eamdem rationem. Quaeratur ergo unde hoc.

8 Item, si unio humanae naturae ad divinam [est] quiddam creatum et correlativum, debet respondere correlativo et aliquid creatum, scilicet unio divinae naturae ad humanam. — Contra: Nihil creatum est in divina natura.

9 Solutio: Extrema sunt duae naturae, medium uniens hypostasis, et persona tenet rationem unientis et ejus quod unitur et ejus in quo fit

---

64 *aliud]* Buyt., *om.* D   65 *vel] add.* ut (*om.* ut *var.*) Buyt. *idem]* eadem Buyt.   *Nam] add.* ex Buyt.
67 *confitemur] DeFideOrth* III, 3; PG 94, 989A; Buytaert, p. 174.   71 *personae] Ibid.* III, 3; PG 94, 988B-989A; Buytaert, pp. 173-174: "Si igitur secundum haereticos unius compositae naturae Christus post unionem exstitit (existit *var.*), ex simplici natura versus est in compositam; et neque Patri, simplicis existenti (existentis *var.*) naturae, est homousios (id est consubstantialis), neque matri. Non enim ex deitate et humanitate ipsa composita est, neque utique in deitate est et humanitate; neque Deus nominabitur neque homo, sed Christus solum (solus *var.*); et erit hoc nomen 'Christus' non hypostaseos (id est personae) eius nomen, sed unius secundum ipsos naturae."
83 *est] om.* D

unitio. Medium est illa persona, quia utramque naturam uniens; et est
illud in quo fit unitio, quia sibi univit humanam naturam; et in hoc 90
quod sibi univit, extremum est illius, et ita tenet rationem ejus quod
unitum est humanae naturae.

10   Ad illud de puncto respondeo quod in aliquo est simile, in
aliquo dissimile: simile quantum ad hoc quod punctus est conjungens
duas lineas sub duplici ratione, nam unius est terminus, alterius vero 95
initium, et ita quasi compositus est punctus. Sic illa personalis
hypostasis composita est ex diversis naturis, quae duae naturae in una
hypostasi conveniunt; unde Joannes Damascenus: *Non est dicere unam
naturam in Domino nostro Jesu Christo. Ideo utique ex duabus perfectis naturis, et
divina et humana, inquimus generatam esse unionem.* Et infra: *Substantialem* 100
*autem, non ut in duabus naturis perficientibus unam compositam naturam, sed
unitis invicem secundum veritatem in unam hypostasim compositam Filii Dei, et
servari earum substantialem differentiam decernimus;* et bene dicit "naturis
perfectis" ad differentiam corporis et animae, quorum neutrum sine
altero perfectum est, immo unum est materia et alterum forma. 105
Dicimus ergo quod divina natura in quantum est unibilis tenet
rationem naturae; in quantum uniens rationem personae quae sibi
univit humanam naturam: non quod divina essentia supponat pro persona (hoc numquam accidit), sed in hoc dicitur tenere rationem personae quod sibi univit naturam humanam, et ita sub ratione alia est ex- 110
tremum et medium, et sic patet solutio ad secundam objectionem.

11   Si autem quaeratur quae istarum magis propria: "Istae duae
naturae uniuntur in hypostasi" vel "uniuntur in persona," respondeo
quod magis proprie dicitur "in hypostasi" quam "in persona." Dicuntur
tamen uniri in unitate personae propter haereticos qui ponebant in 115
Christo pluralitatem personarum sicut diversitatem naturarum. Est
enim differentia inter personam et hypostasim, quia persona dicit excellentem proprietatem, hypostasis vero tenet locum medium inter personam et individuum. In divinis est persona; ex parte humanae naturae
est individuum quod habet naturam universalem in se et individuatur 120
duplici individuatione, ut dictum est. Facta unione Verbi ad humanam
naturam, fuit ibi hypostasis persona quantum ad proprietatem excellentem, et individuum, nam Jesus individuum est et illud individuum
fundatum est supra hypostasim Filii Dei; unde Damascenus, capitulo

93 puncto] See par. 6   100 *unionem*] unitionem (unionem *var.*) *Buyt.; DeFideOrth* III, 3; PG 94,
993A; Buytaert, pp. 176-177.   101 *in*] *om. (add.* in *var.) Buyt.*   103 *decernimus*] determinamus
Buyt.; DeFideOrth III, 3; PG 94, 993C; Buytaert, p. 178,   121 est] *Supra,* par. 3

praedicto, ante finem parum: *Ratione quidem [qua] differunt ab invicem* 125
naturae Christi, id est, ratione substantiae, inquimus ipsum copulari extremis:
secundum quidem deitatem et Patri et Spiritui Sancto, secundum autem
humanitatem et Matri et omnibus hominibus. Qua autem ratione copulantur
naturae ejus, differre [ipsum] inquimus et a Patre et a Spiritu Sancto et Matre et
reliquis hominibus; copulantur autem naturae ejus hypostasi (id est, persona), 130
unam hypostasim compositam habentes, secundum quam differunt a Patre et
Spiritu Sancto et Matre et nobis; et ita patet quod ibi individuum secundum
rationem differentiae supra positam erit.

12 Ad aliud dicendum quod unio ex parte humanae naturae est
quid creatum, sed non habet ex alia parte correlationem creaturis 135
respondentem, et hoc est quia unum extremum est natura, alterum
supra naturam, et hujus ratio est sic: Est in creaturis convenientibus in
accidente aliquo quod una creatura possibilis est respectu alterius, et
secundum causam similitudinis utraque immutatur; sed hic, ubi unum
extremum est creatura, alterum Creator, utrumque non est possibile 140
respectu alterius, immo in uno est tantum potentia activa. Ubi aliud est
possibile respectu alterius, immutatur ab illo. Quando autem utrumque
est possibile respectu utriusque, utrumque immutatur ab altero, ut in
conjunctione animae ad corpus, quia ex parte animae multas recipit
dispositiones corpus, et anima ex parte corporis, quia *corpus quod corrum-* 145
pitur aggravat animam, nec ita libera est in corpore sicut si esset separata.
In Creatore Christo non est hujusmodi possibilitas; unde dicitur in *Sym-*
bolo Athanasii: Non conversione deitatis in carnem, sed assumptione humanitatis
in Deo.

[2 (c): *De gratia unionis.*]   150

13 Item, quaeritur utrum aliquid circa animam factum sit, secundum quod fit unio. Exemplum: Duo sunt pares in naturalibus et
gratuitis; ponatur quod uni deitas unitur: aut aliquid ibi (propter quod
unitur) ei factum est, alteri non, aut nihil. Videtur quod aliquid, cum

125 *qua*] Buyt., *om.* D (cf. *infra*, q. 3, 54; p. 187).   126 *ipsum*] cum D, ipsum Buyt. Cf. *infra*, q. 3, 54;
p. 187.   127 *Sancto*] *om.* Buyt.   128 *Matri*] *add.* et nobis. Consubstantialis est enim idem, secundum quidem deitatem Patri et Spiritui, secundum humanitatem autem et matri (*om.* et nobis ...
matri *var.*) Buyt.   129 *ipsum*] Buyt., *om.* D (cf. *infra*, q. 3, 54; p. 187).   a²] *om.* (a *var.*) Buyt.   Sancto]
om. (Sancto *var.*) Buyt.   130 *autem*] enim (autem *var.*) Buyt.   131 *differunt*] *add.* et (*om. var.*) Buyt.
132 *Sancto*] *om.* Buyt.   nobis] *DeFideOrth* III, 3; PG 94, 996B; Buytaert, pp. 178-180.
133 positam] Cf. *supra*, 11, ll. 121-124   134 aliud] See par. 8   est] *s.s.* D1   146 animam] Wis
9, 15   149 *Deo*] Symbolum "*Quicumque*"; in H. Denzinger and A. Schönmetzer, edd., *Enchiridion*
Symbolorum ..., 34th ed. (Barcelona: Herder, 1967) no. 76: "... unus autem non conversione divinitatis
in carnem, sed assumptione humanitatis in Deum."   153 quod²] quid D

ante pares essent et nihil sit sine causa et ratione a Deo. Si nihil sit fac- 155
tum, qua ergo ratione unitur uni et [non] alteri? Si dicat: Ratio est quia
vult Deus; — sed voluntas ejus semper ordinata est ad sapientiam et ita
rationabilis.

14 Item, unio est consequens rem naturalem. Ergo in uno praecedit
aliqua natura vel aliquid quod non est in alio. Quaeratur quid sit illud. 160
Si dicatur aliqua excellens gratia, quae est illa, vel quae ratio con-
ferendi illam? Dicit Damascenus, capitulo *De modo inceptionis Verbi Dei*,
sic: *Post assensum igitur semper Virginis, Spiritus Sanctus supervenit super eam*
secundum Domini sermonem quem dixit angelus, purgans ipsam et virtutem
susceptivam Verbi Dei tribuens, simul autem et generativam. Et superobumbravit 165
super ipsam, Dei hypostasim habens altissimi. Ex hoc infertur, quia si carni
vim generativam contulit, et animae vim aliquam [contulit] qua ei
uniretur.

15 Item, in quibusdam est vestigium, quod dicit comparationem ad
Deum secundum aliquid, scilicet unitatem, veritatem, bonitatem; in aliis 170
imago secundum memoriam, intelligentiam, et voluntatem; in aliis
similitudo secundum gratiam. Igitur in natura divina et humana unio
erit per aliquid et videtur quod secundum gratiam excellentem. Ergo
unio ad illud, quod dictum est similitudo, reducetur, quae similiter
secundum gratiam. 175

16 Item, illa gratia aut erit potentia aut passio aut habitus; non
potentia vel passio; ergo virtus vel scientia; cum sit habitus et non scientia, igitur virtus. Ergo mediante virtute est unio. — Contra: Immo, omnis virtus consequenter ex unione est et unionem sequens.

17 Praeterea, si gratia est causa unionis, qualis erit error illius qui 180
dicit: *Non invideo Christo Domino, quia possum fieri Filius Dei?*

18 Praeterea, gratia facit qualem, non quid, et ita Filius Dei, secundum quod homo, non erit aliquid.

19 Solutio: Anima creata ad imaginem et similitudinem Dei, quae
est substantia incorporea, unibilis Deo fuit, ut supra dictum est, sed non 185
quaelibet, immo illa quae habuit gratiam praeelectionis, quam Deus ab

---

156 non] *om.* D   alteri] alii D   163 *eam*] ipsam (eam *var.*) *Buyt.*   165 *Verbi Dei*] deitatis Verbi
(Verbi Dei *var.*) *Buyt.*   *Et*] *add.* tunc (*om.* tunc *var.*) *Buyt.*   *superobumbravit*] superumbravit
(superobumbravit *var.*) *Buyt.*   166 *hypostasim ... altissimi*] altissimi enhypostatos (id est hypostasim
habens) *Buyt.; DeFideOrth* III, 2; PG 94, 985A-B; Buytaert, p. 171.   167 contulit] *om.* D   181 *Dei*]
In his *Summa* Praepositinus of Cremona ascribes the statement to Julian the Apostate: "Unde
Julianus Apostata: 'Non invideo Christo facto Deo, quia et ego possum esse Deus si volo'" (text
established from *MS.* London, British Museum Royal 9.E.XIV, fols. 176va, and *MS.* Tours, Ville 142,
fol. 112va). Cf. *GlossaAlex* III, 11, 3 (E); p. 121, ll. 22-24.   182 quid / et] I 82rb D   185 est²] Cf.
Philip, *DeIncarn*, 1-i & 1-ii, 9-12; pp. 161-164.

aeterno prae aliis elegit; unde: *Beatus quem elegisti et assumpsisti*: haec est
electio Domini Dei quae praeparavit hanc animam, in qua fuerunt
naturalia priora meliora, antecedentia omnia alia naturalia cujuslibet
animae. Sic ergo est gratia unionem antecedens naturaliter, quae est ad 190
fieri et ad assumere: est enim ad esse animae ut assumatur. Est et alia
quae sequitur unionem naturaliter, et est ad bene esse, quae est
plenitudo omnium bonorum et charismatum; unde dicit Damascenus,
III libro, capitulo *Quoniam omnis divina natura: Unitum est carni per medium
intellectum Verbum Dei mediante Dei puritate et carnis grossitie: higemonicon (id* 195
*est, dux principalis) animae et carnis intellectus; [intellectus] [autem] quod
animae purissimum*, etc. Cum igitur illa anima potentias [et] vires in
natura sua habuit transcendentes alias creaturas, et bonitatem
naturalem excedentem, recte fuit praeelecta et deitati unita, et ad idem
facit auctoritas Damasceni supra posita: *Post assensum*.   200

20   Ad hoc etiam facit quod Deus tripliciter dicitur esse in rebus:
primo modo essentialiter, praesentialiter, potentialiter; secundo modo
per gratiam; tertio modo per unionem. Ut igitur fiat transitus conveniens de primo modo in ultimum, fiet per modum medium, scilicet
per gratiam. Sic ergo anima illa, condigna per hujusmodi gratiam 205
praeparata, unita fuit Verbo; unde Augustinus, libro *De Divinitate et
Humanitate Christi: Non ita fuit Filius Dei in anima Christi sicut in anima
alterius hominis. "Uncta" enim fuit "oleo laetitiae prae consortibus suis" et peccati incapax; ideoque et unum cum ipso atque ejus vocabulis nuncupatur. Christus
enim prae aliis unctus, anima ejus Verbo inseparabiliter inhaerens, totum tota* 210
*recipiens, spirituali substantia animae inter Deum et hominem mediante. Non
enim fuit possibile sine mediatione uniri illam Christi animam quae, quasi ferrum
in igne, sic semper in Verbo, omne quod agit, quod sentit, quod intelligit, ut Deus
sentit et agit et intelligit.*

187 *assumpsisti*] Ps 64, 5   189 priora] puriora D   194 *Unitum*] unita D, unitum *Buyt.; add.*
igitur *Buyt.*   195 *puritate*] puritati D, puritate (puritati *var.*) *Buyt.*   *carnis*]
carni D, carnis *Buyt.*   *higemonicon*] *add.* enim (*om.* enim *var.*) *Buyt.*   196 *principalis*] *add.* quidem et
Buyt.   *intellectus²*] *om.* D, intellectus (*om.* intellectus *var.*) *Buyt.*   *autem quod*] quidem D, autem quod
Buyt.   197 etc. *DeFideOrth* III, 6; PG 94, 1005B; Buytaert, p. 189   197 et] *om.* D   200 *assen-*
sum] See par. 14   203 unionem] unienem D   208 *suis*] Ps 44, 8   213 *sentit*] sapit D   214 *in-*
telligit] This quotation is a summary of passages from a compilation of excerpts from Origen's *De*
Principiis called *De Incarnatione Verbi ad Januarium*. This quotation summarizes II, 19; PL 42, 1189-
1190 & 1192: "Nec tamen ita dicimus fuisse Filium Dei in illa anima, sicut fuit in anima Petri vel
Pauli caeterorumque sanctorum, in quibus Christus similiter ut in Paulo loqui creditur ... Haec
vero anima quae in Christo fuit, priusquam sciret malum, elegit bonum (*Isai.* VII, 15): et quia dilexit
justitiam, et odio habuit iniquitatem, propterea unxit eam Deus oleo laetitiae prae participibus suis
(*Psal.* XLIV, 8). Oleo ergo laetitiae ungitur, cum Verbo Dei immaculata foederatione conjuncta est:
et per hoc sola omnium animarum peccati incapax fuit quia Filii Dei bene et plene capax fuit:
ideoque et unum cum ipso est, atque ejus vocabulis nuncupatur, et Jesus Christus appellatur, per

21   Item, anima Christi simul tempore creata, infusa, corpori juncta, 215
et deitati fuit unita; tamen, si naturalem ordinem attendamus, prius fuit
unio animae ad corpus quam animae et carnis ad deitatem, et anima sic
considerata non habuit ut uniretur divinae naturae, et caro anima
mediante, sed dignitatem et congruitatem suscepit a Filio Dei ut, talis et
tam digna facta, uniretur, et ipsa anima fuit principale medium unionis 220
carnis ad divinam naturam, scilicet quod tanta et tam digna fuit. Ex incidenti autem medium [est] conjunctio corporis ad animam. Unde in
triduo, licet cessaret medium ex incidenti, scilicet conjunctio corporis et
animae, quia tamen principale medium mansit (anima talis et tanta),
ideo Verbum non fuit separatum a carne et anima, sed manserunt unio 225
animae ad Deum et [unio] carnis ad deitatem.

22   Ad illud quod objicitur quod, si secundum gratiam est unio,
ergo et secundum assimilationem gratiae, ergo et nos possumus uniri,
respondeo: Unionem causat, secundum quod diximus, gratia quae est
ad esse, et tu objicis de gratia quae est ad bene esse, et ideo non valet 230
argumentatio.

[2 (d): *De comparatione unitatum.*]

23   Ultimo quaeritur utrum major sit unitas in Trinitate personarum qua illa sit quam facit unio naturarum in hypostasi Verbi, et
proceditur sic.   235

24   Ens non ab alio, ens ab alio summe distant. Ergo maxime differunt. Ubi autem maxima differentia, est minima convenientia. Ergo
quae summe differunt conveniunt in minimam unitatem. Sed conveniunt ens non ab alio et ens ab alio in unitate personali. Ergo unitas
personalis minima convenientia.   240

25   Contra: Ubi minima differentia, ibi maxima convenientia. Sed in
Trinitate est minima differentia, quae est in personis, et minima
discretio personalis. Ergo maxima convenientia erit in persona.

26   Item, ubi minima differentia, ibi maxima convenientia. Sed in

---

quem omnia facta esse dicuntur (*Joan.* I, 3). ... Illa anima ... inseparabiliter atque indissociabiliter
inhaerens, utpote Verbo et sapientiae Dei et veritate ac luci verae, et tota totum recipiens, atque in
ejus lucem splendoremque ipsa cedens, facta est cum ipso principaliter unus spiritus ... Hac ergo
substantia animae inter Deum carnemque mediante (non enim possibile erat, Dei naturam corpori
sine mediatore misceri) nascitur, ut diximus, Deus homo, illa substantia media existente, cui utique
contra naturam non erat corpus assumere ... Hoc ergo modo etiam illa anima, quae quasi ferrum
in igne; sic semper in Verbo, semper in sapientia, semper in Deo posita est: omne quod agit, quod
sentit, quod intelligit Deus est." I have not found a medieval work with the title given by Philip.
222 est] *om.* D   226 unio] *om.* D   228 uniri] See par. 17 and also par. 15.

Trinitate est minima differentia. Ergo in Trinitate est maxima con- 245
venientia, et haec est in natura divina. Ergo maxima convenientia est in
natura divina, non persona.

27   Contra: Unum subjecto sunt Filius Dei et Filius Virginis, et supposito Filio Dei, supponitur Filius Virginis, et quicquid dicitur de Filio
Dei dicitur de Filio Virginis. In personis autem sunt tria supposita quae 250
sunt divina natura. Ergo major est unitas quam facit unio naturarum in
unitate personae quam unitas in Trinitate.

28   Solutio: Multiplex est unitas, scilicet in genere, quae secundum
[eandem] figuram praedicati dicitur; item, unitas in specie; item, in
numero, quae est secundum formam; accidens proprium et differentia 255
non faciunt numerum cum eo cui conveniunt. Juxta unitatem in specie
est unitas in natura divina; juxta unitatem in numero unitas personalis
Filii Dei. Unum in natura est Pater cum Filio, quoniam paternitas et
filiatio non numerant naturam, cum sint proprietates. Unum in
hypostasi sunt quae non numerant hypostasim, ut duae naturae in 260
Christo et duae in homine, scilicet anima et corpus. Unum naturâ
numerat personas, quod est contra unum in hypostasi. Dicimus ergo
quod in hypostasi major est unitas respectu personae, minor vero
respectu naturae. — Item, maxima convenientia in hypostasi secundum
quod habetur respectus ad personam, minima vero respectu naturae. E 265
converso, maxima convenientia in tribus personis respectu naturae,
minima respectu hypostasis.

29   Sic patet solutio ad tres objectiones. Ad illud quod objicit de
subjecto, respondeo quod revera major est convenientia respectu
hypostasis, sed non respectu naturae: unitas in persona non numerat 270
hypostasim, et ideo non numeratur praedicatio nec multiplicatur, sed
unitas naturae numerat hypostasim, et ideo praedicatio multiplicatur.

30   Si tamen quaeritur quae unitas simpliciter major, respondeo
quod unitas naturae. Unitas tamen in persona completior est respectu
gradus, quod patet sic: Triplex est esse: naturae, individui, et esse per- 275
sonale. Esse naturae respicit subjectum, esse individui hypostasim; esse
personae est morale et respicit dignitatem; et ita secundum hos tres
gradus persona completior est.

---

254 eandem] *om.* D : supplied from text of Aristotle (see 2nd note following)   praedicati]
praedicationis in Latin translations of Aristotle   255 formam] Cf. Aristotle, *Metaphysics*, Delta, 6;
passim, esp. 1016b 31-34. Aristotle, however, says that numerical unity is based on oneness of matter rather than on oneness of form as in Philip. The *reportator* seems to have corrupted the whole
passage.   269 subjecto] See par. 27   275 sic] sicut D   278 est] Cf. *Glossa Alex* III, 2, 14i (L); p. 30:
"Completior tamen modus est dicendi in persona quam in subiecto, ubi unum adicitur super
alterum; nam individuum dicitur in ratione, subiectum in natura, persona in moribus."

[Quaestio 3]

Secundum Cancellarium: De Homine Assumpto.

[3 (a): *De subjecto actus assumendi.*]

1 Quaeritur cujus est actus assumendi, naturae scilicet an personae; et videtur quod natura naturam assumpsit quia idem est divina natura et substantia, et assumere actus est substantiae; ergo et naturae.   5

2 Item, Augustinus dicit: *Forma Dei accepit formam servi*, et forma est natura. Ergo natura accepit formam servi.

3 Item, creare et unire est ejusdem. Ergo creare et assumere est ejusdem. Sed creare est naturae, et inde ut prius. Quod creare sit naturae probatur, quia natura communis est tribus personis et tota   10 Trinitas creat, et inde ut prius.

4 Item, quid est assumere nisi assumptionem facere? Et hoc totius Trinitatis, et ita naturae.

5 Si concedatur, contra: Si natura assumit, communicat actum tribus personis. Ergo tres personae assumunt humanam naturam, quod   15 falsum est.

6 Solutio: "Assumere" quandoque dicitur "in se sumere": si convenit hic actus soli Filio; quandoque dicitur "ad se sumere": si convenit naturae divinae; quandoque dicitur "ad aliquid sumere": sic est totius Trinitatis. Secundum primam acceptionem haec est falsa: "Divina natura assumpsit humanam naturam," et haec vera: "Persona assumpsit   20 humanam naturam." Juxta secundam haec vera: "Divina natura assumpsit humanam naturam." Juxta tertiam haec est vera: "Tota Trinitas assumpsit humanam naturam." Et primo modo propriissime sumitur "assumere," secundo modo proprie, tertio minus proprie.

7 Ad aliud respondeo quod assumere est ad aliquid sumere et   25 assumptionem facere: sic convertuntur; in aliis acceptionibus non convertuntur.

8 Ad aliud quod divina natura sibi humanam univit, et cujus est creare, ejus est unire, ergo et assumere ejusdem erit, respondeo: Non sequitur, quia "unire" et "creare" dicunt actus sine accedente,   30

Quaestio 3: I, 82vb-83rb D

7 servi] *De Trinitate* I, 7, 14; PL 42, 828; CorChrSerLat 50/ 1, 45: "Neque enim sic accepit formam serui ut amitteret formam dei in qua erat aequalis patri." *Ibid*. I, 11, 22; PL 42, 836; CorChrSerLat 50/1, 60: "... ut distinguamus quid in eis sonet secundum formam dei in qua est et aequalis est patri, et quid secundum formam serui quam accepit et minor est patre ..."   25 aliud] See par. 4 28 aliud] *add*. respondeo D   29 erit] See par. 3.

"assumere" vero dicit actum cum accedente, scilicet in se sumere, [quod est solius Filii], et ad se sumere, quod est naturae, et ad aliquid sumere, quod est totius Trinitatis.

9 Item, cujus est actus unire, cum dicat actum pure? Videtur quod naturae divinae. — Contra: Actus dicuntur de natura divina secundum 35 proportionem ad inferiora. Sed in inferioribus dicitur habens naturam agere, non ipsa natura. Ergo in divinis eodem modo debet dici habens naturam agere, et si ita est, unire est actus personae vel substantiae, non naturae; quod si verum, natura non univit naturam sibi.

10 Solutio: Quattuor consideranda sunt: natura, essentia, sub- 40 stantia, hypostasis. In divinis igitur cum sit substantia natura, habens naturam est natura. Unde ea ratione actus bene dicitur naturae qui respicit naturam et rationem essentiae, proprie tamen dicitur actus substantiae. In inferioribus non est ita quoniam ibi habens naturam non est eadem natura; Deus vero habens naturam est eadem natura, ideoque 45 frequenter actus qui proprie substantiae est attribuitur naturae, ut creare, unire.

11 Item, in naturis idem est esse quid et esse quis. In divinis non est idem dicere "quis" et "quid"; unde supposita persona, non supponitur essentia et e converso, et tamen persona est essentia et e converso. 50

12 Item, quidam actus dicuntur de Deo secundum proportionem organi, et potius debet fundari in substantia quae quasi per modum organi se habet, ut sumere. Sed unire est actus spiritualis non habens se per modum organi. Ergo non eadem ratione attribuuntur. — Quod concedimus, et dicimus quod actus sumendi proprie secundum sub- 55 stantiam dicitur, actus vero uniendi de natura dicitur proprie.

13 Item, haec est vera: "Divina natura est unita carni," ut dicunt omnes, et haec vera: "Humana natura est unita divinae naturae"; tamen "unita" diversimode sumitur, quoniam in prima dicit increatum, in secunda creatum. — Sed videtur haec falsa: "Divina natura est unita 60 carni": sensus enim est: "Divina natura univit carnem"; in neutra illarum positum est verbum aliquod vel aliquis terminus per quem unio retorqueatur ad personam, et constat quod locutio falsa est ubi non reducitur, quoniam in persona facta est unio. Ergo prima falsa, et hoc patet: Divina natura tribus personis communis est et ei attribuitur unio, 65 et non specificatur per aliquid ibi positum [per] quod reducatur ad personam Filii. Ergo falsa est, cum unio sit in persona et actus tribus attribuitur.

14   Item, haec est vera: "Divina natura univit sibi humanam." —
Contra: Divina natura communis est tribus personis, et unire ad unam   70
personam tantum pertinet.

15   Item, divina natura est homo. [Ergo] divina essentia [est] nata,
passa, mortua.

16   Solutio: Ubi ponitur verbum unionis, distinguendum est utrum
sumatur active vel passive; quando active, significat increatum, quando   75
passive, creatum. Dicimus ergo quod in hac: "Divina natura univit sibi
humanam naturam," praedicatur persona Filii et sic per aliquid ibi
positum fit reductio ad personam.

17   Ad aliud respondeo quod divina natura unita est carni, sed
"unita" non dicit ibi actionem sed ostendit factum, et hoc ipsum dicit   80
personam Filii; sed "univit" dicit actionem, et ideo dicit naturam. Cum
autem dicitur: "Divina natura univit humanam," non est ibi
reciprocatio vera et expressa; sed cum apponitur "sibi," expressior est
reciprocatio et copulatur divina natura, et quia natura est communis
toti Trinitati et Filius est divina natura, propter connotatum quod est   85
Filius vera est haec: "Divina natura univit sibi humanam."

18   Ad illud: "Divina natura est homo," respondeo quod vera est,
quoniam *quicquid convenit Filio Dei per naturam convenit Filio Hominis per
gratiam*; tamen, supposita divina natura, non supponitur Filius Dei.
Haec est vera: "Divina essentia est nata, passa, mortua," si praedicatur   90
substantive; si adjective, falsae sunt, et sic dicunt aliqui simpliciter falsas
esse praedictas; unde Damascenus, libro III, titulo *De ea quae in specie
dominica,* etc., capitulo *Natura vel nuda,* ultra medium: *Naturam Verbi
passam in carne neque umquam audivimus; Christum autem passibilem in carne
edocti sumus. Quare non hypostasim manifestat dicere "naturam Verbi."*   95
*Relinquitur ergo dicere quoniam incarnatum esse quidem unitum esse est carni;
carnem autem generatum esse Verbum, ipsam Verbi hypostasim invertibiliter
generatam esse carnis hypostasim. Et quoniam quidem Deus homo generatus, et
homo Deus dictum est: Deus enim Verbum generatus intransmutabiliter homo.*

---

72 Ergo] *om.* D   est²] *om.* D   79 carni] See par. 13   80 factum] factam D   87 homo] See
par. 15 89 *gratiam*] The closest text I have found in Augustine is in his *Contra Sermonem Arianorum,* 8;
PL 42, 688: "Ipse namque unus Christus et Dei Filius semper natura, et hominis Filius qui ex tempore assumptus est gratia ..." See the remarks in *HypUnion* I, 280, n. 56, and the thorough study by
J. Châtillon, "'Quidquid convenit Filio Dei per naturam convenit Filio Hominis per gratiam': A
propos de Jean de Ripa, *Determinationes,* I, 4, 4," in *Miscellanea André Combes* II (Rome-Paris 1967) 319-
331.   93 *dominica*] *om. Buyt.*   *Naturam*] *add.* autem *Buyt.*   94 *in¹*] *om. Buyt.*   umquam] *add.* et
nunc *Buyt.*   *in²*] *om. Buyt.*   96 *ergo*] igitur (ergo *var.*) *Buyt.*   est] et D, est *Buyt.*   97 *carnem*] carne
D, carnem *Buyt.*   98 *generatus*] *add.* est (*om.* est *var.*) *Buyt.*

Quoniam autem deitas homo generata est vel incarnata est vel humanata est,   100
[nequaquam audivimus. Quoniam autem deitas unita est humanitati] in una
ejus hypostaseon, didicimus.

19   Item, dicit Damascenus, libro III, titulo *Quoniam omnis divina*
natura, capitulo *Communia,* ante finem: *Et quando dicimus naturam Verbi in-*
carnatam esse, secundum beatos Athanasium et Cyrillum deitatem dicimus esse   105
unitam carni. Ideo non possumus dicere: "Natura Verbi passa est": non enim
passa est deitas in ipso. Dicimus humanam naturam passam esse in Christo.
Similiter, quotiens aliqua praedicatio fit de divina substantia quae notet
definitionem, falsa est, sicut haec: "Divina essentia est nata." Haec est
vera: "Divina essentia est incarnata," quoniam dicit rem suam ut ad ter-   110
minum sive ad finem; "unita" vero dicit terminum incarnationis; hoc
est, planis verbis dicere, "incarnata" significat rem suam ut sine
praeexistentia hominis, "unita" vero ut cum praeexistentia hominis, ut
dicit Damascenus.

[3 (b): *Utrum persona assumpsit personam.*]   115

20   Item, quaeritur utrum persona assumpsit personam, et dicunt
omnes quod non.
21   Tamen objicitur in contrarium: dicit enim Damascenus, libro III,
capitulo *Natura vel nuda*, circa principium: *Deus igitur Verbum incarnatum*
neque eam quae nuda contemplatione consideratur naturam assumpsit: non enim   120
incarnatio haec, sed deceptio et fictio incarnationis; neque eam quae in specie con-
sideratur: non enim omnes hypostases assumpsit, sed eam quae in atomo, quae est
in specie. Ex hoc videtur quod persona, quia persona in atomo est.
22   Item, tres sunt distinctiones personales: secundum originem,
secundum proprietatem essentiae, et secundum proprietatem originis.   125
Sed hujusmodi proprietas in incarnatione est assumpta; ergo persona.

101 *nequaquam ... humanitati*] *Buyt.,* om. D   102 *didicimus*] *DeFideOrth* III, 11; PG 94, 1025B-C;
Buytaert, pp. 206-207.   104 *Communia*] Communio D, Communia *Buyt.*   105 *beatos*] add.
Anastasium vel D, add. et (*om.* et *var.*) *Buyt.*   *Cyrillum*] Curillum D   107 *Dicimus*] add. autem (*om.*
autem *var.*) *Buyt.*   *Christo*] *DeFideOrth* III, 6; PG 94, 1008B; Buytaert, pp. 190-191.
114 Damascenus] Cf. *DeFideOrth* III, 11; PG 94, 1024B-C; Buytaert, p. 205: "Igitur aliud quidem est
unitio, et aliud incarnatio. Nam unitio quidem solum demonstrat copulationem; ad quid autem
facta est copulatio, non adhuc. Incarnatio autem, idem autem dicere et inhumanatio, eam quae ad
carnem, scilicet ad hominem copulationem demonstrat, quemadmodum et ignitio eam quae ad
ignem unitionem." 118 III] I D   119 *incarnatum*] incarnatus (incarnatum *var.*) *Buyt.*   120 con-
sideratur] cogitatur (consideratur *var.*) *Buyt.*   121 *haec*] hoc *Buyt.*   122 *quae²*] add. eadem (*om.*
eadem *var.*) *Buyt.*   123 *specie*] *DeFideOrth* III, 11; PG 94, 1024A; Buytaert, pp. 203-204.   125 originis]
Cf. Philip the Chancellor, *DeDiscrPers*, 3-4 (pp. 155-156); *DeIncarn,* 1-i, 1 (p. 158), 1-i & 1-ii, 8 (p. 161);
Richard of Saint-Victor, *DeTrin* IV, 13-15 (Ribaillier, pp. 175-178).

23 Item, quid deest huic ut non sit persona in assumptione?

24 Item, persona est nomen dignitatis sive excellentiae, sed nihil destruxit deitas assumens quod esset dignitatis vel excellentiae.

25 Item, in ordinibus non tollitur minor character propter 130 majorem; eadem ratione et hic.

26 Item, anima ordinem habet: creatur in corpore. Item, separatur a corpore et, separata, non acquirit personalitatem. Sic nec, conjuncta divinae naturae humana [natura], personalitatem amittet.

27 Item, ex creatione animae in corpore homo est in forma sua 135 habens completum esse. Ergo est persona.

28 Item, ubi terminatur actus creationis, ibi incipit actus assumendi. Sed in termino creationis est homo completus; ergo persona. Et ita persona personam assumpsit.

29 Solutio: Damascenus bene dicit *non eam quae nuda* est, id est, ab- 140 stractam ab accidentibus et proprietatibus, *sed eam quae in atomo*, id est, cum proprietatibus suis singularem naturam, non quae prius in atomo esset, sed in ipsa hypostasi sua existentem. Est enim individuatio duplex: prima per esse particulare solum sine proprietatibus: sic non assumpsit naturam individuatam, sed secundum secundam individuationem, quae 145 est in atomo cum collectione proprietatum individuantium ipsam ab omni alia re.

30 Ad aliud respondeo quod non assumpsit discretionem personalem secundum originem, sed secundum proprietatem essentiae quae est in habente naturam assumpsit, quae non est tamen natura. 150

31 Item, nativitatem non assumpsit, sed naturam consequentem nativitatem.

32 Ad aliud respondeo quod nihil destruxit in humana natura divina natura, sed quia "persona" dicitur quasi "per se sonans," id est, unum per se et habens esse absolutum et excellentiam dignitatis, ut 155 patet in ejus definitione: *Persona est rationabilis naturae substantia individua* — "individua substantia" dicit ut "quid," "rationabilis naturae" ut "quis," et humana natura unita divinae non habet hoc — ideo non dicitur persona.

33 Ad sequens respondeo quod non valet processus, quia creationis 160 terminus non dicit esse personae quod sit conjunctum aut conjungibile, sed dicit esse inconjunctum et inconjungibile actu et potentia.

---

129 excellentiae] essentiae D   134 natura] *om*. D   138 persona / Et] I 83ra D   141 *atomo*] See par. 21   147 re] Cf. *DeIncarn*, 2, 3 (p. 170, ll. 37-38) and *infra*, 44 (p. 184)   148 aliud] See par. 22   153 aliud] See par. 24   156 *individua*] Boethius, *ContraEut*, 3 & 4; Rand, pp. 84 & 92.   157 naturae] creaturae D   160 sequens] See par. 28.

34   Ad illud, scilicet quod anima exuta a corpore non acquirit, etc., respondeo quod ideo hoc contingit quia ejus esse non est absolutum sed dependens a corpore, cui naturaliter appetit uniri. Sed ubi unitur 165 divina natura humanae, ejus esse, scilicet humanae naturae, non est per se unum et absolutum nec habens dignitatem excellentiae; ideoque non est persona, nec tamen tollitur ei aliquid quoniam illud numquam habuit.

[3 (c): *De hypostasi composita.*]   170

35   Postmodum quaeritur de hoc quod dicit Damascenus, libro III, [titulo] *De duabus naturis*, capitulo *Inconvertibiliter*, circa medium: *In Domino nostro Jesu Christo ideo utique ex duabus perfectis naturis, et divina et humana, inquimus generationem*, etc., et titulo *De modo retributionis*, capitulo *Igitur quoniam aliud*, post medium: *In Domino igitur nostro Jesu Christo, quia* 175 *duas naturas cognoscimus, unam quidem hypostasim ex utrisque compositam, quando quidem naturas respicimus, deitatem et humanitatem [vocamus; quando autem eam quae ex naturis compositam hypostasim, quandoque quidem ex utroque Christum] nominamus, et Deum et hominem secundum idem, et Deum in-carnatum;* et capitulo sequenti: *Unam autem hypostasim ex duabus naturis* 180 *perfectis compositam*; et quando ex utrisque Christum nominamus et Deum, quaeritur quo genere compositionis et cujusmodi sint partes, et utrum duae naturae faciant alterum perfectum.

36   De primo quaeritur an sic composita sit sicut homo componitur ex corpore et anima, et hoc videtur per illud quod dicitur in Symbolo: 185 *Nam sicut anima rationalis et caro unus est homo*, etc.; haec enim manent in-confusa et propter hoc fit una persona, et hoc cognoscimus per ac-tiones, quae inseparabiles sunt. A simili, hic manent duae naturae et est una persona, et actiones sunt inseparabiles in Christo.

37   Si hoc concedatur, contra: Filius Dei est divina natura et ita 190 "divina natura" dicit totum. Sed hypostasis composita est ex duabus

163 etc.] See par. 26   172 titulo] *om.* D   174 etc.] *DeFideOrth* III, 3; PG 94, 993A; Buytaert, pp. 176-177: "Hinc non est dicere unam naturam in Domino nostro Iesu Christo. Ideo utique ex duabus naturis perfectis, et divina et humana, inquimus generatam esse unitionem ..." The Latin translation omits a line of the corresponding Greek text between *Christo* and *Ideo.*   titulo] capitulo D   175 *quoniam] add.* quidem *Buyt.*   176 *duas] add.* quidem (*om.* quidem *var.*) *Buyt.*   quidem] autem (quidem *var.*) *Buyt.*   177 *deitatem*] divinitatem (deitatem *var.*) *Buyt.*   177-179 *vocamus ... Christum] Buyt., om.* D   179 *secundum idem, et*] et secundum idem D, secundum idem, et *Buyt.*   179-180 *incarnatum] DeFideOrth* III,.4; PG 94, 997B; Buytaert, p. 181   181 *perfectis*] perfectam *Buyt.* *compositam] DeFideOrth* III, 5; PG 94, 1000C; Buytaert, p. 184.   186 etc.] *Symbolum "Quicumque"*; in H. Denzinger and A. Schönmetzer, edd., *Enchiridion Symbolorum* ..., 34th ed. (Barcelona: Herder, 1967) no. 76.

naturis. Ergo divina natura non venit in compositionem ut pars, cum
ipsa sit totum.

38   Item, haec hypostasis est composita ex his duabus naturis. Ergo
totum venit in compositionem. At hoc falsum est de divina natura.   195

39   Item, quaeritur quid notatur per hanc praepositionem "ex" cum
dico "ex utrisque"; non habitudinem partium integralium ad suum
totum, nec talem compositionem qualis est inter animam et corpus,
quoniam anima venit in compositionem quasi forma corporis: sic non
est de divina natura.   200

40   Item, partes rei compositae non sunt actu. Ergo divina natura
non erit actu si venit in compositionem: quod falsum est. Non igitur
venit in compositionem ut pars.

41   Item, Damascenus, capitulo *De duabus naturis: Si secundum
haereticos unius compositae naturae Christus post unionem existit, ex simplici*   205
*natura versus est in compositam, et neque Patri simplicis existentis naturae est
homousios (id est, consubstantialis) neque Matri. Non enim ex divinitate et
humanitate ipsa composita est, neque utique in deitate [est] et humanitate, neque
Deus vocabitur neque homo, sed Christus solum.* Si haec ratio sufficiens est:
quod si dicitur unius compositae naturae, neque Patri consubstantialis   210
est neque Matri, ergo, eadem ratione, si dicatur unius compositae
hypostasis, [non] erit Deus aut homo, vel non dicetur hypostasis composita, quia est Deus et est homo.

42   Item, quid vult dicere "composita ex his"? Si sensus est: id est, in
his, ergo potius debuit dicere "composita his," non "in his," et si ita est,   215
potius debuit dici "juxtaposita" quam "composita" hypostasis.

43   Item, non est assignare quo modo compositionis sit composita, et
sic nullo modo composita dici debet.

44   Solutio: Tria consideranda sunt: persona; hypostasis; individuum
in suo esse distincto, et juxta hoc in divinis tres personae dicuntur tres   220
entes; secunda individuatio est per *collectionem proprietatum quas impossibile
est in alio quolibet reperire.* Hypostasis vero sic potest describi: Hypostasis
est incommunicabilis existentia secundum proprietatum collectionem
distincta; persona vero est incommunicabilis existentia secundum

---

195 compositionem] compositione D   204 *Si*] add. igitur *Buyt.*   205 *existit*] exstitit (existit *var.*)
Buyt.   206 *existentis*] existenti (existentis *var.*) *Buyt.*   207 *divinitate*] deitate (divinitate *var.*) *Buyt.*
208 *est²*] *Buyt.; om.* D   209 *vocabitur*] *nominabitur* Buyt.   *solum*] *DeFideOrth* III, 3; PG 94, 988B-989A;
Buytaert, pp. 173-174.   212 non¹] *om.* D   217 quo modo] quomodo quo D   221 entes] Cf.
Damascene, *DeFideOrth* III, 5; PG 94, 1000B; Buytaert, p. 183: "Quemadmodum autem in deitate
unam naturam confitemur, tres autem hypostases (id est personas) secundum veritatem entes infimus ..."   222 *reperire*] See *DeIncarn,* 2, 3; p. 170, n. to l. 38.

proprietatem dignitatis distincta. Juxta hanc notificationem hypostasis 225
media est inter personam et individuum, quod tamen, proprie sump-
tum, in divinis non est; hypostasis vero, secundum quod est Filius Dei,
est persona, et' non secundum quod Filius Virginis. Cum autem
hypostasis [est] individuum secundum quod est Filius Virginis et non
secundum quod est Filius Dei, hac ratione hypostasis quasi media et in- 230
dividuum dicitur, composita ex duabus et in duabus naturis, quoniam,
ut patet, ex una parte respicit personam et ex altera respicit individuum, et individuum in atomo, de quo supra diximus.

45 Ad primum respondeo quod hypostasis dicitur composita
quoniam substat illis duabus naturis, unde dicitur ab "hypo," quod est 235
"sub." Continet ergo utramque naturam sive (quod melius dictum est)
supposita est utrique naturae, et est divina natura et est res humanae
naturae sive homo; non tamen dicimus quod aliquo istorum modorum
proprie sit composita, sed quoniam est sub illis; unde Damascenus: *Non*
enim idiosystatos (id est, separabiliter) substituta est Dei Verbi caro, neque altera 240
hypostasis generata est praeter Dei Verbi hypostasim, sed in ipsa subsistens
enhypostatos (id est, in indivisa) magis et non secundum seipsam idiosystatos (id
est, separatim subsistens) hypostasis generata est. Ideo neque anhypostatos (id est,
in non individuo) est, neque alteram in Trinitate infert hypostasim.

46 Substat ergo utrique naturae, et secundum divinam naturam non 245
incipit esse quis, sed secundum humanam naturam incipit esse quis vel
quid, non tamen simpliciter, quoniam incipit esse divina persona quae
fuit ab aeterno. Humana natura in Petro facit quis vel quem simpliciter:
non autem sic in Christo, quoniam etsi anima sit incommunicabilis
existentia, tamen non facit quis aut quem simpliciter, cum ejus [cor- 250
poris] dependerat, quoniam in conjunctione invenit esse completum.
Unde, cum sit ibi prima individuatio, secunda adveniens non facit quis
vel quem, sed quale, quia invenit completum esse. Facit tamen quis et
quid secundum quod Filius Virginis; facit, dico, non simpliciter sed
secundum quid: advenit enim hypostasi Filii Dei humana natura juxta 255
secundam individuationem, quae non facit quem, sed facit praeinventam

---

225 distincta] Cf. *GlossaAlex* III, 6, 13 (A); p. 78: "Nota quod persona est hypostasis distincta per
proprietatem dignitatis; hypostasis est exsistentia incommunicabilis ex quibuscumque in-
dividuantibus, supposita essentia. Unde omnis persona est hypostasis, et non convertitur."
227 Filius] Filii D   229 est¹] *om.* D   233 diximus] See par. 29   234 primum] See par. 35
237 divina] individua D (cf. *infra*, par. 51)   240 *substituta*] suscituta D, subsistura (substituta *var.*)
Buyt.   242 *in indivisa*] in individuo (indivisa *var.*) *Buyt.*   *idiosystatos*] idiosysta. D, idiosystatos *Buyt.*
243 *separatim*] separate *Buyt.*   *subsistens*] consistens (subsistens *var.*) *Buyt. generata*] facta (generata
var.) *Buyt. neque*] *Buyt., om.* D   *anhypostatos*] anpostatos D, anhypostatos *Buyt.*   244 *hypostasim*]
DeFideOrth III, 9; PG 94, 1017B; Buytaert, pp. 198-199 249 incommunicabilis] communicabilis D; cf.
supra, par. 44 (p. 184)   250-251 corporis] *om.* D

individuationem quae fuit secundum primum modum individuationis et
habuit completum esse; facit tamen quem hujus naturae qui prius erat
quis ab aeterno, et in quantum incipit esse quis hujus naturae, in tantum dicitur hypostasis composita. 260

47 Et ideo dicit Damascenus *in duabus et ex duabus naturis compositam,*
ita inquiens: *In omnibus igitur et super omnia erat, [et] in utero existens sanctae
Dei Genitricis, sed in ipso actu incarnationis. Incarnatus igitur est, ex ipsa
assumens primitias nostrae massae, carnem animatam anima rationali et in-
tellectuali, ut ipsa existeret carni hypostasis [quae Dei Verbi hypostasis], et com-* 265
*posita generatur quae prius erat simplex Verbi hypostasis; composita vero ex
duabus perfectis naturis, et deitate et humanitate, et ferat ipsa divinae Dei Verbi
filiationis characteristicum [et determinativum idioma, secundum quod divisa
sunt a Patre et Spiritu, et carnis characteristica] et determinativa idiomata, secundum quod differunt a Matre et reliquis hominibus.* 270

48 Ex hoc patet quod compositio est ex parte humanae naturae;
unde cum divina natura totaliter activa sit et nullo modo in potentia, et
omnis pars in quantum hujusmodi habeat esse potentiale, ipsa non erit
pars. Possumus tamen qualitercumque assimilare partes in hac compositione partibus quae veniunt in definitione generis; illae enim non 275
numerant definitum. Similiter divina natura et humana dicuntur partes
hypostasis secundum quod Christus dicitur Deus et homo, et tamen
Christus non numeratur cum Deo aut homine.

49 Illud autem de anima et carne: Non est simile de carne et anima,
et hoc ideo quoniam non veniunt in unam rationem ut dicatur: "Anima 280
est caro," sicut dicitur: "Deus homo" et "Homo Deus."

50 Item, anima pars potentialis et corpus similiter, sed divina natura
activa tantum, humana vero passibilis; unde humana natura immutatur
in melius, divina natura manente immutabili.

---

261 *ex*] sub D, ex *Buyt.* *compositam*] Cf. the text immediately following, and *DeFideOrth* III, 3; PG
94, 989A; Buytaert, p. 174: "Nam ex deitate quidem et humanitate Deum perfectum et hominem
perfectum eundem esse et dici, et ex duabus et in duabus naturis confitemur." Cf. also *ibid.* III, 3
(PG 94, 993A-B; Buytaert, p. 177, ll. 66-81), III, 4 (PG 94, 997B; Buytaert, p. 181, ll. 18-24: quoted
supra, par. 35; p. 183). 262 *et²*] *Buyt., om.* D 263 *ipso*] ipsa (ipso *var.*) *Buyt.* 264 *anima*] *add.* et
(*om.* et *var.*) *Buyt.* 265 *quae ... hypostasis*] *Buyt., om.* D & *var. Buyt.* 268 *characteristicum*] charac-
teristicam D & *var. Buyt.,* characteristicum *Buyt.* 269 *et²*] ea quae (et *var.*) *Buyt.* The original Greek
shows that the variant reading in Buytaert (and Philip's reading, which agrees with the variant) is
preferable. Many manuscripts omit both *ea quae* and *et*: this also gives a more faithful rendering of
the Greek than Buytaert's reading. On his method of editing, see C. Vansteenkiste, "Le versioni
latine del *De Fide Orthodoxa* di San Giovanni Damasceno," *Angelicum* 35 (1958) 91-98. 268-269 *et
determinativum ... characteristica*] *Buyt., om.* D 270 *quod*] quae (quod *var.*) *Buyt.* *differunt*] differt
(differunt *var.*) *Buyt., add.* et *Buyt.* *hominibus*] *DeFideOrth* III, 7; PG 94, 1009A-B; Buytaert, p. 192.
279 *carne¹*] See par. 36.

51 Item, divina natura non est simpliciter forma sed quasi, in quan- 285
tum trahit humanam naturam ad personam sive hypostasim. Dicitur
ergo pro tanta composita hypostasis ex duabus et in duabus naturis,
quia est divina natura et res humanae naturae, ut dictum est.

52 Ad secundum objectum dicimus quod Filius, in eo quod differt a
Patre, scilicet in hypostasi, dicitur compositus; quare ex eo non sequitur 290
quod Pater sit compositus si Filius est compositus.

53 Si autem quaeratur sic: Non est nisi duplex genus compositionis
secundum Damascenum: unum genus est secundum quod aliquid componitur ex partibus manentibus, ut homo ex anima et corpore, aliud
secundum quod aliquid componitur ex partibus transeuntibus, ut cor- 295
pus ex quattuor elementis; secundum aliquam harum compositionum
non praedicatur pars componens de composito; ergo, cum hypostasis
Filii Dei sit Deus et homo, non debet dici composita ex his naturis vel in
his; respondeo quod in hac compositione fit hoc hujus naturae et hoc
illius, et ideo composita dicitur, et est aliud genus compositionis a 300
praedictis: loquitur enim Damascenus de compositione rerum
naturalium.

54 Ad aliud: "Quo modo ex his," etc., respondeo quod non est in-
conveniens hypostasim componi, cum sit illius naturae et hujus, et sit
natura haec et illa. Damascenus: *Hypostasis secundum quod divina natura* 305
convenit cum Patre, secundum quod humana convenit cum Matre. Ergo ratione
quidem qua differunt ab invicem naturae Christi, id est, ratione substantiae,
inquimus ipsum copulari extremis: secundum quidem deitatem Patri et Spiritui
Sancto, secundum autem humanitatem Matri et omnibus hominibus. Qua autem
ratione copulantur naturae [ejus], differre ipsum [et] a Patre inquimus et [a] 310
Spiritu Sancto, et Matre et reliquis hominibus; copulantur autem naturae ejus in
hypostasi (id est, persona), unam hypostasim compositam habentes, secundum
quam differunt a Patre et Spiritu, et Matre et nobis.

288 est²] *Supra*, pars. 44 & 45; pp. 184-185   289 objectum] Cf. pars. 38, 40, 41   297 com-
posito] Cf. Damascene, *DeFideOrth* III, 3; PG 94, 988B-989B; Buytaert, pp. 173-174. 299 his] Cf. pars.
41 & 42   303 etc.] Cf. par. 43   306 *Matre*] *DeFideOrth* III, 3; PG 94, 996A-B; Buytaert, p. 179:
"Scimus enim quemadmodum unam eius hypostasim, ita et naturarum substantialem differentiam
servari. Qualiter autem servabitur differentia, non servatis hiis quae differentiam habent ad invicem ? Differentia enim differentium est differentia." *Ergo*] igitur *Buyt.* 307 *ab*] ad D, ab *Buyt.*
(cf. Philip, *De Incarn*, 2, 11; p. 173)   308 *deitatem*] divinitatem D, deitatem (divinitatem *var.*) *Buyt.* (cf.
Philip, De Incarn, 2, 11; p. 173); *add.* et *Buyt.*   309 *Sancto*] *om. Buyt. humanitatem*] *add.* et *Buyt.*
Matri] *add.* et nobis. Consubstantialis est enim idem, secundum quidem deitatem Patri et Spiritui,
secundum humanitatem autem et matri (*om.* et nobis ... matri *var.*) *Buyt.*   309-310 autem /
ratione] I 83rb D   310 *naturae*] nec D, naturae *Buyt. ejus*] *Buyt., om.* D (cf. Philip, *DeIncarn*, 2, 11;
p. 173)   *et¹*] *Buyt., om.* D & *var. Buyt.* (cf. Philip, *DeIncarn*, 2, 11; p. 173)   *a*] *om.* (a *var.*) *Buyt., om.* D
311 *Sancto*] *om.* (Sancto *var.*) *Buyt.*   *et¹*] a D, et *Buyt.* (cf. Philip, *DeIncarn*, 2, 11; p. 173)   *autem*]
enim (autem *var.*) *Buyt.*   *in*] *om.* (in *var.*) *Buyt.*   313 *differunt*] differt D, differunt *Buyt.* (cf. Philip,
DeIncarn, 2, 11; p. 173); *add.* et *Buyt.*   *et²*] a D, et *Buyt.* (cf. Philip, *loc. cit.*)   *nobis*] *DeFideOrth* III, 3;
PG 94, 996B; Buytaert, pp. 179-180.

55   Item, objicitur: Diversae perfectiones diversorum diversa faciunt perfecta in naturis; ergo eadem ratione in divinis. Ergo Christus erit 315 duo neutraliter.

56   Item, sunt diversae naturae et manent diversae. Ergo potius faciunt diversas compositiones duae naturae quam unam hypostasim compositam.

57   Solutio: Damascenus: *Custodit alterutra natura sui ipsius naturam in-* 320 *transmutabilem. Ideoque et numerantur, et numerus non inducit divisionem. Unus enim est Christus in deitate et humanitate perfectus: numerus enim non divisionis vel unionis causâ aptus natus [est] esse, sed quantitatis numeratorum significativus, sive unitorum sive divisorum: unitorum quidem, quoniam quinquaginta lapides habet unus murus, divisorum autem, quoniam quinquaginta* 325 *lapides sunt et jacent in campo hoc; et unitorum, quoniam duae naturae sunt in carbone, ignis dico et ligni; divisorum autem, quoniam natura ignis alia est a natura ligni. Quemadmodum igitur impossibile est tres hypostases deitatis, etsi unitae sunt ad invicem, unam hypostasim dicere, propterea ut non confusionem et destructionem hypostaseon differentiarum operemur, ita et duas naturas Christi,* 330 *quae secundum hypostasim unitae sunt, impossibile est unam naturam dicere, ut non destructionem et confusionem et inexistentiam operemur .earum differentiarum.*

318 duae naturae quam] quam duae naturae D   320 *Custodit*] add. enim *Buyt.*   natura] om. (natura *var.*) *Buyt.*   naturam] naturalem *Buyt.*, add. proprietatem *Buyt.*   321 *inducit*] introducit *Buyt.*   323 *unionis*] unitionis *Buyt.*   est] *Buyt.*, om. D   325 *unus*] om. *Buyt.*   divisorum] diversorum D, divisorum *Buyt.*   326 *sunt¹*] om. *Buyt.*   et¹] om. *Buyt.*   et ... hoc] in campo et jacent hoc D   unitorum] add. quidem *Buyt.*   327 *divisorum*] diversorum D, divisorum *Buyt.*   327-328 *a ... ligni*] et ligni alia *Buyt.*, add. alio modo uniente et dividente ea, et non numero *Buyt.*   est] om. (est *var.*) *Buyt.*   tres ... deitatis] hypostases deitatis tres D   329 *ad*] om. (ad *var.*) *Buyt.*   330 *differentiarum*] differentiae (differentiarum *var.*) *Buyt.*   331 *est*] om. (est *var.*) *Buyt.*   332-333 *differentiarum*] differentiae (differentiarum *var.*) *Buyt.*; *DeFideOrth* III, 5; PG 94, 1001A-B; Buytaert, pp. 185-186.

THE THEOLOGY OF THE HYPOSTATIC UNION
IN THE
EARLY THIRTEENTH CENTURY

GENERAL CONCLUSION

1. SYNOPSIS

In the summaries and conclusions given at the end of each volume a detailed review has been given of the individual doctrines of William of Auxerre, Alexander of Hales, Hugh of Saint-Cher, and Philip the Chancellor. This final conclusion, therefore, will limit itself to a synoptic view of the common and contrasting elements of their teaching on the main topics of discussion and to the more general results of this study.

In their theology of the Hypostatic Union these four authors present a panorama of the state of this doctrine in the important third and fourth decades of the thirteenth century. In examining their writings on this subject, we find a general homogeneity of thought coupled with many striking contrasts in detail.

The general philosophical outlook of these authors is basically the same. The Augustinian and Boethian traditions combine to form the overall background, but added to this background in varying degrees and at different points are elements from twelfth-century authors, from Pseudo-Denis the Areopagite, and from Aristotelian and Arabic philosophy. The philosophy of being of these four theologians is a type of essentialism that views the metaphysical perfection of a thing in terms of its form, essence, or *quo est*; in a creature the various forms or essential perfections coalesce to constitute the concrete subject or *quod est*, so that the metaphysical structure of a being often seems to correspond to the logical pattern of genus, species, difference, properties, and accidents. With varying degrees of explicitness the different authors think of essential being as the object of metaphysics, which for them is aided by and patterned on logic, whereas they put existential being, or rather the mere fact of existence, on the level of nature along with matter and physical form; this view seems present in all our authors, but is especially evident in certain statements of Philip the Chancellor. Thus the individual is regularly defined as a collection of properties or accidents, and the person is usually distinguished from the individual by the addition of a new characteristic of the same logico-metaphysical order. Alexander of Hales and Philip the Chancellor, however, also teach a prior and more fundamental type of in-dividuation, and William of Auxerre hints at the same thing.

This Boethian metaphysics, whose remarkable endurance in this period is an important conclusion arising from the present study, is penetrated in varying degrees by the philosophical concepts coming from the contact of the West with the "new" Aristotle and with Arabic philosophy. Here to some extent the homogeneity of outlook breaks down, and the four authors are seen to divide into two pairs. William of Auxerre and Hugh of Saint-Cher, although they accept various elements of the new thought, remain somewhat more conservative in their use of philosophers such as Aristotle and Avicenna. In comparison with predecessors such as Praepositinus or Stephen Langton they do indeed move toward a more widespread use of these new philosophical concepts, especially in the realm of the causes and of the virtues, but by comparison with Alexander of Hales and Philip the Chancellor they appear more closely attached to the methods of these immediate predecessors. Thus the use of speculative grammar and dialectical arguments is more pronounced in their method than in that of Alexander or Philip, even though it plays a less prominent role than in their predecessors.

Alexander of Hales and Philip the Chancellor, on the other hand, appear much more open to the new ideas. They know Aristotle and the Arabian authors better than William or Hugh do; they quote Aristotle more frequently, and refer explicitly or implicitly to his *Physics* and *Metaphysics* more often than do William or Hugh, who seem to have at best a slight acquaintance with these works. Both Alexander and Philip evidence a certain intellectual rigor and critical faculty, a more profound penetration of the concepts they use, little resort to speculative grammar as a means of solving problems, a more constant awareness of the degrees or levels of being extending from the lower creatures to God and consequently a greater recourse to proportionality or analogy in their analyses. In these respects Alexander of Hales stands out as the innovator, whereas Philip, who follows Alexander but also manifests remarkable originality, often develops the same material more completely and more explicitly. Among the philosophical ideas emphasized more strongly by Alexander and Philip than by William or Hugh are the transcendental properties of being, various potency-act relationships, Aristotelian concepts of nature and of unity, and the analogical structure of reality. Thus it seems that Alexander and Philip, who were so influential in founding the Franciscan school of philosophy and theology, were also the ones most open to the influence of the newer philosophical movements; William of Auxerre, who strongly influenced the Dominicans, and Hugh of Saint-Cher, one of the earliest Dominican masters, followed a more conservative path: this difference may be partly explained by the relatively earlier date of William's *Summa Aurea* and by Hugh's tendency to follow and expose the work of his predecessors rather than, with important exceptions, to strike out in new directions.

In their theology of the Hypostatic Union these authors seldom employ Scripture or the Fathers at any length. St. Augustine continues to dominate the scene, and most other patristic texts are those found in the *Sentences* and the *Collectanea* of Peter Lombard or in the *Glossa Ordinaria*. One important exception, however, is St. John Damascene, who exercises a beneficial influence on all these authors, but especially on Alexander of Hales and Philip the Chancellor; in the questions of the latter the quotations from Damascene's *De Fide Orthodoxa* are particularly abundant and lengthy. In the use of patristic sources and writings of earlier theologians Alexander of Hales once again surpasses the rest: of his more immediate predecessors, St. Anselm, St. Bernard, Richard of Saint-Victor, and Alan of Lille appear more frequently in his writings than in those of the other three. As for the discussion of heresies or for traditional statements of Catholic faith concerning the Incarnation, Alexander of Hales and Hugh of Saint-Cher present more texts: this reflects the form of their writings, works orientated to the *Sentences* of Peter Lombard, where such discussions and statements are fairly frequent; William and Philip, on the other hand, organize their own treatises, so that they are not compelled by a text in front of them to engage in such discussions.

Each author teaches that the Incarnation is a mystery of faith transcending reason. William of Auxerre brings this out most clearly in his treatise on free will, Philip in his analysis of the virtue of faith. William, however, also makes some important statements on the matter in his treatise on the Incarnation; there, applying an original and important intuition that helped theology to come to view itself as a science, he compares the Incarnation as a mystery of faith to the indemonstrable first principles of a natural science.

Alexander of Hales shows the influence of twelfth-century theologians by developing interesting arguments of fittingness for the Incarnation; neither Hugh nor Philip do so, and William of Auxerre's chief concern with such arguments is to oppose them to the extent that they claim to prove apodictically the necessity of the Incarnation. Alexander's arguments reveal his vision of the order and symmetry of the cosmos; they are also, along with similar arguments in Robert Grosseteste, early examples of the conviction that even without the redeeming passion and death of Christ, the Incarnation would have been most fitting and useful: although Alexander does not say explicitly that the Incarnation would have taken place in such circumstances, the force of his arguments tends in that direction.

Alexander of Hales also surpasses the rest in his defence of the rational possibility of the Incarnation against arguments seeking to prove its impossibility. Philip the Chancellor has similar arguments, but they are not developed so extensively as in Alexander: Philip's questions on this topic may precede the questions of Alexander. By comparison with these two, William and Hugh have practically nothing on this topic. Alexander and Philip also take the lead in the comparison of angelic and human nature as to their suitability for being assumed in the Incarnation. They compare the two natures as likenesses of God and as possible subjects of redemption. At this stage Philip advances beyond Alexander through one of his most penetrating analyses, comparing personal distinction in angels and men by applying the concepts of potency and act to their being and becoming.

With respect to the three opinions on the Hypostatic Union, the evolution of their interpretation observable in late twelfth-century authors continues and, in fact, is systematized and permanently fixed for subsequent authors by William of Auxerre, Alexander of Hales, and Hugh of Saint-Cher; Philip the Chancellor, at least in his extant writings, has little on the subject. William of Auxerre constantly reduces the three opinions to a dispute about the unity or duality of Christ, and both Alexander and Hugh follow him in this. According to William, because the third opinion wishes to maintain that Christ is one, it rejects a human *aliquid* in Christ; the first opinion says that Christ is two, so that it maintains that there is a twofold supposition or a duality of subjects in Christ, and rejects the communication of properties or idioms; the second opinion maintains that Christ is both *aliquid* as a man and yet is one, so that it teaches a unity of supposition and subject in Christ as well as the communication of properties or idioms. The other three authors join William in rejecting the third opinion as a heresy making the humanity of Christ an accident and the union of natures an accidental union. What is most significant, however, is that by stating the opinions in terms of unity or duality, William, Alexander, and Hugh set forth the first opinion in such sharply dualistic terms that it was rendered more patently objectionable than it might otherwise have been. It is, indeed, their very analysis and critique of the first opinion in terms of a duality in Christ that appear to have led to the universal abandonment of the first opinion in the thirteenth century. In this development the influential teachers, William, Alexander, Hugh, and perhaps Philip, seem to have played the decisive role, so that the unanimity of the great doctors of the middle of the century is to be explained largely by the intervention of the authors we have studied and the direction they gave to the interpretation of the opinions. For our authors both the dualistic position of the first opinion and its doctrine of the *assumptus homo* related to this duality are viewed as implying an accidental union in Christ; hence their insistence that it was not a man but a human nature that was assumed; hence, too, their insistence that Christ is one rather than two or several.

Within this general unanimity concerning the opinions subtle differences of emphasis appear in our four authors. William of Auxerre's schematization of the opinions and his stress on the unity-duality question lead him to neglect certain other aspects of the opinions that both Alexander and Hugh preserve. Here the literary form chosen by the authors is again a probable influence: whereas William organizes his own treatise on the Incarnation, Alexander and Hugh are forced, by commenting on the *Sentences* of Peter Lombard, to a closer consideration of his original statement of the opinions. But because they are influenced by William of Auxerre, they also interject the unity-duality question into their presentation of the opinions.

Alexander of Hales shows his usual philosophical interest by analyzing the three opinions according to the three degrees of natural, rational, and moral being that he constantly discerns in reality; he also interprets the third opinion as an expression of Nominalist philosophy. Even while rejecting the first and third opinions, Alexander is more sympathetic to certain of their intuitions than are William or Hugh; he tries to find the element of truth contained in these opinions. Hugh of Saint-Cher stresses the duality of subject taught by the first opinion and is somewhat more concerned than the rest about the priority by nature of its "assumed man." The lack of information about Philip the Chancellor's analysis of the opinions may simply mean that we do not possess all the questions that he discussed concerning the Incarnation; in those we do possess Philip links the *non-est-aliquid* doctrine, which for him touches on matters of faith, with an accidental union: he rejects the one and the other. Because Philip teaches the unity of Christ and the doctrine of the "composed hypostasis" characteristic of the second opinion, he evidently holds the same opinion as the other authors.

The rejection of the first and third opinions, interpreted in the way described above, constitutes the main opposition of these four theologians to an accidental union in Christ. They are equally opposed to a union of the two natures in which one new nature becomes common to or is produced from the divine and human natures, or in which the human nature becomes so identified with the divine nature that human properties belong to the divine nature. The perfection, simplicity, and impassibility of the divine nature are given as basic reasons why such a union is impossible. In this question the second redaction of Alexander's *Glossa* and the analysis by Philip the Chancellor present the most interesting arguments, including one that rejects any attempt to explain the union by a multiplication of entities.

The union of the natures, being neither accidental nor in one nature, is a union of two distinct natures in the person of the Son: all our authors defend this position by attempting to show theologically how the human nature of Christ can be complete as an individual substantial nature and yet lack human personality, thereby making possible the second person's assumption of this individual nature. William of Auxerre's systematization of the three distinctions that he finds necessary for personality, namely, the distinctions of singularity, incommunicability, and dignity, is utilized by the other authors as well as William himself to explain the union in Christ. The human nature of Christ, having both singularity and incommunicability (which makes it whole as a nature rather than a part of a nature), is an individual substantial nature; since, however, it lacks the distinction of dignity, it is not a human person. Because the human nature is assumed by the Son of God, it lacks that perseity and completeness of being which would make it a person; according to William and Hugh, the nobler "form" of the Son replaces it. Three of the authors fail to state explicitly the extent to which the crucial property of dignity is or is not a special perfection: William of Auxerre simply links it with perseity in being; Alexander views it as something of the moral order, but also associates it with incommunicable being; Philip the Chancellor describes it in terms of perseity, but seems to stress the concrete existential reality of the person more than the others do. Hugh of Saint-Cher, however, explicitly states that the perfection of personality is a "privation," that is, the fact of not being assumed by a nobler being. From certain discussions in William of Auxerre and in the *Glossa* of Alexander of Hales, especially in its second redaction, it could be inferred that in both cases the distinction of dignity is looked upon in this negative fashion: thus the second redaction of the *Glossa* maintains, as William of Auxerre implies and Hugh of Saint-Cher teaches explicitly, that if the union were dissolved, the individual human nature of Christ would at once be a human person without the addition of any positive perfection.

Both redactions of the *Glossa* of Alexander of Hales speak of a hypostasis of human nature, which seems to be distinct from the divine person. This is not meant to be a concrete subject or supposit existing distinctly from the divine person, such as the first opinion was held to teach, but rather a logical individual, an entity of the logical order, a name of second intention.

Our authors link their position on the Hypostatic Union with the second opinion, as they understand it, not only by their use of a philosophy of subject and form or of *quod* and *quo* that is implicit in the doctrine of individuation and personality already referred to, but also by their acceptance of the concept of Christ as a "composed hypostasis." This expression, coming from St. John Damascene, expresses a characteristic teaching of the second opinion, one that brings out forcefully for these theologians the physical reality of the union in Christ. William of Auxerre, it is true, does not use the term, but he seems to align himself with this position by his discussion of parts with respect to Christ, whom he sometimes calls a whole in relation to either the two natures in him or to the parts of human nature; in speaking of parts William, of course, rejects any composition in the divine nature or person. For Hugh of Saint-Cher the word "composed" expresses solely the composition of the *human nature*, whereas the term "composed hypostasis" refers to the union of the divine person to this composed human nature. For Alexander of Hales and Philip the Chancellor, however, the expression "composed hypostasis" denotes the *divine person* or *hypostasis* as composed by being a person or hypostasis of two natures: he exists in two natures. Philip the Chancellor attaches great importance to this concept, making it his central theme in exposing the Hypostatic Union. He even prefers to say that the union took place in hypostasis rather than in person. According to Philip the hypostasis is a medium between the divine person and the human individual, a medium identified with each of these under different aspects; thus in the union, he teaches, the divine hypostasis or person becomes a hypostasis or person of human nature in that he is qualified by the human nature united to him; when the divine hypostasis or person becomes a hypostasis or person of human nature, he is then a "composed hypostasis." All these authors deny a composition of the person from the natures as from parts; they differ as to whether one should speak of parts in Christ.

As has been said, the first opinion is universally rejected because of its denial of the unity of Christ. Three of our authors discuss the theological explanation of Christ's unity at considerable length; Philip the Chancellor alone gives it less attention, both because he presents little material on the opinions and also because he stresses the "composed hypostasis" as his main concept in analyzing the mystery. For all four authors the basic reason for Christ's unity is the unity of person or hypostasis or subject or *quod est* or supposit: the authors use now one, now the other of these terms, but in every case the principle they invoke states that Christ is numbered according to person or hypostasis, etc., rather than according to nature. Here the basically Boethian metaphysics is again strongly influential.

As for the problem of apparent duality in Christ raised by the requirement to speak of a human *aliquid* in him along with the divine *aliquid*, various solutions are proposed. William of Auxerre applies to this problem the idea, used by earlier authors in other contexts, that the human nature is quasi-accidental to the divine nature or person so that, like all accidents, the human *aliquid* is not numbered with the divine nature or person so as to make Christ two. This argument finds no echo in the two redactions of Alexander's *Glossa* when they deal with this problem; Hugh of Saint-Cher relegates it to a secondary place among his solutions of this question. Alexander applies to this problem Aristotle's concept of the one as undivided being. While repeating this, the second redaction of his *Glossa* adds further important arguments; these stress the unity in concrete physical being of the two distinct natures or essences in Christ: Christ should be said to be *of* two substances or natures, but he *is* one; although the two essences or substances as such are distinct in him, they are not divided in reality, but are united to make Christ one being.

This same concept reappears in an important and apparently quite original analysis made by Hugh of Saint-Cher. Although Hugh uses William of Auxerre's concept of quasi-accidentality as one solution of this problem, he quite evidently prefers to say that the human *essentia* or *esse* in Christ is identical with the divine *essentia* or *esse*: by this terminology Hugh does not teach any destruction of the distinction of natures, but rather Christ's unity in being or reality in his two natures. As one of the first to use the term *esse* in this question of Christ's unity or duality, he may have influenced the terminology if not the theology of later discussions, which asked not only whether Christ is one or two, but whether he is one or two in *esse*.

An important contribution made by these theologians to the subsequent theology of the Hypostatic Union is their gradual clarification of the manner in which the two natures stand with respect to one another in the union; this question is closely linked with the explanation of how God does not change in the union and of how only one divine person can become incarnate. William of Auxerre says little concerning the problem of change, and speaks frequently of the union simply as an association of the natures in the person of the Son. In passing, however, he mentions the concept of relation; this relation he apparently locates in both God and the human nature as subjects. More penetrating in their analyses are the second redaction of Alexander's *Glossa* and his *Quaestiones*: the same is true of Hugh of Saint-Cher and Philip the Chancellor. They all reject a change in God and maintain that only the human nature is properly the subject of any change in the union and so of the created relation by which the two natures are compared to one another. Alexander and Philip teach that we may think of and predicate a relation in God, but, they say, this is to be understood only as a mental or logical relation imposed by our minds; the real and created relation is in the human nature. In these analyses Philip applies the concepts of potency and act as an aid to his solution.

The greater interest shown by Alexander and Philip in the new philosophical currents helps to explain why they introduce two questions that fail to occupy the attention of William of Auxerre or Hugh of Saint-Cher. These are the questions how the Hypostatic Union is to be classified among the categories of unity, and how it compares in dignity and greatness with other types of union. The categories of unity analyzed by Aristotle in his *Metaphysics* are referred to explicitly in the first of these investigations; they are probably the occasion of the whole question. Both Alexander and Philip maintain that the Hypostatic Union transcends all the categories of unity listed by Aristotle; Philip, however, puts its unity in hypostasis in the category of *per se* unity by giving the latter an extended, analogical sense.

The comparison of this union with other types of union in order to see which is the greatest brings out the preeminence of the Hypostatic Union with respect to all created unions. Alexander stresses the notions of potency and act and also the simplicity of God in order to assert the superiority and inseparability of the Hypostatic Union. However, he places the Hypostatic Union below the unity in nature of the three persons of the Trinity; Philip agrees with him in this comparison, except when the unions are looked at from the viewpoint of hypostasis — then, he says, the union in Christ is greater than that in the Trinity.

Another major contribution of these four authors to the development of the theology of the Hypostatic Union is found in the elaboration and enrichment they give to the concept of the grace of union. They appear to be the first to state clearly that the grace of union is not only the divine will or operation gratuitously effecting the union, but also the personal union itself, considered as a gift or grace flowing from the divine will and operation. For all these theologians the grace of union, considered as the reality itself conferred, is different from both the grace of adoption found in ordinary man and from the sanctifying grace in the soul of Christ himself. Alexander of Hales explores certain aspects in greater detail: the grace of union, he maintains, is in some respects infinite; it is supreme among all graces of men and angels, beyond the other graces of Christ himself; it raises Christ above all creatures, although it does not make him, as man, equal to God; it is one reason for the inseparability of the union.

Both the second redaction of the *Glossa* and Philip the Chancellor agree that the grace of union, although not a medium or new entity standing between the human and divine nature, is or implies some kind of disposition in the human nature ennobling it and disposing it for immediate union to the divine nature. William of Auxerre does not mention this aspect of the question. Hugh of Saint-Cher indicates that he does not consider the grace of union a medium; he seems to imply as well that it is not a disposition in the nature. Philip the Chancellor's discussion of this aspect of the grace of union is especially noteworthy for its amplitude; for him the dispositions it involves appear to belong to the orders both of natural qualities and of supernatural gifts. All four authors deduce certain other prerogatives of Christ either directly from the grace of union or from the equivalent fact that his human nature is united to the divine nature in a personal union.

With respect to the divine participant in the union, only Alexander of Hales refuses to say that the divine nature is *incarnate*: his reason is that the term "divine nature" designates no person or subject for the Incarnation. The other three authors accept such a statement, but interpret it in various ways; all ensure the independence of the divine nature with respect to human properties: thus the divine nature's being incarnate differs from the Son's being incarnate, for in his case human properties are properly predicated of him. Alexander joins the others in accepting propositions saying that the divine nature is *united* or is *united to flesh*. With respect to these and similar propositions Hugh of Saint-Cher prefers William of Auvergne to William of Auxerre as a guide, seeing in the different predicates designations of various relations on the side of the human nature with respect to the divine nature. William of Auxerre speaks simply of the association of the natures. Philip the Chancellor distinguishes being incarnate from being united: the former is the process by which the union is achieved, the latter the accomplished union itself. In his *Quaestiones* Alexander of Hales, alone among these authors, compares the divine nature and the divine person as to unitability: it belongs primarily to the nature to be united, he holds, because it is the nature that is said to be united in the person; he adds, of course, that the person too is united.

When the divine nature and person are considered according to their active role in the Incarnation, Alexander of Hales again separates himself from the other three authors with respect to the term "assume." He says that because "to assume" implies that the terminus of the act of assuming is the same as the subject of that act, neither the divine nature nor the other persons but only the Son can be said to assume the human nature. For their part, William, Hugh, and Philip maintain that the divine nature can be said to assume human nature by taking that nature into union with itself in the person of the Son. They all go on to point out, however, that the Son assumes human nature in a more proper and complete sense than do the divine nature or the other persons acting in common: only the Son takes the human nature into himself in such a way that it is his and that its properties and attributes are his. Thus their more specialized, more proper use of the term "assume" corresponds to the only meaning that Alexander of Hales recognizes for it. With respect to the act of uniting, Alexander of Hales agrees with William, Hugh, and Philip that the divine nature *unites* the human nature: this term expresses the efficient activity involved in the Incarnation, which proceeds from the divine nature, so that the verb "unites" can be predicated of it. In this period, then, we see a gradual clarification of terminology taking place with respect to the notions of assumption and union; these advances were to be useful for subsequent theologians.

In this matter of the divine nature's uniting the human nature, Alexander of Hales and Philip the Chancellor add certain specialized conclusions as a result of questions they alone consider. For Alexander, it is the divine *nature* rather than the divine essence that most properly unites, in that to unite, being an activity, is more properly related to the order of operation connected with the term "nature" than to the order of being expressed by the term "essence". Philip, comparing the divine *nature* and the divine *person* as to which is the most proper subject of the act of uniting, concludes that because this activity is common to the three persons and so proceeds from the nature, the divine nature is more properly the subject of the act of uniting than the divine person.

The principles established in the discussions of assumption and union provide our authors with the means of showing how only one divine person can become incarnate. All three persons act in common to effect the union, they teach, but only the Son, distinct from the Father and Holy Spirit, is terminus of the act of uniting. In this question Alexander of Hales' analysis is less consistent than that of the others. After merely hinting at the solution just summarized, he argues as if only the second person has the property of being able to be united; thus, although he is most insistent on the strictly reflexive use of the term "assume," he fails to draw out the implications of his own position in this particular question.

With respect to the divine participant in the union Alexander characteristically introduces an analysis that none of the others mention. He assumes as a hypothesis that we may abstract from the three persons of the Trinity and consider the divine being without the personal properties; in such a case, he asks, would a union of the two natures be possible? If only the two natures remained, he replies, they could not be united without the destruction of one or both; however, he adds, since even without the Trinitarian persons there would still be a unique hypostasis in God, the union could take place in this hypostasis.

As to the nature assumed by the Son of God, in addition to the points previously mentioned our authors discuss the question whether Christ is as truly a man as other men are. William of Auxerre and Hugh of Saint-Cher answer in the affirmative, but add that in Christ human nature differs in condition from that in ordinary men: in Christ, William says, human nature does not comprise his whole being; in Christ, Hugh says, human nature does not unite with the other nature to form one nature, whereas in other men the various "natures" in them, that is, body and soul, unite to form one nature. Redaction L of the *Glossa* of Alexander introduces no such qualifications: as man, it teaches, Christ belongs to the common species "man," understanding this univocally of Christ and other men. Although Philip the Chancellor does not discuss this question, by certain statements he shows he would agree that Christ is as truly a man as is any man. William and Hugh reinforce their conclusions by declaring that if the union in Christ were dissolved, the same man would exist after the union as existed before, with no alteration being needed in the transition from a united human nature to an ordinary man.

In discussing various names or terms applied to Christ, William, Alexander, and Hugh indicate that certain terms have some kind of double supposition whereby they stand for both the divine person and the individual man; Philip does not seem to hold such a position, but speaks only of a unique supposition for terms applied to Christ. Among the first three authors, only Hugh states explicitly the difference between this position and that of the first opinion: for the first opinion, he says, the name "Jesus" — one of those which for him has a twofold supposition — stands only for the individual human in Christ; Hugh, however, maintains that it also stands for the divine person in an accidental or secondary sense. William of Auxerre's use of the expression "*quasi*-twofold supposition" undoubtedly means the same thing. These authors do not intend to teach the first opinion; they are struggling with methods of predication, especially in the face of perplexing dialectical problems put to them by their opponents.

All four of these authors expressly teach the union of body and soul to each other in Christ as well as the union of each to the divine nature. Only Alexander of Hales adds reasons, related to man's need for complete redemption, why all the parts of human nature should be assumed. All four authors also teach that the union of body and soul to each other has a certain priority by nature over the union of each to the Divinity: William, Alexander, and Hugh state that this priority is necessary in order that the Son of God be truly a man and that human properties truly belong to him. Alexander of Hales also relates this mutual union of body and soul to the Redemption: by reason of it, he says, Christ, although sinless, was ordered to the sinful race of Adam and so could make fitting satisfaction on its behalf. Alexander also discusses the role of the Divinity and the soul in giving life to the body: in the *Glossa* he denies that the Divinity gives physical life, this being the function of the soul; in the *Quaestiones*, although he assigns to the Divinity some function of giving life to the body, his statements seem to refer to the conservation and concursus of God in governing and disposing the soul and body of Christ. Both Alexander and Philip teach that among the various unions in Christ the union of the soul to the Divinity is first in dignity; the other unions are ordered to this union. At this point Hugh of Saint-Cher introduces a description of the third opinion in which he says it taught that the body and soul were not united at any time in Christ; this inaccuracy in reporting the original teaching of the third opinion was to be repeated by subsequent authors of the thirteenth century and by modern authors as well.

An important patristic theme spoke of the soul as medium of union for the body and the Divinity. William of Auxerre seems to have passed over this topic; Alexander, Hugh, and Philip all agree that the soul's role as medium is not that of a physical cause linking or joining the divine nature and the body: hence in the three days of Christ's death, when his soul and body were separated from each other, the body remained united to the Divinity. Each author explains the soul's role as medium in a similar, yet slightly different, fashion. Alexander speaks of both soul and spirit as media according to nature or dignity, that is, as natures standing in the scale of being between the purely spiritual divine being and the entirely material body; Hugh calls the soul a "medium of assimilation" or "likeness" because it resembles each of the extremes more than either extreme resembles the other; Philip speaks of the soul as a medium of fittingness: the grace of union disposes the soul of Christ for its union with the Divinity, and since this soul is united, the body to which it happens to be joined will also be united to the Divinity. But the physical union of soul and body with one another is only incidental to the soul's role as medium; it is the soul's fittingness for union that makes it principally a medium.

The expression "communication of properties" seems to owe its introduction into theology to Alexander of Hales, who uses it several times. Although Alexander does not use the corresponding expression "communication of idioms," he does say that in Christ "the idioms are common," and he also interchanges the terms "idiom" and "property"; thus he is the immediate forerunner of those who first used the latter expression. Since all four of our authors adhere to the second opinion as they understand it, they teach that properties of the individual man in Christ may be predicated of the Son of God and that properties of the Son of God may be predicated of the individual man; in this they oppose the first opinion, which, they say, taught that there were two supposits in Christ and that such communication of properties or idioms is invalid unless it is merely figurative. However, William, Alexander, and Hugh qualify their position to some extent by saying that certain concrete terms such as *iste homo, iste, Filius Dei*, and *Jesus* have a twofold supposition according to which they stand for both the divine person and the individual man. The authors predicate certain properties only according to one or the other of these suppositions. This qualification of their doctrine, which seems to weaken their position on the unity of supposit in Christ and on the communication of properties resulting therefrom, may, however, represent an attempt on their part to express the nature according to which the attribution in question takes place. Alexander of Hales introduces a further and rather curious qualification. He maintains that properties belonging to the human nature of Christ by reason of created grace are predicated of the individual man in Christ rather than of the Son of God; again, however, there are indications in the texts that in saying this he means that the phrase "according to human nature" must be added when such properties are predicated of the Son of God.

Concerning the procedure to be followed in the communication of properties, Hugh of Saint-Cher gives the most precise account of the rules used by the two opinions and formulates certain grammatical rules to guide the procedure: this is in keeping with Hugh's greater emphasis on grammatical and dialectical method. Philip the Chancellor, who speaks only of unity of supposition when referring to predication concerning Christ, formulates the rule that if only the human nature and not the concrete individual man is included in the supposition of a term, that term may not be predicated of the Son of God; but, he adds, if a term stands for the concrete individual man, it may be predicated of the Son of God and vice versa. This statement seems to represent a clarification and advance in the practice of the communication of idioms. Later authors such as St. Thomas Aquinas would say that abstract terms such as rationality or mortality, which refer to the humanity of Christ and do not stand for the hypostasis in that nature, cannot be predicated of the Son of God;[1] this seems to be the intent of Philip's remarks, which introduce a distinction not adverted to by the other authors.

2. EVALUATION

The preceding synopsis should indicate the interest and importance of the doctrine of William of Auxerre, Alexander of Hales, Hugh of Saint-Cher, and Philip the Chancellor both for its own sake and for the development of the theology of the Hypostatic Union in the thirteenth century. Not only do these authors transmit the acquisitions of previous generations of theologians, at times with modifications that are themselves worthy of note, but they also introduce new methods of inquiry, present different ways of looking at the basic problems of the Hypostatic Union (particularly with respect to the three opinions), add new topics of discussion, give original solutions to certain problems, and clarify terminology in various areas. It is beyond our purpose to trace the later influence of these authors: one of the results of the present study will be to make more evident the extent to which the analyses of subsequent authors are original and how much they inherit from the theologians we have studied. Coming from a study of the texts of these four theologians to even a cursory reading of the *Summa Fratris Alexandri*, the *Commentary* of Richard Fishacre, the *Summae* or *Com-*

---

1 *Summa Theologiae* III, q. 16, a. 5c.

mentaries of St. Albert, St. Bonaventure, and St. Thomas, to name but a few, one realizes how basic a structure for this tract, how uniform an outlook concerning the three fundamental opinions on the Hypostatic Union, how many particular arguments and solutions these later authors inherited, either directly or at most through one or two intermediaries, from William of Auxerre, Alexander of Hales, Hugh of Saint-Cher, and Philip the Chancellor. The same world is present, the same outlook, too, only brought to fuller development. To pass from our authors to the great theologians of the following generation is like first examining a garden in its springtime promise and then later revisiting the same spot at its midsummer maturity and again seeing the same plants and flowers, but now in full bloom. Although the great doctors of the middle of the thirteenth century made important and decisive contributions, in doing so they did not begin from a previous intellectual vacuum, but rather built on, adapted, and perfected the important preparatory work of these earlier men.

The preceding analyses and summaries have brought out the common elements and the individual differences among the four authors we have studied. In the investigation of the Hypostatic Union Alexander of Hales unquestionably holds front rank among them for the extent and originality of his discussions, whether in dealing with the standard problems of this tract of theology, in proposing new questions for inquiry, or in solving the various questions raised by himself or others. Undoubtedly, however, Alexander profited greatly from William of Auxerre's new work, which preceded his and which continued its own influence well into the thirteenth century, particularly among the Dominican theologians. Thus the following remark, made by the editors of Alexander of Hales' *Quaestiones* about both Alexander and William of Auxerre, is not exaggerated: "Indeed, these two can perhaps deservedly be considered the true creators or originators of 'High Scholasticism,' especially Alexander, who more than others reveals himself a bold and felicitous innovator."[2]

By the wide use made of Hugh of Saint-Cher's clearer and more extensive, if less original, treatise, the influence of William of Auxerre (and of William of Auvergne on a few individual points) was furthered; moreover, as has been indicated, Hugh himself makes a number of distinctive contributions of his own in this tract. Philip the Chancellor, some of whose material on the Hypostatic Union seems to have passed

---

2 *QuaestAlex*, Prologus, p. 6*.

into or directly influenced the compilation known as the *Summa Fratris Alexandri*, shows an affinity with Alexander of Hales in method, outlook, and profundity of thought. It remains uncertain whether his questions on the Hypostatic Union precede or follow the questions of Alexander on this topic; in any case, when the two sets of questions deal with the same topics, Philip reveals an independence and originality that serves to restore some of the luster taken from his reputation by the discovery of his extensive copying from Alexander's *Glossa* for certain parts of his *Summa de Bono*.

At various points in this study, particularly in the conclusions to the individual volumes, questions have been raised concerning the adequacy of the theology of the Hypostatic Union presented by these authors. Beyond various details that would be rectified and clarified subsequently by further analysis and discussion, the most basic question concerns the philosophy of essence and form used by these theologians, and in particular its consequences for their doctrines of individuation and personality as applied to the Hypostatic Union. If, when the individual is viewed as a collection of forms or formal perfections, personality is said to be constituted by a final form added to other forms, in such an essentialist philosophy this form or perfection would seem to belong to the order of the essence (or at least to be a property necessarily flowing from the essence), or else it would seem to be an accident. Since the latter alternative would be generally unacceptable, one would be left with the former. But then it is difficult to see how the lack of human personality in Christ would not diminish the perfection of his human essence or nature by taking from it something that should be there. Our authors may have sensed this dilemma; this may explain why they frequently indicate or even state expressly, as Hugh of Saint-Cher does, that personality is simply a "privation", the negation of assumption by a higher being: the perseity linked with the distinction of dignity would then simply be the perfection of an integral human nature with the added qualification, purely negative in character, that it has not been assumed by a nobler being.

If this is the case, one might ask how such a doctrine contributes to that positive, albeit partial and analogical, understanding of the mystery of the Hypostatic Union that is legitimately accessible to reason when, "enlightened by faith, it seeks earnestly, devoutly, and moderately" to attain "by God's gift some understanding of the mysteries ..."[3] Such a

---

3 First Vatican Council, Sessio III, *Constitutio dogmatica de fide catholica*, c. 4; in H. Denzinger and A. Schönmetzer, *Enchiridion Symbolorum ...*, 34th ed. (Barcelona 1967) no. 3016: "Ac ratio quidem, fide

doctrine can and in these theologians did render good service in a negative fashion, that is, by showing it is not intrinsically impossible to have a perfect human nature united to a divine person without there being a human person present; it seems, however, to make the union a sort of juxtaposition of the two natures, a juxtaposition effected by the divine will but without there being in the constituted union itself a positive principle in the order of being causing the union to be physical or substantial.

To see in some obscure way how, positively, there can be such a principle supplied by the divine person, in no way detracting from the perfection of human nature as such, it appears necessary to be aware of the real distinction between essence and the act of existing and to see both as intrinsic principles of being itself. With this distinction in mind, it becomes easier to attain some grasp of how a human nature, complete and perfect in the order of nature, can, by being without its own intrinsic perfection of human existence, lack human personality without being impoverished in its human nature, and at the same time find in the divine personal being the positive principle of union that makes the joining of the two natures a physical or substantial reality. In this study it has been suggested that in some instances these theologians, in their attempts to explain human individuality and personality, grope beyond the order of essence toward the concrete order of *physical* existence, without, to be sure, seeing in the act of existing a positive and intrinsic *metaphysical* principle of being.[4] If our interpretation is correct, they were perhaps already vaguely aware of the inadequacy of a philosophy of essence and form as a tool for investigating the mystery of the Hypostatic Union. Perhaps, too, their groping and the problems they raised may have focused attention on the issue of existence and contributed to later and, in our opinion, happy developments in this respect.

---

illustrata, cum sedulo, pie et sobrie quaerit, aliquam Deo dante mysteriorum intelligentiam eamque fructuosissimam assequitur tum ex eorum, quae naturaliter cognoscit, analogia, tum e mysteriorum nexu inter se et cum fine hominis ultimo ..."

4 A perhaps too hasty reading of our third volume, together with a neglect of what had been clearly stated in the first two volumes and was referred to in the third, led two reviewers of the third volume to think we were asserting that Hugh of Saint-Cher had achieved this metaphysical advance. To avoid further misunderstandings, let us say that this was neither our intention nor our statement: we were speaking on the one hand of existence on the *physical* and not on the *metaphysical* level, while suggesting that attention might have been thereby focused on existence without explicit exploitation of its deeper possibilities; we were speaking on the other hand of the *terminology* of *esse* in the question of the unity of Christ and not of the *metaphysics* of *esse*.

It is beyond the scope of this series of historical studies, though not beyond our intention in undertaking it, to enter into current debates about the theology of the Hypostatic Union. It might at least be said here, however, that many of the current criticisms made against the theology that developed on the basis of the Chalcedonian pronouncements proceed from authors who, like the theologians we have studied, think of it from an essentialist viewpoint. Using such a viewpoint in their analysis, they soon run into the very difficulties experienced by the theologians we have studied or that we have found in them. But, in our opinion, a good many of these criticisms, justified with respect to these early thirteenth-century theologians (and others of later times), are beside the point if one is able to grasp the profound revolution introduced into the theology of the Hypostatic Union by Thomas Aquinas' penetration into the properly metaphysical value of the act of existing and his application of it to the theology of Christ.[5]

Such considerations, it is acknowledged, arise from a doctrine that was to be developed only in times after the authors we have studied. One cannot expect a single generation of theologians to meet and solve every problem. As we have indicated, William of Auxerre, Alexander of Hales, Hugh of Saint-Cher, and Philip the Chancellor made important contributions to the transmission and development of the theology of the Hypostatic Union, and, by forming a strong link in the chain of successive generations of theologians, merit the study and recognition we have sought to give them here.

---

5 These remarks are intended as a corrective of shallow and unfounded criticisms of the more traditional theology. They are not meant to indicate opposition to legitimate developments based on a solid hermeneutic, and this not only in theology but even in any possible future dogmatic formulation. Our sympathy with and even enthusiasm for such development can be seen from our article: "The Hermeneutic of Roman Catholic Dogmatic Statements," *SR: Studies in Religion/Sciences Religieuses* 2 (Toronto 1972) 157-175. For a profound discussion of the contemporary hermeneutical problem in relation to Chalcedon see Alois Grillmeier, "Die altkirchliche Christologie und die moderne Hermeneutik," *Theologische Bericht* 1 (1972) 69-169 (a copy of which was graciously sent to me by the distinguished author).

BIBLIOGRAPHY

I. Manuscript Sources

Bruges. Ville 236.
Douai. Ville 434. 2 vols.
Florence. Bibl. Laurenziana, Plut. 36, dext. 4.
London. British Museum Royal 9. E. XIV.
Paris. Bibl. Nat. *Lat.* 3146; 15,749; 16,387.
Padua. Bibl. Antoniana, Scaf. VIII°, Cod. 56; Scaf. X°, Cod. 214.
Pisa. Bibl. Seminarii S. Catharinae 143.
Toulouse. Ville 192.
Tours. Ville 142.
Vatican. Lat. 7669.

II. Published Sources

A. *Primary Sources*

Sources quoted by Philip the Chancellor or referred to in the edition but not otherwise used are not included. These may be found in the index.

Alan of Lille. *Theologicae Regulae.* In PL 210, 617B-684C.

Alexander of Hales. *Glossa in Quatuor Libros Sententiarum Petri Lombardi.* Edd. PP. Collegii S. Bonaventurae. Bibliotheca Franciscana Scholastica Medii Aevi, 12-15. 4 vols. Quaracchi: Collegium S. Bonaventurae, 1951-57.

—. *Quaestiones Disputatae "Antequam Esset Frater."* Edd. PP. Collegii S. Bonaventurae. Bibliotheca Franciscana Scholastica Medii Aevi, 19-21. 3 vols. Quaracchi: Collegium S. Bonaventurae, 1960.

[Alexander of Hales (?)]. *Summa Theologica* ([Vol. IV adds]: *seu Sic ab Origine Dicta "Summa Fratris Alexandri"*). Edd. PP. Collegii S. Bonaventurae. 4 vols. Quaracchi: Collegium S. Bonaventurae, 1924-48.

Analecta Hymnica Medii Aevi. Vols. XX, XXI, L. Edd. Guido Maria Dreves and (with him for vol. L) Clemens Blume. Leipzig: Reisland, 1895 (for vols. XX, XXI) and 1907 (for vol. L).

Anselm of Canterbury. *Opera Omnia.* Ed. Franciscus Salesius Schmitt. 6 vols. Seckau, Styria, 1938 (Vol. I); Rome: Sansaini, 1940 (Vol. II); Edinburgh: Nelson, 1946 (reprints of Vols. I-II), 1946-61 (Vols. III-VI).

Aristotle. *Opera.* Ed. Academia Regia Borussica. 5 vols. (Vols. I-II: *Aristoteles Graece.* Ed. Immanuel Bekker.) Berlin: Reimer, 1831-70.

—. *Opera Omnia Graece et Latine cum Indice Nominum et Rerum Absolutissimo.* Paris: Firmin-Didot, 1848-73. Used in reprint of 1927-30.

Augustine of Hippo, St. Aurelius. *Opera Omnia.* In PL 32-46.

—. *De Trinitate Libri XV.* Cura et studio W. J. Mountain, auxiliante Fr. Glorie. CorChrSerLat, 50-50a. 2 vols. Turnhout: Brepols, 1968.

Boethius, Anicius Manlius Severinus. *The Theological Tractates*. [Latin text ed. E. K. Rand.] Trans. H. F. Stewart and E. K. Rand. The Loeb Classical Library. London: Heinemann; New York: Putnam's Sons, 1918.

Denis (or Dionysius) the Areopagite (Pseudo-). *De Divinis Nominibus*. In PG 3, 585A-995B. Latin trans. John Scotus Erigena. In PL 122, 1111B-1172B.

—. *Dionysiaca: Recueil donnant l'ensemble des traductions latines des ouvrages attribués au Denys de l'Aréopage*. Edd. [Philippe Chevallier *et al*.]. 2 vols. Bruges: Desclée de Brouwer, [1937-50].

Denzinger, Henricus, and Adolfus Schönmetzer, edd. *Enchiridion Symbolorum, Definitionum et Declarationum de Rebus Fidei et Morum*. 34th ed. Barcelona: Herder, 1967.

Glossa Ordinaria. In *Biblia Sacra cum Glossa Ordinaria primum quidem a Strabo Fuldensis collecta, et Postilla Nicolai Lyrani* ... Edd. F. Franciscus Feu-ardentium Ordinis Minorum, Ioannes Dedraeus and Iacobus de Cuilly, 7 vols. Paris-Lyons, 1590.

Hugh of Saint-Cher. *Scriptum super III Sententiarum*, distinctiones 2, 5-7, 10-12, 21-22. Ed. Walter H. Principe, *The Theology of the Hypostatic Union in the Early Thirteenth Century*, Vol. III: *Hugh of Saint-Cher's Theology of the Hypostatic Union*. Studies and Texts, 19. Toronto: Pontifical Institute of Mediaeval Studies, 1970, pp. 153-243.

John Damascene, St. *De Fide Orthodoxa*. In PG 94, 781-1228.

—. *De Fide Orthodoxa: Versions of Burgundio and Cerbanus*. Ed. Eligius M. Buytaert. Franciscan Institute Publications: Text Series, 8. St. Bonaventure, N.Y.: Franciscan Institute; Louvain, Nauwelaerts; Paderborn: Schöningh, 1955.

Peter Lombard. *Collectanea in Omnes D. Pauli Apostoli Epistolas*. In PL 191, 1297A-1696C; PL 192, 9A-520A.

—. *Libri IV Sententiarum*. Edd. PP. Collegii S. Bonaventurae. 2 vols. 2nd ed. Quaracchi prope Florentiam: Collegium S. Bonaventurae, 1916.

—. *Sententiae in IV Libris Distinctae*, Vol. I: *Prolegomena, Liber I et II*. Edd. PP. Collegii S. Bonaventurae Ad Claras Aquas. 3rd ed. Grottaferrata (Romae): Editiones Collegii S. Bonaventurae Ad Claras Aquas, 1971.

Philip the Chancellor. *In Psalterium Dauidicum CCCXXX. Sermones*. 2 tomes in 1 vol. Paris: J. Badius, 1523.

—. *Summa de Bono: Quaestiones de Anima*. Ed. Leo W. Keeler, *Ex Summa Philippi Cancellarii Quaestiones de Anima*. Opuscula et Textus: Series Scholastica, 20. Münster i. W.: Aschendorff, 1937.

—. *Summa de Bono: Quaestiones de Fide*. Ed. Victorius a Ceva, *De Fide: Ex Summa Philippi Cancellarii* († 1236). Rome: Pontificia Universitas Gregoriana, 1961.

Richard of Saint-Victor. *De Trinitate: Texte critique avec introduction, notes et tables*. Ed Jean Ribaillier. Textes Philosophiques du Moyen Age, 6. Paris: Vrin, 1958.

William of Auxerre. *Summa aurea in quattuor libros sententiarum: a subtilissimo doctore Magistro Guillermo altissiodorensi edita, quam ... magister Guillermus de quercu ... emendavit*. Paris: Philip Pigouchet, Nicolas Vaultier, and Durandus Gerlier, 1500.

—. *Summa Aurea*, Liber Tertius, Tractatus 1, Exordium, Quaestio 1 (*De Incarnatione*) and Quaestio 10 (*De Statu Christi in Triduo*). Ed. Walter Henry Principe, *The Theology of the Hypostatic Union in the Early Thirteenth Century*, Vol. I: *William of Auxerre's Theology of the Hypostatic Union*. Studies and Texts, 7. Toronto: Pontifical Institute of Mediaeval Studies, 1963.

B. *Secondary Sources*

Auer, Johann. *Die Entwicklung der Gnadenlehre in der Hochscholastik.* Freiburger Theologische Studien, 62 & 64. 2 vols. Freiburg: Herder, 1942, 1951.

—. "Textkritische Studien zur Gnadenlehre des Alexander von Hales," *Scholastik* 15 (1940) 63-75.

Backes, Ignaz. "Die christologische Problematik der Hochscholastik und ihre Beziehung zu Chalkedon," in Vol. II of Aloys Grillmeier and Heinrich Bacht, edd., *Das Konzil von Chalkedon: Geschichte und Gegenwart.* Würzburg: Echter-Verlag, [1953] pp. 923-939.

Bertola, Ermenegildo. "Alano di Lilla, Filippo il Cancelliere ed una inedita 'quaestio' sull'immortalità dell'anima umana," *Rivista di Filosofia Neo-scolastica* 72 (1970) 245-271.

Bettoni, E. "Filippo il Cancelliere," *Pier Lombardo* 4 (1960) 123-135.

Beumer, Johannes. *Theologie als Glaubensverständnis.* Würzburg: Echter-Verlag, 1953.

Bouvy, Jean. "La nécessité de la grâce dans le Commentaire des Sentences d'Odon Rigaud," *Recherches de Théologie ancienne et médiévale* 28 (1961) 59-96.

—. "Les questions sur la grâce dans le Commentaire des Sentences d'Odon Rigaud," *Recherches de Théologie ancienne et médiévale* 27 (1960) 290-343.

Callus, Daniel A. *Introduction of Aristotelian Learning to Oxford.* Extracted from *Proceedings of the British Academy* 29 (1943). London: H. Milford, 1944.

—. "Philip the Chancellor and the *De Anima* Ascribed to Robert Grosseteste," *Mediaeval and Renaissance Studies* 1 (1941-43) 105-107.

—. "Robert Grosseteste as Scholar," in D. A. Callus, ed., *Robert Grosseteste: Scholar and Bishop: Essays in Commemoration of the Seventh Centenary of His Death.* Oxford: Clarendon Press, 1955, pp. 1-69.

—. "The Function of the Philosopher in Thirteenth-century Oxford," in Paul Wilpert and Willehad Paul Eckert, edd., *Beiträge zum Berufsbewusstsein des mittelalterliche Menschen.* Vol. III of Paul Wilpert, ed., *Miscellanea Mediaevalia.* Veröffentlichungen des Thomas-Instituts an der Universität Köln. Berlin: W. de Gruyter, 1964, pp. 152-162.

—. "The Origins of the Problem of the Unity of Form," *The Thomist* 34 (1961) 257-285.

—. "The Powers of the Soul: An Early Unpublished Text," *Recherches de Théologie ancienne et médiévale* 19 (1952) 131-170.

Carra de Vaux Saint-Cyr, Bruno. "Une source inconnue de la *Summa fratris Alexandri*," *Revue des Sciences Philosophiques et Théologiques* 47 (1963) 571-605.

Ceva, Victorius a. *De Fide: Ex Summa Philippi Cancellarii († 1236).* Rome: Pontificia Universitas Gregoriana, 1961.

Châtillon, Jean. "'Quidquid convenit Filio Dei per naturam convenit Filio Hominis per gratiam': A propos de Jean de Ripa, *Determinationes* I, 4, 4," in Vol. II of *Miscellanea André Combes.* Rome: Pont. Università Lateranense; Paris: Vrin, 1967, pp. 319-331.

Chenu, M.-D. *La théologie au douzième siècle.* Pref. by Étienne Gilson. Études de Philosophie Médiévale, 45. Paris: Vrin, 1957.

—. *La théologie comme science au XIIIᵉ siècle.* Bibliothèque Thomiste, 33. 3rd ed. Paris: Vrin, 1957.

Conlon, Walter M. "The Certitude of Hope," *The Thomist* 10 (1947) 75-119, 226-252.

Crowe, M. B. "The Term *Synderesis* and the Scholastics," *The Irish Theological Quarterly* 23 (1956) 151-164, 228-245.

Crowley, Theodore. *Roger Bacon: The Problem of the Soul in His Philosophical Commentaries.* Louvain: Éditions de l'Institut Supérieur de Philosophie; Dublin: James Duffy, 1950.

da Cruz Pontes, J. M. "Le problème de l'origine de l'âme de la patristique à la solution thomiste," *Recherches de Théologie ancienne et médiévale* 31 (1964) 175-229.

Daunou, M. "Philippe de Grève, Chancelier de l'Église de Paris," in *Histoire littéraire de la France*, Vol. XVIII. Paris: Firmin-Didot, 1835, pp. 184-191.

Davy, M.-M. *Les sermons universitaires parisiens de 1230-1231: Contribution à l'histoire de la prédication médiévale.* Études de Philosophie Médiévale, 15. Paris: Vrin, 1931.

de Contenson, P.-M. "Avicennisme latin et vision de Dieu au début du xiiiᵉ siècle," *Archives d'Histoire Doctrinale et Littéraire du Moyen Age* 26 (1959) 29-97.

Deman, Th. "Le 'De moribus Ecclesiae catholicae' de S. Augustin dans l'œuvre de S. Thomas d'Aquin," *Recherches de Théologie ancienne et médiévale* 21 (1954) 248-280.

de Vaux, R. "La première entrée d'Averroës chez les Latins," *Revue des Sciences Philosophiques et Théologiques* 22 (1933) 193-245.

De Wulf, Maurice. *Le treizième siècle.* Vol. II of his *Histoire de la philosophie médiévale.* 6th ed. Louvain: Institut Supérieur de Philosophie; Paris: Vrin, 1936.

Doucet, Victorin. "A travers le manuscrit 434 de Douai," *Antonianum* 27 (1952) 531-580.

Englhardt, Georg. "Adam de Puteorumvilla: Un Maître proche d'Odon Rigaud. Sa psychologie de la foi," *Recherches de Théologie ancienne et médiévale* 8 (1936) 61-78.

—. "Das Glaubenslicht nach Albert dem Grossen," in Johann Auer and Herman Volk, edd., *Theologie in Geschichte und Gegenwart* [Festgabe Michael Schmaus]. Munich: Karl Zink, 1957, pp. 371-396.

—. *Die Entwicklung der dogmatischen Glaubenspsychologie in der mittelalterlichen Scholastik vom Abaelardstreit (um 1140) bis zu Philipp dem Kanzler (gest. 1236).* Beiträge, 30, 4-6. Münster i. W.: Aschendorff, 1933.

Fabro, Cornelio. "La distinzione tra 'quod est' e 'quo est' nella 'Summa de Anima' di Giovanni De La Rochelle," *Divus Thomas (Piacenza)* 41 (1938) 508-522.

Feckes, Carl. "Die Behandlung der Tugend der Keuschheit im Schriftum Alberts des Grossen," in Heinrich Ostlender, ed., *Studia Albertina: Festschrift für Bernhard Geyer zum 70. Geburtstage.* Beiträge, Supplementband IV. Münster Westf., 1952, pp. 90-111.

Feret, P. *La faculté de théologie de Paris et ses docteurs les plus célèbres: Moyen Age*, Vol. I. Paris: Picard, 1894.

Ferté, J. "Rapports de la somme d'Alexandre de Halès dans son 'De Fide' avec Philippe le Chancelier," *Recherches de Théologie ancienne et médiévale* 7 (1935) 381-402.

Filthaut, Ephrem. *Roland von Cremona O.P. und die Anfänge der Scholastik im Predigerorden: Ein Beitrag zur Geistesgeschichte der älteren Dominikaner.* Vechta i. O.: Albertus-Magnus-Verlag, 1936.

Galot, J. *La Nature du Caractère Sacramentel: Étude de Théologie Médiévale.* Museum Lessianum: Section Théologique, 52. [Bruges]: Desclée de Brouwer, [1957].

Gauthier, R.-A. *Magnanimité: L'idéal de la grandeur dans la philosophie païenne et dans la théologie chrétienne.* Bibliothèque Thomiste, 28. Paris: Vrin, 1951.

Gillon, L.-B. *La théorie des oppositions et la théologie du péché au XIIIᵉ siècle.* Paris: Vrin, 1937.

Gilson, Étienne. *History of Christian Philosophy in the Middle Ages.* New York: Random House, [1955].

Glorieux, P. "La Summa Duacensis," *Recherches de Théologie ancienne et médiévale* 12 (1940) 104-135.

—. *La "Summa Duacensis" (Douai 434): Texte critique avec une introduction et des tables.* Textes Philosophiques du Moyen Age, 2. Paris: Vrin, 1955.

—. "L'enseignement au moyen âge. Technique et méthodes en usage à la Faculté de Théologie de Paris au xiiie siècle," *Archives d'Histoire Doctrinale et Littéraire du Moyen Age* 35 (1968) 65-186.

—. "Les années 1242-1247 à la Faculté de Théologie de Paris," *Recherches de Théologie ancienne et médiévale* 29 (1962) 234-249.

—. "Les 572 Questions du manuscrit de Douai 434," *Recherches de Théologie ancienne et médiévale* 10 (1938) 123-152, 225-267.

—. *Pour revaloriser Migne: Tables rectificatives.* Cahier Supplémentaire to *Mélanges de Science Religieuse* 9 (1952). Lille: Facultés Catholiques, 1952.

—. *Répertoire des maîtres en théologie de Paris au XIIIe siècle.* Études de Philosophie Médiévale, 17-18. 2 vols. Paris: Vrin, 1933.

Gössmann, Elisabeth. *Metaphysik und Heilsgeschichte: Eine theologische Untersuchung der Summa Halensis (Alexander von Hales).* Mitteilungen des Grabmann-Instituts der Universität München, Sonderband. Munich: Hueber, 1964.

Graf, Thomas. *De Subiecto Psychico Gratiae et Virtutum secundum Doctrinam Scholasticorum usque ad Medium Saeculum XIV.* 2 vols. Studia Anselmiana, 2-4. Rome: Herder, 1934-35.

Grillmeier, Alois. "Die altkirchliche Christologie und die moderne Hermeneutik," *Theologische Bericht* 1 (1972) 69-169.

Gründel, Johannes. *Die Lehre von den Umständen der menschlichen Handlung im Mittelalter.* Beiträge, 39/5. Münster Westf.: Aschendorff, 1963.

Guindon, Roger. *Béatitude et Théologie morale chez saint Thomas d'Aquin: Origines-Interprétation.* Ottawa: Éditions de l'Université d'Ottawa, 1956.

Hansen, Joseph. "Zur Frage der anfanglosen und zeitlichen Schöpfung bei Albert dem Grossen," in *Studia Albertina* [see supra, sub Feckes], pp. 167-188.

Hödl, Ludwig. "Articulus fidei. Eine begriffschichtliche Arbeit," in Joseph Ratzinger and Heinrich Fries, edd., *Einsicht und Glaube* [Gottlieb Söhngen zum 70. Geburtstag am 21. Mai 1962]. Freiburg: Herder, 1962, pp. 358-376.

—. *Die neuen Quästionen der Gnadentheologie des Johannes von Rupella OM († 1245) in Cod. lat. Paris 14726.* Mitteilungen des Grabmann-Instituts der Universität München, 8. Munich: Hueber, 1964.

Kaepelli, Th. "Un recueil de sermons prêchés à Paris et en Angleterre conservé dans le MS. de Canterbury, Cathedr. Libr. D 7 (Jourdain de Saxe O.P., Thomas de Chabham etc.)," *Archivum Fratrum Praedicatorum* 26 (1956) 161-191.

Keeler, Leo W. *Ex Summa Philippi Cancellarii Quaestiones de Anima.* Opuscula et Textus: Series Scholastica, 20. Münster i. W.: Aschendorff, 1937.

Korošak, Bruno. *Mariologia S. Alberti Magni eiusque coaequalium.* Bibliotheca Mariana Medii Aevi: Textus et Disquisitiones, 8. Rome: Academia Mariana Internationalis, 1954.

Künzle, Pius. *Das Verhältnis der Seele zu ihren Potenzen: Problemgeschichtliche Untersuchungen von Augustin bis und mit Thomas von Aquin.* Studia Friburgensia, Neue Folge, 12. Freiburg (Schweiz): Universitätsverlag, 1956.

—. "Hat Philipp der Kanzler die Summa Duacensis verfasst?" *Freiburger Zeitschrift für Philosophie und Theologie* 2 (1955) 469-473.

Landgraf, Artur. *Dogmengeschichte der Frühscholastik.* 4 parts, each of 2 vols. Regensburg: Pustet, 1952-56.

—. *Einführung in die Geschichte der theologischen Literatur der Frühscholastik unter dem Gesichtspunkte der Schulenbildung.* Regensburg: Pustet, 1948.

Lang, Albert. "Die Bedeutung Alberts des Grossen für die Aufrollung der fun-

damentaltheologischen Frage," in *Studia Albertina* [see *supra, sub* Feckes], pp. 343-
373.

Leclercq, J. "Sermon de Philippe le Chancelier sur S. Bernard," *Cîteaux* 16 (1965) 205-
213.

Lecoy de la Marche, A. *La chaire française au moyen âge, spécialement au XIIIᵉ siècle, d'après
les manuscrits contemporains*. 2nd ed. Paris: Renouard, H. Laurens, successeur, 1886.

Lerner, R. E. "Weltklerus und religiose Bewegung im XIII. Jahrhundert. Das Beispiel
Philipps des Kanzlers," *Archiv für Kulturgeschichte* 51 (1969) 94-108.

Lottin, Odon. *Psychologie et Morale au XIIᵉ et XIIIᵉ siècles*. 6 tomes in 8 vols. Gembloux:
Duculot, 1942-60 (2nd ed. of Vol. I, 1957).

—. "Quelques 'Quaestiones' de maîtres parisiens aux environs de 1225-1235," *Recherches de Théologie ancienne et médiévale* 5 (1933) 79-95 (abridged version in *Psychologie et
Morale* VI, 137-148).

Lynch, Kilian F. "The Theory of Alexander of Hales on the Efficacy of the Sacrament of
Matrimony," *Franciscan Studies* 11, nos. 3-4 (Sept.-Dec. 1951: St. Bonaventure
University Commemorative Volume) 69-139.

McDevitt, Augustine. "The Episcopate as an Order and Sacrament on the Eve of the
High Scholastic Period," *Franciscan Studies* 20 (1960) 96-148.

Meier, Annaliese. "Filippo il Cancelliere," *Enciclopedia Cattolica* 5 (1950) cols. 1315-16.

Meylan, Henri. "Les 'Questions' de Philippe le Chancelier, Chancelier de l'Église de
Paris (*Tractatus de bono nature et de bono in genere*): avec une introduction sur la vie et
les œuvres théologiques de l'auteur," [Summary of his dissertation] in *École
Nationale des Chartes: Positions des thèses soutenues par les élèves de la promotion de 1927*.
Paris: Presses Universitaires, 1927, pp. 89-94.

Michaud-Quantin, P., and M. Lemoine, "Pour le dossier des 'philosophantes'," *Archives
d'Histoire Doctrinale et Littéraire du Moyen Age* 35 (1968) 17-22.

Minges, Parthenius. "Philosophiegeschichtliche Bemerkungen über Philipp von Grève
(†1236)," *Philosophisches Jahrbuch* 27 (1914) 21-32.

Natalini, Valentinus. *De Natura Gratiae Sacramentalis iuxta S. Bonaventuram*. Studia Antoniana, 17. Rome: Pontificium Athenaeum Antonianum, 1961.

Pinckaers, Servais. "La nature vertueuse de l'espérance," *Revue Thomiste* 58 (1958) 405-
442, 623-644.

Pouillon, Henri. "La Beauté, propriété transcendantale chez les Scolastiques (1220-
1270)," *Archives d'Histoire Doctrinale et Littéraire du Moyen Age* 15 (1946) 263-329.

—. "Le premier Traité des Propriétés transcendantales: La 'Summa de bono' du
Chancelier Philippe," *Revue Néoscolastique de Philosophie* 42 (1939) 40-77.

Princìpe, Walter H. "The Theology of the Hypostatic Union in the Early Thirteenth
Century: The Doctrines of William of Auxerre, Alexander of Hales, Hugh of Saint-
Cher, and Philip the Chancellor," *Mediaeval Studies* 24 (1962) 392-394.

—. *The Theology of the Hypostatic Union in the Early Thirteenth Century*, Vol. I: *William of
Auxerre's Theology of the Hypostatic Union;* Vol. II: *Alexander of Hales' Theology of the
Hypostatic Union*; Vol. III: *Hugh of Saint-Cher's Theology of the Hypostatic Union*. Studies
and Texts, 7, 12, 19. Toronto: Pontifical Institute of Mediaeval Studies, 1963, 1967,
1970.

Raby, F. *A History of Christian Latin Poetry from the Beginnings to the Close of the Middle Ages*.
2nd ed. Oxford: Clarendon Press, 1953.

—. *A History of Secular Latin Poetry in the Middle Ages*. 2 vols. Oxford: Clarendon Press,
1934; reprint, 1957, 1967.

Rohof, Jan. *La sainteté substantielle du Christ dans la théologie scolastique: Histoire du problème.* Studia Friburgensia, Nouvelle Série, 5. Fribourg (Suisse): Éditions St-Paul, 1952.

Saffrey, Henri-Dominique. "L'état actuel des recherches sur le Liber de causis comme source de la métaphysique au moyen âge," in Paul Wilpert and Willehad Paul Eckert, edd., *Die Metaphysik im Mittelalter: Ihre Ursprung und ihre Bedeutung.* Vol. II of Paul Wilpert, ed., *Miscellanea Mediaevalia.* Veröffentlichungen des Thomas-Instituts an der Universität Köln. Berlin: W. de Gruyter, 1963, pp. 267-281.

Salman, D. H. "Jean de La Rochelle et les débuts de l'averroïsme latin," *Archives d'Histoire Doctrinale et Littéraire du Moyen Age* 16 (1947-48) 133-144.

Schneyer, Joh. Baptist. *Beobachtungen zu lateinischen Sermoneshandschriften der Staatsbibliothek München.* Bayerische Akademie der Wissenschaften, Philosophisch-historische Klasse: Sitzungsberichte, Jahrgang 1958, Heft 8. Munich: Beck, 1958.

—. "Die Erforschung der scholastischen Sermones und ihre Bedeutung für die Homiletik: Ein Hinweis auf die Bedeutung der scholastischen Sermones für die Theologie," *Scholastik* 39 (1964) 1-26.

—. "Einige Sermoneshandschriften aus der früheren Benediktinerbibliothek des Mont Saint-Michel," *Sacris Erudiri* 17 (1966) 150-211.

—. "Entstehung und Überlieferung eines mittelalterlichen Predigtsexempels," *Tübingen Theologische Quartalschrift* 146 (1966) 329-347.

—. "Philipp der Kanzler — ein hervorragender Prediger des Mittelalters," *Münchener Theologische Zeitschrift* 8 (1957) 174-179.

—. *Repertorium der lateinischen Sermones des Mittelalters für die Zeit von 1150-1350 (Autoren L-P).* Beiträge, 43, 4. Münster Westf.: Aschendorff, 1972.

—. *Die Sittenkritik in den Predigten Philipps des Kanzlers.* Beiträge, 39, 4. Münster Westf.: Aschendorff, 1962.

Smalley, Beryl. "A Commentary on the Hexaemeron by Henry of Ghent," *Recherches de Théologie ancienne et médiévale* 20 (1953) 60-101.

—. "Gilbertus Universalis, Bishop of London (1128-34), and the Problem of the 'Glossa Ordinaria'," *Recherches de Théologie ancienne et médiévale* 7 (1935) 235-262; 8 (1936) 24-60.

Smith, Gerard. "Avicenna and the Possibles," *The New Scholasticism* 17 (1943) 340-357.

Spitzmuller, Henry. *Carmina Sacra Medii Aevi Saec. III-XV / Poésie latine chrétienne du moyen âge: IIIe-XVe siècle.* [Bruges]: Desclée de Brouwer, 1971.

Stegmüller, Friedrich. *Repertorium Commentariorum in Sententias Petri Lombardi.* 2 vols. Würzburg: Schöningh, 1947.

Torrell, Eugène J.-P. *La connaissance prophétique dans le manuscrit de Douai 434: Édition critique et commentaire des textes.* Dissertation, Université de Montréal, 1973.

Van den Eynde, Damien. *Les Définitions des Sacrements pendant la première période de la théologie scolastique (1050-1240).* Rome: Antonianum; Louvain: Nauwelaerts, 1950.

Vande Wiele, Joseph. "Le problème de la vérité ontologique dans la philosophie de saint Thomas," *Revue Philosophique de Louvain* 52 (1954) 521-571.

Vanneste, Alfred. "La théologie de la pénitence chez quelques maîtres parisiens de la première moitié du XIIIe siècle," *Ephemerides Theologicae Lovaniensis* 28 (1952) 24-58.

Vansteenkiste, G. "Le versioni latine del De Fide Orthodoxa di San Giovanni Damasceno," *Angelicum* 35 (1958) 91-98.

—. Review of P. Glorieux, ed., *La "Summa Duacensis" (Douai 434): Texte critique ...,* in *Angelicum* 34 (1957) 331-334.

Vicaire, M. H. "Les Porrétains et l'Avicennisme avant 1215," *Revue des Sciences Philosophiques et Théologiques* 26 (1937) 449-482.

Vugts, Ant. *La grâce d'union d'après S. Thomas d'Aquin: Essai historique et doctrinal.* Tilburg, Drukkerij Missiehuis, 1946.

Wicki, Nikolaus. *Die Lehre von der himmlischen Seligkeit in der mittelalterlichen Scholastik von Petrus Lombardus bis Thomas von Aquin.* Studia Friburgensia, Neue Folge, 9. Freiburg, Schweiz: Universitätsverlag, 1954.

—. "Philipp der Kanzler," *Lexikon für Theologie und Kirche.* 2nd ed. Vol. 8 (1963) cols. 452-453.

—. "Philipp der Kanzler und die Pariser Bischofswahl von 1227/1228," *Freiburger Zeitschrift für Philosophie und Theologie* 5 (1958) 318-326.

—. "Philip the Chancellor," *New Catholic Encyclopedia* 11 (1967) 274-275.

Zavalloni, R. *Richard de Mediavilla et la controverse sur la pluralité des formes.* Louvain, 1951.

ANALYTICAL INDEX

Heavy type: most important analyses of the topic (including notes). 21: page 21. 21n: note on page 21. 21&n: page 21 and note on page 21. 21&nn: page 21 and two or more notes on page 21. 21-25nn: from page 21 to page 25, in the notes only. 21-25 passim: scattered references on pages 21-25 (including notes). HypU: Hypostatic Union (index title under H).

Distinction(s): 37, 51, 62, 67, 72, 73, 75, 82n, 83, 90, 91, 112, 127, 142, 196, 198; of natures: 92, 103, 113, 144, 171, 184; personal: *see* Person, distinction.

Divinity: *see* God, essence.

Dominicans: 17, 192, 206.

Ens: 26n, **27-33**, 35; *ab alio*: 111, 176; *communiter dictum*: 27n, 28, 31, 44; *compositum*: 32, 36; *creatum* and *increatum*: 30&n, 111, 142; distinct from *esse* in creatures: 27n; distinct from *id quod est*: 27, 28; equivalent to *esse*: 27-30 passim, 33; equivalent to *id quod*: 27n, 28; includes *esse* and *id quod est*: 27, 28; and material and formal multiplication: 31-32; *non ab alio*: 111, 176; and *non-ens*: 28; predication of: 31, 58; *Primum*: 30, 33; *simplex*: 32, 36; *Summe*: 30; *see also*: Being; *Esse*.

Esse: 27-30 passim, **32-42**, 52, 53, 54n, 60, 61, 67, **81-85, 182, 185**, 198; absolute: **67**, 84, 85, 95, 96, 144, **157**, 159, 162, 163, **182**, 183; *in actu*: 29, 41, 42; *animae*: 175; as being in general: 32-34, 142; and *bene esse*: 34&n, 116&n, 118, 119, 146, 174, *caritatis*: 34; complete: 101, 182, 185, 196; composite: 36, 52; conjoined: 85, **96**, 157, **182**; *corporale*: **162**; distinct: 60-62, 184; *divinum*: 34, 35, 36n, 40n, 198, 202, 204, 208; as essence or form (*quo est*): 32, **34-40**, 142; *exemplare* and *spirituale* (of angels): 34; as existence: 32, 40-42; formal: 39n, 53; generic, specific, and individual: 34, 170 (*speciei*); *gratiae*: 34n; identical with *posse* in simple beings: **81-85** passim, **156, 157**; *individui*: 34, 46, 67, 113, 162, 163, **177**; *latriae*: 34; material: 53; *miraculorum*: 34; *morale*: 34, 40n, 46, 67, 113, **177**; *naturae*: 46, 113, 177; *naturale, morale, gratuitum*: 34, 46, **177**; *naturale, morale, rationale*: 34, 40n, 195; *non-esse in actu*: 29, 41, 42; particular: 60, 61, 95, 144, 182; *per se*: **58-59**, 67, **85**, 157, **163**, 196; personal: 67, 84n, 95, **96**, 113, 159, **163**, 177, 182; physical: 40, 61&n, **80-85**, 96, 142, 148, 208&n; of physical (natural) order: 40&n, 46; *potentiale*: 186; prior to the one, the true, the good: 33&n; and *quod est*: 34-40, 52; and "reflex predication": 35; *secundum quid*: **85**, 156, **163**, 185; *simpliciter*: **85**, 156, **163**; *spirituale*: 34, **162**; substantial: 62; in *Summa de Bono*: 32-42; *virtutis*: 34.

Essence: 27, 29, 32, **34-40**, 45, 46, **48-51**, 58n, 59n, 64n, 65, 81&n, 83, 85, 97, 142, 155, 157, 158, 161, 164, 165, 179, 191, 198, 201, 207, 208; distinction from existence: 38n; equivalent to *esse*: 34-40; exemplary cause: 49; formal cause: 49, 56-57; incorruptible, 48; and nature: 49; object of metaphysics: 40n, 46, 49, 191; relationship with power and act: 49n; simple (*essentia simplex*): 37, 64n; *see also*: *Quo est*.

Eternity: 34n, 83, 90, 101n, 105, 156, 163, 169, 175, 185, 186.

Evil: 28, 69, 82n, 121, 122n, 165, 175n; *see also*: Angel, devil.

Existere/ existence: 27, 32, 38&n, **40-42, 43-44**, 66, 89, 97, 98, 142, 144, 184, 185, 191, 208, 209; natural/ physical: 40, 42, 43, 65, 142, 144, 148, 208&n; in some state: 43, 44; somewhere: 43, 44; *see also*: *Esse*.

Factus: *see* Becoming.

Faith: 59&n, 69, **71-76**, 89, 114&n, 193, 195, 207; and the Incarnation: **71-76**, 142-144, 193; necessity and contingency in objects of: 71-73.

Father (in God): 41, 73n, 92, 104, 112, 126, 131, 147, 155, 161, 171, 173, 177, 178, 184, 186, 187&n, 202; *see also*: Trinity.

Fieri: *see* Becoming.

Filius Dei: *see* Son of God.

Filius Hominis: *see* Son of Man.

Filius Virginis: *see* Son of the Virgin.

First opinion: *see* HypU, opinions.

NAME INDEX

ADAM: 58, 122, 203.

ALAN OF LILLE: 193, 52n.

ALBERT, ST.: 206.

ALEXANDER OF HALES: philosophy of: 32, 34&n, 37, 38, 43, 44, 46, 52, 56, 61-63 passim, 67, 171, 141, 142, 191, 193, 195, 197-199; theology of: 19-20&nn, 26, 29&n, 36&n, 41, 60, 77, 86, 90-92, 99, 109, 111&n, 113, 117, 119, 141, 143, 146, 148, 193, 194, 196, 200-209 passim.

ALGAZEL: 25n.

AMBROSE, ST.: 165n.

ANASTASIUS: 181n.

ANSELM, ST.: 26, 73, 74n, 165n, 193.

AQUINAS, ST. THOMAS: 140n, 205, 206, 209.

ARISTOTLE: 25&nn, 28n, 49-50&nn, 57&n, 59&n, 82, 143, 157n, 169n, 170n, 177n, 191, 192, 198, 199.

ATHANASIUS: 102, 109, 173, 181.

AUGUSTINE, ST.: 26, 56, 58, 74, 76nn, 114&nn, 115n, 118, 126n, 134&n, 138, 142, 165n, 166&n, 167&n, 175, 178, 180n, 191, 193.

AUGUSTINE, PSEUDO-: 166n.

AVERROES: 25&n.

AVICEBRON: 25&n.

AVICENNA: 25&n, 32, 41, 42, 57n, 83, 84, 143, 192.

BEDE, VENERABLE: 165n.

BERNARD, ST.: 26, 159n, 193.

Bettoni, E.: 17nn, 19n.

BOETHIUS: 26, 28, 32, 34-36, 38, 39, 59, 60, 67, 83, 95n, 142, 155n, 170n, 182n, 191, 198.

BONAVENTURE, ST.: 206.

Callus, Daniel A.: 17nn, 19n, 25nn, 82n.

Ceva, Victorius: 17n, 18n, 21n, 47n, 59nn, 71-74nn, 76n, 77n, 115nn, 126n, 151n.

CHALCEDON: 209&n.

Châtillon, Jean: 180n.

Chenu, M. D.: 82n.

Collectanea in Omnes D. Pauli Apostoli Epistolas: 76&n, 114n, 115n, 193.

Commentaria in Porphyrium a Se Translatum of Boethius: 170n.

Contra Sermonem Arianorum of Augustine: 114n, 180n.

Cur Deus Homo of Anselm: 73, 74n, 165n.

CYRIL, ST.: 181.

DAMASCENE, ST. JOHN: 26, 59n, 60, 65, 71, 77, 86n, 90, 92, 94, 96n, 98, 99, 100, 102-106 passim, 109, 116n, 123, 124n, 125, 133&n, 138, 142, 145, 148, 154, 164-166 passim, 169, 171, 172, 174, 175, 180-188 passim, 193, 197.

Davy, M.-M.: 17n.

De Anima of Aristotle: 25n.

Quaestiones de Discretioni Personali of Philip: 54n, 62n, 65n, 68n, 69n, 77n, 81n, 83-85nn, 93n, 151, 154, 155-157, 181n.

Quaestiones de Incarnatione of Philip: 46n, 54n, 59n, 60-63 passim, 65&n, 68n, 69, 70&n, 76&n, 77&n, 79-86 passim, 89-117nn, 123-130nn, 132-140 passim, 142, 147, 148, 151, 152-154, 158-188.

Raby, F.: 17n.
RICHARD OF SAINT-VICTOR: 43, 62&n, 68, 156n, 158n, 161n, 181n, 193.
RIGAUD, ODON: 20n.
Rohof, J.: 118n.

Schneyer, J. B.: 17nn.
SCRIPTURAL REFERENCES:
  Ps 64, 5: 175.
  Eccli 27, 10: 158.
  Wis 9, 15: 173.
  Is 11, 2: 115n, 121n.
  Mt 28, 18: 120.
  Lk 10: 165; 18, 19: 55.
  Jn 1, 3: 176n.
  Rom 1, 2-3: 115.
  I Cor 11, 7: 162.
  Col 2, 9: 120.
  Heb 4, 12: 159.
Scriptum super Sententiis of Hugh of Saint-Cher: 19n, 44n.
Sentences of Peter Lombard: 26, 36, 89, 114n, 134n, 142, 166n, 193, 195.
Sermo of "Augustine": #236: 76n; #246: 76n.
Smith, Gerard: 83n.
Spitzmuller, H.: 18n.
Stegmüller, F.: 18n.
Summa Aurea of William of Auxerre: 19n, 82n, 192.
Summa de Bono: 17, 18-21, 25-69 passim, 71, 76-77, 79, 81-83, 86n, 87, 114&n, 117, 119&n, 126&n, 133, 135, 138-142 passim, 147, 148, 151, 152n, 154, 207; contents of: 21; date of composition of: 18-19, 19n; editions of: 18n, 152n; and HypU: 21; manuscripts of: 18n, 151-152; originality of: 19-20&nn; other names for: 18n; and relationship with theological questions: 21, 141, 142.
Summa Duacensis: 19&n, 20&n, 26n.
Summa Fratris Alexandri: 20, 62, 63, 85, 94n, 98n, 148, 205, 207.
Summa Theologiae of Thomas Aquinas: 140n, 205n, 206.
Summa Theologica of Alexander of Hales: 20.
Summas: of Albert: 205-206; of Bonaventure: 205-206; of Praepositinus of Cremona: 174n.
Symbolum "Quicumque": 173&n, 183.

Theologicae Regulae of Alan of Lille: 52n.
Torrell, Eugène J.-P.: 19n.

UNIVERSITY OF PARIS: 17.

GENERAL BOOKBINDING CO.
274NY3   340
75   4   340   A   6752
QUALITY CONTROL MARK